Fate's Gambit

THREADS OF FATE BOOK ONE

Mariah Killian

Copyright © 2024 by *Mariah Killian*. All rights reserved.

No part of this book may be reproduced, distributed, or transmitted in any form or by any means, including photocopying, recording, or other electronic or mechanical methods, without the prior written permission of the publisher, except in the case of brief quotations embodied in critical reviews and certain other noncommercial uses permitted by copyright law.

Names: Mariah Killian., author.

Editors: Mariah Killian, Marla Esposito

Illustrator: Henry Klassen

Title: Fate's Gambit / Mariah Killian

Description: First edition.| Panda Publishing, 2024. | Series: Threads of Fate; 1 | Audience: Ages 20-30 | Summary: Six heroes become the new fates of Eckris, while an ancient evil breaks free from its prison. In a race against time, they must band together and use their new gifts to defeat this evil before it threatens to end the world they call home.

Subjects: ADF: Magic-fiction | Royalty- Fiction | Dark-Fiction

Table of Contents

Tristan. I am sorry you never got the chance to read my book. May the next life treat you more kindly, my friend.

About the Author

Mariah Killian is an emerging fantasy-fiction voice, passionate about weaving together intricate worlds, compelling characters, and epic tales of magic, heroism, and destiny. Exploring the depths of human nature, relationships, and the power of unlikely friendships; Mariah draws her inspiration from her everyday life. Born with a love for storytelling, Mariah has spent countless hours as a teenager creating imaginary worlds, filling notebooks with story ideas, world-building, and intricate plotlines.

"Fate's Gambit," invites readers into the realm of Eckris, where mystic forces, ancient curses, and courageous champions stand against a rising evil that threatens to consume the world.

When not writing, Mariah enjoys drawing, reading, and Dungeons & Dragons, which often spark new ideas for characters and worlds. Mariah is working on the next book in the Threads of Fate series, "Kings Quandry," expanding the epic saga introduced in their debut.

Connect with Mariah Killian

- Instagram: @killianmariah

- Twitter: @killianmariah

- Email: authorkillian.mariah@gmail.com

Chapter One

<u>Clovis</u>

Clenching and unclenching his hands as he walked, Clovis thought, *How could she be so reckless?*

Inhaling, he focuses on the castle's architecture instead of the footsteps padding softly behind him. The walls of Aebruthey's castle were clad in rich, mahogany wainscoting, rising from the floor to about waist height, intricately carved with scenes of ancient motifs. Above, the plastered expanse is painted a deep, velvety shade of indigo, reminiscent of the night sky. Flickering sconces lined the walls, casting a warm, amber glow that lit the polished wooden floor, creating pools of light amidst the shadows.

An ornate Persian runner carpet stretched the length of the hallway, absorbing the prince's footfalls as he walks towards his room. Alongside the carpet, tall bookshelves stood sentinel, their mahogany shelves filled with leather-bound tomes.

A magnificent arched doorway stood at the far end of the hallway, its timeworn oak door adorned with iron filigree and a gleaming brass handle. Above the entrance, an elaborate transom window filtered in a muted, ethereal light, casting a halo-like glow around the threshold.

"Honestly, if you're going to be an idiot, do not include me," a mocking voice sounded off from behind Clovis.

Spinning on his heels, Mika ran into his chest, startling him. Her icy blue eyes stared into his.

"Mika." Clovis sighed, touching his younger sister's head and leaning down to meet her stare.

"If you don't leave me alone, I will ensure you have the worst time during the Auro's Festival." Before Mika could respond, Clovis stepped into his room and slammed the door in his sister's face.

I shouldn't have slammed the door. I want to be left alone for a while.

After a second, he re-opened his door and said, " Listen, next time you sneak out, tell me so I can properly cover for you. but seriously, if you're going to be an idiot, do it alone."

"I'll be more careful next time, I just wanted to get a gift for Ethan."

"You could have said something; I'd have gone with you."

"Okay, I get it," Mika said, tugging at her skirt.

Raising an eyebrow, he said, "Okay, well, I am going to spend some time alone now."

Closing the door, Clovis hesitantly began stripping himself of his garments. "Do this, Clovis, do that Clovis; the kingdom will fall and perish if you don't smile at that infant, Clovis." A mocking smirk curled on the young prince's face as he said the words aloud. Peering down at his black fingertips, his smile disappeared. There were more pressing matters to attend to, though he wasn't sure how he would tend to what he didn't understand. The memories of the other week replayed in his head.

***

Clovis stood in the ruins of an old Aurami town between Aeberuthey and Tarrin, setting up to perform a protection spell at a checkpoint for merchants who frequented the forest. It was a simple spell: four runes on the main pathways into the ruins, pine wood buried below the entrances, and a piece of wither-root buried in the cross-section of the paths. A simple spell and done. At least that's how it was supposed to go until Iathos Casxes showed up. He was a well-known war general for Kamouraska in the eastern country.

"Clovis, what are you doing?" Iathos questioned, taking a careful approach toward the prince.

"I am placing protection runes for travelers," Clovis quipped back.

Iathos drew his sword in response to the prince. "I don't believe you."

A deafening silence overtook both men as they looked upon one another with tensed jaws. Only a few seconds passed before Iathos reached for his side and flung a dagger in the prince's direction. With no other choice, Clovis split his concentration on his spell to use another, blocking the dagger with a force field; the spell shattered after deflecting Iatho's dagger. Meanwhile, the knight made a race toward his target, and one cut was all it took to send everything sideways. Iathos got into Clovis's space, slashing his hand as Clovis conjured a blade to fight back. staring down at his now bloodied hand, the prince let out a hiss. "You bastard."

Standing up from the spell's blast, Iathos prepared for another charge at the wizard.

"I don't suggest that, knight."

Before Iathos could respond, he watched as Clovis lifted his hand. Shadows materialized from the air, flowing around his hand. With a snap of his fingers, the knight was pulled into the air as three shadowy blades sliced his arm, then dropped him to the ground. As he landed, the whole world seemed to suddenly shift as if being plunged into the deepest depths of the sea.

Darkness surrounded both men while orbs of light flickered around like fireflies. A low, cold voice spoke to them, "Ah, a wondrous meal has been placed before me. A man of magic and a man of fear. What a combination you will make." Beside him, Clovis heard Iathos reaching for his sword.

"It won't save you. Stand up, idiot," Clovis stated angrily. "If we don't find a way out, we are going to die here, so get off your knees unless that's the man you wanna die as."

Slithering sounds suddenly came from around them as heavy sludge-feeling tendrils wrapped around their arms and legs. Haunting laughter filled their ears as pain seared through their bodies. Clovis knew they were being drained of life force.

Briefly, Clovis thought of his sister. Who would protect her?

As he did, the light came flooding into the scenery. The monster screeched and let both men go, dropping them with a thud. A hand grabbed Clovis, dragging him somewhere in his blindness. Coming from somewhere else, he could hear Iathos shouting at someone.

Screaming, the monster's voice echoed, "They'll be mine! I've cursed them, and in turn, you shall be mine also."

Hearing a sigh from the man dragging him, they responded, "Better be worth it then."

The dragging stopped; Clovis's vision was blurry at this point. He finally spoke, "What's going on?"

Above him, his savior spoke in a gruff voice, "You've been chosen by Echo, the fate of death and destruction, and myself, the fate of darkness. You will potentially be taking our place one day."

Dumbfounded, Clovis said, "What does this have to do with us?"

Feeling a sharp kick to his side, fate cursed, then said, "It was just you, but now you are tied together because he was a fool to attack you during that spell, and you a bigger one for doing the spell, to begin with."

Pinching his nose and dropping Clovis, he continued, "We can slow down the curse on you. We don't know how it works yet, so you two will have to help figure that out before killing all of us, got it?"

"I will try," Clovis responded, still confused by the rush of events that had just happened.

As he began to make sense of his situation, the world around him turned, and suddenly, both men were back in the quiet ruins. staring at Iathos before him, Clovis knew, without a doubt, that they were cursed. The knight's face was slashed open, the cut barely missing his eye. Black magic stained his fingertips, and his long black hair now held a few gray streaks. Looking down at his fingers, they, too, were stained black.

Throwing his hands up, Clovis said openly, "Let's not kill each other today, you need medical attention, and we need to go see the Vulocri before this gets worse." Wiggling his fingers, the prince put his hands down while waiting for the knight's response.

"Yeah," Iathos said with a curtness to his voice. "No magic until we can meet again. I don't like this a bit, but with the festival coming up, we will be busy."

Turning to walk away, the prince said, "Not a bad idea to be safe, but no promises. I'll see you in a few weeks; we will leave together after the festival." With that, the knight and wizard went different ways.

Still frowning down at his stained fingertips, Clovis let out another frustrated sigh. Lifting his head toward the ceiling, he said, "I don't like this." Pushing himself off the desk, the prince grabbed a change of clothes and cleaned up for the evening.

***

As morning rolled around, Clovis was woken by a loud banging on his door.

"Clovis, get up! We got to leave soon or we won't make it to Colkirk on time!" Mika yelled in between her banging. "It's a day's journey on the airship and I want to be early!" the princess continued.

"I am up, go away!" The tired prince groaned.

"Be ready in ten minutes!" Mika yelled back before knocking again.

A few hours later, Clovis found himself, Mika, and his parents standing in front of one of their family airships. This ship was called *Izzy* per the request of Mika and it was one of the Gorkem family's ships. The craft had the general shape of a water-based ship, with standard sails on the side of the ship shaped like a bird's wings and a fin sail on the back for maneuvering. *Izzy* was a magic-powered airship, while most other ships ran off of heat. This ship, however, had a kist crystal installed in the steering wheel, giving the ship access only to those whose genetics were within the crystal.

The *Izzy* was a boast of his parents' wealth. Anyone who saw it wouldn't doubt the money it came from. The ship was lined with a rifilium metal, a rare but malleable material with a surprising resistance to breaking. There are rumors that the fates themselves wore armor made from the metal when fighting the great demon Velron.

Boarding the ship, a tense silence followed the family as parents separated from their children, doing anything but conversing with one

5

another. Mika spoke up first after their parents left for one of the private rooms.

"Mom and Dad sure have been weird since they learned about your curse."

"Well, it's not every day your kid gets sucked into a void, gets cursed, and spits back out into the world within two minutes," Clovis stated sarcastically.

He stared at his sister pointedly. "I can't even use magic without my fingers turning black, so for now, magic use is a no-go. It's not like I asked for this to happen, so Mom and Dad will have to also deal with it."

"Maybe it's because your eyes are gold now. Maybe they are just scared you'll be the embarrassment for once instead of me." Mika laughed and poked her brother's shoulder. "It's going to be fine; you're the smartest wizard I know, so of course, things will turn out for the better!"

Clovis chuckled before speaking back, "I want to know what drug you're on because it's not sypher."

"Hey! It's not my fault you suck in the morning. You just need some happy juice."

"All right, get. Give me some space and I don't want any of your happy juice. I don't want to be sick again, I'm pretty sure you put fish scales in your last concoction."

"You'll never know."

As Colkirk emerged on the horizon, bathed in the gentle hues of a setting sun, the city's illumination gradually sparked to life. The sprawling expanse of golden sands stretched out, culminating in a majestic zenith at its heart, rivaling even the stature of a modest mountain.

The lower tiers bustled with activity, hosting vibrant market districts and the vital operations of coastal trade—a hub for imported treasures and the meticulous processes of water filtration and purification. On the desert-facing flank, artisans meticulously sifted the Oraburn sands, unearthing their arcane secrets, known for their profound healing properties.

In the middle reaches, stately bridges arched gracefully, facilitating the passage of merchants, while the more commonplace paths were paved with smooth limestone walkways and adorned with regal staircases. Encircling this district, fountains adorned with noble statues bestowed the gift of free water upon the city's populace, paying homage to the brave heroes of wars past.

High above, a more intimate enclave awaited, the upper echelon of Colkirk. Here, nestled amidst verdant gardens, the opulent mansions of the city's aristocracy stood sentinel, surrounding the regal palace of King Hawkore. His reign, marked by tireless efforts in preserving the unity of Eckris, earned him the mantle of a peerless sovereign. Amidst this lofty expanse, an intricate aqueduct network flowed, bridging the divide between the upper and lower realms, gifting life-sustaining waters through the city's ever-flowing fountains. The city itself was charming for being made of mostly sand, but it was where all the nations met a few times a year to celebrate their peace since the war in the Anu era.

"Put on a smile, Clovis. You can't let the people see you as weak," the prince's mother said sternly as she walked by.

Following their parents, Mika and Clovis put on smiles, waving at the crowd as they made their way to their carriages. Along the way, he felt an arm slip through his, and a sickly-sweet voice pierced his ears. "Long time no see, Prince."

"Vivian, let go of my arm, we are not a pair." Clovis's voice rang low and cold.

Vivian's tanned hand held tighter to his arm. "We can be, I'll treat you right."

"You'll put my money to waste just like the air you're using now."

"So cold, you know by now I like it when you play hard to get. It was love at first sight and you and I know it." Vivan pouted.

Stopping at Vivan's carriage, Clovis stared down at her; she was beautiful with her long black curly locks, brown eyes, and pouty lips. "However beautiful you may be, Lady Vivan, you are not for me. Love at first sight is a sad excuse to justify being with anyone, and your cunning is not for me but for my money. The whole scandal with Jasper, when we were twenty, proved that to me long ago."

"Honestly, Clovis, times have changed, you can't judge me for how I was five years ago."

"Oh, on the contrary, Viv, I can do whatever I want," Clovis smirked. "Now, get in your carriage."

Pouting, Lady Vivan got into her carriage, but before the door closed, she said, "One dance at the ball, and I will consider leaving you alone."

No, you won't.

Clovis closed the door and went straight for his respective carriage. Once inside, he slumped against the seat and ran his fingers through his hair. "Don't," he warned his little sister. A smile broke out on her face, but she remained quiet not wanting to let the coachmen hear any more gossip than they just had. Leaning his head against the carriage window, the memories from the ruins flashed through his head, and a pain pricked up his fingers. peering down, he saw the black start swirling, burning pain began running up his arms, and a voice rang in his head.

"Your trial begins soon, you will bear my mark now."

Hot flashes ran over his body. Falling forward, his sister caught him the best she could.

"Clovis, what's wrong, what's happening." Mika panicked.

"Curse," he grunted out. "Keep the carriage moving."

"Clovis?" Mika said, sounding scared.

"I'll be okay," Clovis hissed out before passing out.

When Clovis awoke, he was in the palace medical wing, his sister sitting beside him, bouncing her knee. Sitting up, he asked, "What happened after I passed out?"

Startled, Mika sprung from her chair and ran into her brother's arms to hug him. "I'm glad you're okay, I was terrified."

Taking a deep breath, she continued, "You've never had anything like that happen before, and I panicked, and your body was covered in shadows. It ate you up, then dug itself into your left arm."

"I hope he isn't possessed by something," Mika's voice whispered in his mind.

Pausing, the princess said, "You reached out for your spell book and it turned black, when you touched it your body returned to normal and you stopped moving. I thought you died and it was going to be my fault."

"I don't want you to die," her voice whispered again.

"Okay, Mika, calm down. I am alive, and it's not your fault. Please slow down when you talk; you are hard to keep up with," Clovis said calmly. He lifted his arm to find a king chess piece wrapped in thorns marked on his arm. He could feel three different magics swirling within it.

Focusing on his sister, the prince asked, "Where is the spell book?"

"Uh, well, it's over on the desk, covered. None of us could pick it up without getting attacked by some dark magic," Mika said shyly, showing her bruised arm to her brother.

"Mika? Why didn't you let a healer take care of you?" he said, taking the hurt arm into his hands.

"I am okay. I was more worried about you. I will get it taken care of," Mika said proudly, pulling her arm from him. "I am nineteen now. I can take care of myself, don't baby me."

"I'm not, but I am allowed to care about you," he said rudely.

"Yeah, I guess you can, but don't ruin my chances to have fun this weekend."

Letting out a laugh, Clovis lay back and said, "Okay, go get the doctor so I can leave this bed."

"Why am I hearing her voice in my head? Am I losing my mind?"

After a few minutes, Mika returned with her parents and the doctor. Sitting back up, Clovis prepared himself for the onslaught of questions the doctor would surely ask. He studied at his parents, who wore blank faces. The bit of emotion shown between the two was the wringing of his mother's hands. Pushing his hair out of his face, the prince turned to the doctor and said, "Well, am I dying?"

Laughing, the doctor replied, "I can't say for certain, but it is quite the nasty curse you have."

"Well, I could have told you that," Clovis stated.

Ignoring the prince's curtness, he continued, "You're free to go, you're in overall good health, though I would suggest seeing a Vulocri who is more suited to your problem."

Clovis finally took notice of the blue metal band around his neck, swinging his legs over the edge of the bed, Clovis asked, "You're a common healer; where would I find one of your rare healers?"

Smiling at the prince, he replied, "You can check at the temple in Three Crows Mountain, but I doubt you will find one of our rarest lingering there."

Glancing at his family and then back at the doctor, Clovis said, "I'll take my chances. Thank you, doctor."

Walking past everyone, Clovis headed to the hall with his family in tow. Trying to drown out their pestering about his well-being and mannerisms. As Clovis did, he came to the realization he had no idea where he was supposed to be staying. As he continued, lost in his thoughts, he felt a strong grip grab his arm and yank him to a stop.

"Clovis Gorkem, you will listen to your parents when they're speaking to you," his father's rasped voice said sternly.

Clovis took in the sight of his father; he had darker blond hair, blue eyes, and wrinkles that had made their way onto his face in recent years. gazing down at the slightly shorter man, Clovis responded coldly, "I have listened to the same speech with different wording for the last twenty-six years whenever something happened that neither of you likes."

"Clovis," his father warned.

Laughing, the prince pushed on, "You can't control everything, I know having your prodigal son cursed is an embarrassment to you, but shit happens. We'll be lucky if I live through it."

Cutting in, his mother spoke, "Clovis, you need to control your temper; that's what's embarrassing to this family. We can write your curse off as something non-problematic."

"Oh, I see. Yes, mother dearest, I shall continue to be your most perfect son." Bowing to his parents, he straightened himself and walked away.

Once again, he went to tune out the words of the people who called themselves his parents when he heard them say, "Mika, stay away from him."

A rush of anger came and went as he heard his sister say, "Clovis, wait up."

Slowing beside him, she reached over and squeezed his hand before silently showing him where their rooms were. As they reached the rooms, Mika finally spoke, "Clovis, you know I'm always on your side, you're the best brother."

Sighing, she continued, "Though they are right with this curse, you need to be more careful."

"What if you hurt someone?" her voice whispered.

Putting his hand on his sister's head, the prince said, "Thank you, Mika. Now, go have fun."

Giving Mika a soft push in one direction, Clovis took off in another, in need of fresh air. The prince strolled through the upper sector's enchanting gardens, a symphony of refined beauty. Limestone pillars rose proudly, cradling the ornate canopies that sheltered the walkways. Each pillar cradled baskets brimming with succulents and delicate lilac sunbonnets, lending a touch of vibrant elegance to the stone supports.

Beneath his feet, a velvety tapestry of moss replaced the traditional grass, a verdant expanse adorned with clusters of delicate white blooms. At the corners, where the protective eaves of the houses met the open air, rain barrels stood for both functionality and aesthetic consideration.

Majestic palm trees punctuated the mossy landscape, their towering fronds casting dappled shadows, a lush contrast against the pale stones and delicate flora. The fountains, their cascading waters a melodious rhythm, infused the air with a tranquil serenity, a soothing accompaniment to the prince's contemplative walk.

Surprisingly, no one had bothered the prince for most of his walk, though he knew it would only be a matter of time before someone would seek him out. His hands itched to grab his spell book after hearing what his sister said, but he knew it wasn't smart to do at the moment.

Perhaps I could sneak to the lower levels and find out some information on nasty curses, he thought.

Clovis knew his peace wouldn't last, though; as he turned to make his way toward the lower sectors, he found himself faced with three girls. All of them wore revealing dresses in deep purples and makeup to match. One reached out to grab his shirt and another for his arm. Taking a few steps back, Clovis spun on his heel and began walking as fast as possible. As he went, one of them called out, "Come on, prince, you know you love us."

"All I want is some peace," he grumbled to himself.

"You definitely won't find it in Colkirk." He heard a soft voice come from above him.

Clovis met eyes with a girl sitting on one of the moss-covered rooftops. She had purple hair, gray eyes, and dark olive skin, and wore an amused smile.

"You're a Matuen, how brave of you to be out in the open," the prince said to her.

"How observant of you."

"What are you here for, I know your kind isn't allowed within the upper rings of the city," Clovis said, crossing his arms.

"I am here for work," the Matuen said with a bright smile.

"Careful what your work is, otherwise, I may have to kill you," the prince said to her coldly.

Rising to her feet, the girl said, "Well, prince, I'd like to see you try."

Turning to walk away along the rooftops, she stopped and said, "If you want some peace, you'll find it on the second sector's mist street."

Still staring up at her, the prince asked, "Who are you?"

"Anything you want me to be, prince, for the right price."

Chapter Two

<u>Kilgi</u>

Colkirk, like many other cities, seemed to have a never-dying bustle. There were people everywhere, none seemed to be aware of their surroundings. Kilgi sat along the limestone rooftops, focusing on her current target. She was an upper-class woman named Fira. She had three daughters, a sister, no parents, and a husband. Kilgi was supposed to tail her to see if she was having an affair. Though a boring job, it still gave her money to live.

Kilgi was already wary of Fira because most nobles don't make their way to the lower sectors of Colkirk unless it's to cause trouble or for political campaigns. This woman, however, was down dressed and kept her head down as she walked to the street. Mist Street was a fairly popular place to go as a royal searching for "fun."

Tailing the woman, Kilgi saw her duck into the "The Misty Tortoise Hotel."

Interesting, Kilgi thought to herself.

Turning into the narrow alley beside the inn, Kilgi prepared herself to scale the building. Taking off with a run, Kilgi managed to shift her weight between the neighboring building to give her a good enough jump to catch the railing of one of the inn's balconies. Making her way up the building after that was easy. Landing her feet on the roof with a soft thud, Kigi surveyed the area.

Under the unrelenting blaze of the sun, the city gleamed, its limestone edifices casting forth a radiance unmatched by any in Eckris. Turning toward the beckoning doorway atop the rooftop, Kilgi stepped inside. The hotel's corridors boasted a regal opulence, crafted from the richness of dark oak juxtaposed against the cool expanse of white marbled floors. A procession of orbed lighting adorned the passageways, their gentle glow guiding the way.

Descending to the ground floor, Kilgi claimed a seat in the lobby, her presence already exuding an air of belonging. At its heart, a colossal stone fireplace commanded attention, its ancient stones echoing tales of time. Surrounding this focal point, a series of plush, dark leather couches formed an inviting enclave for guests to gather.

On the opposite side of the hearth, a refined restaurant beckoned, boasting tables of elegant wood and chairs swathed in supple leather, each meticulously spaced in a harmonious arrangement. Above, crystal chandeliers cast a shimmering cascade of light, illuminating the lobby with an aura of refined splendor, lending the hotel an unmistakable air of high-class distinction.

One of the lobby attendants came to Kilgi and asked, "Can I help you with anything?"

"No, I am all right, I am just waiting on my husband." Kilgi smiled at the woman.

"All right, have a good evening, ma'am," the attendant said before walking away.

Keeping herself busy, Kilgi decided to pick up one of the books on the table in front of her. About an hour into her reading, Kilgi spotted her target heading toward the hotel's restaurant. Behind her was an older gentleman with dark blond hair and blue eyes. He was wearing a simple shirt and buttoned it up fully to support the graceful tie he was wearing. On top of the shirt, he was wearing a classy vest with three buttons. It had a fairly deep V-line and was just narrow enough for the top to remain visible, adding another layer of elegance to the suit.

His hand was placed on her lower back, and as Kilgi suspected, she saw a ring on his finger; he was married. Standing, Kilgi went over to the pair, stopping in front of Fria.

I am certain that is King Gorkem.

"Excuse me, I saw your necklace and was wondering where you got such a beautiful piece?" Kilgi asked with a fake enthusiasm.

"Oh, well, I'm not sure it was a gift," she said, smiling up at the man behind her.

"Your husband got it for you, he must be wonderful," Kilgi said, Bowing to the man behind Fria.

"Yes, he is very wonderful," Fria said with a panicked smile on her face.

"I apologize for not introducing myself first. I am Nira Star, and you are?"

"Oh, I'm Fria, and this is Damien," she said, waving between the two.

"It was lovely meeting both of you; thank you for telling me about your necklace," Kilgi said with a wave before taking off.

After making her way back to her inn, Kilgi changed into more comfortable clothes. staring in the mirror before her, she sighed at the black wig on her head and ripped it off. She had on a dark green blouse with a deep V-neck, showing off the wasp tattoo on her chest, black trousers, and a leather belt to hold the outfit together. She tied back her tousled purple hair out of her face and slid on her matching boots. Gray eyes stared back at her in the mirror.

Time to get paid

Knowing her hair would cause a scene, Kilgi stepped out onto her balcony and climbed to the roof. She took the rooftops up to the third sector. The plant life was more prominent on this level. Moss covered most of the ground and rooftops; succulents grew in the moss and planters hung up everywhere. Kilgi could have sat and stared for hours at the natural beauty, but she had business to attend to.

As she returned to her client's home, she happened to hear a conversation between a woman and a man. Peering over the roof, she saw three women and a man with white-blond hair backing away.

"Come on prince, you know you love us," one of the women said, reaching out.

A prince? Kilgi thought to herself as she followed him.

"All I want is some peace," he grumbled to himself.

"You definitely won't find it in Colkirk," Kilgi answered.

Surprised, he said, "You're a Matuen, how brave of you to be out in the open."

"What are you here for, I know your kind isn't allowed within the upper rings of the city."

"I am here for work."

"Careful what your work is, otherwise, I may have to kill you."

"Well, prince, I'd like to see you try," she said, turning to walk away along the rooftops. "If you want some peace, you'll find it on the second sector's mist street."

"Who are you?"

Glancing over her shoulder, she said, "Anything you want me to be, prince, for the right price."

Disappearing out of view, Kigali knew she was sending the prince to find his cheating father. At least, she thought the man was his father; they had similar looks, wore royalty-tier clothing, and she was pretty sure King Gorkem's first name was Damien.

Dropping down onto Duke Lummington's balcony, Kilgi gave a soft knock. She saw his fat fingers grab the handle of the door and usher her inside.

"Well, tell me, is my wife unfaithful?" he asked, taking Kilgi's hands.

Taking her hands back, she said, "Yes, she is."

"That lying little—With who?"

"His name is Damien, I think he is King Gorkem, though I am not certain."

"You don't know what the king of Gorkem looks like?"

"I've only seen some of the Gorkem family in passing, so yes I think it is him, but I have already sent the prince to find out for himself," Kilgi said with a smile to the duke.

"You sent the prince to find out if it's his father or not?"

"Yes, but I need to go and follow him to make sure, so I will take another portion of my pay now, and for the extra work you can pay for my room at my current inn," Kilgi stated.

Nodding he said, "It shall be done, thank you."

"Of course."

Tears threatening to spill down the man's face, he let out a laugh and said, "If it is the king I'd like to hire you to kill one of them at the ball."

"Prices will vary for the lady and king."

***

Kilgi watched as the prince ran for his life from a crowd of people. Rolling her eyes, Kilgi dropped down from where she was and caught up to the prince before tackling him into an alley. Grabbing him by the collar, she hauled him to his feet.

"Run that way, take the first left, then a right. It will spit you out on Mist Street." Kilgi sighed.

He wore a confused expression, but Kilgi ignored him and stepped out into the street and yelled, "Oh my fates! Prince Gorkem just ran that way." Pointing in the opposite direction.

Turning to face the prince as the crowd ran by, Kilgi shooed the prince and took off herself.

Back on track, she thought to herself.

Putting herself back on track, she made her way to the mist street, only to find the prince sitting on a bench as he owned it. With his head toward the sky, he dropped it to meet Kilgi's stare from across the street. Pointing at her, he gestured for her to come to him, to which she stood still. Frowning, the prince then pointed to a restaurant down the street while raising his eyebrow at her. Kilgi shook her head no and entered a dark alley down the road.

"You know it's not wise to disobey royalty," the prince said, entering the alleyway.

"It's also not wise to walk the streets without a disguise as royalty," Kilgi said, rolling her eyes.

Walking closer, the prince said, "What do you want? you led me here for a reason."

"You said you wanted some peace, this street is a getaway for most nobles and royals."

"Yes, most nobles and royals know that by the time they're seventeen."

Teasingly, Kilgi said, "Oh you're an experienced man."

"You're not funny, tell me what you want. Sex, money, information, to kill me?"

"Yes, absolutely, I brought you to a street for secret affairs and black market trades to kill you," she said, with sarcasm.

"Quit playing with me, because I promise you won't like it if I play with you."

"Here, I heard you were a playboy. I need you to tell me if a man at the hotel up the street is your father or not," she said with a more serious tone.

"What?" he asked, confused.

"Yes, you heard me right, I was hired to tail someone, and your father may be involved; I need to know if he is or not. If he is, then I'm backing out because I'm not dumb enough to get involved with royalty more than necessary."

"How much money?"

"Enough for me to pay off my race debt and be declared legally free."

"I thought the race debt was abolished across Eckris."

"Pfft no, if you're not a Krystru then you're anything but holy. Fate forbid, if you're born with any Matuen blood then you're evil itself. Any person born a Matuen is given a race debt until it's paid; we are not allowed to be a part of society at all, and are legally allowed to be hunted down."

"Yes, I know the law, Though it should have been abolished unless it was never published," he said, puzzled.

"It doesn't matter, prince, I need to know if your father is involved in my work or not."

"Fine, but after this, you will be answering me."

"Information for information, that's how this works," she replied.

"Fine, where am I going?" he asked.

"Nowhere, they're coming now."

They watched as Lady Fira and King Gorkem walked out of a shop, Fira holding a few bags. Kilgi glanced over at the prince and watched his stone-cold face dip with anger. He went to move, but Kilgi grabbed his arm.

"Not now," she whispered.

Backing off the prince, Kilgi pulled him further into the alley. Tilting his head to the sky, the prince seemed to have quite a few different emotions filtered across his face. Eventually, his gaze landed on Kilgi, and a deep frown crossed his face.

"Who hired you?" he asked, coming closer to her.

"I can't tell you," she said, taking a step back.

Stopping right in front of her, he said, "It was the duke. He will ask you to kill one of them if he knows the truth, then probably have you killed," the prince said.

"Back off, prince," Kilgi said, putting a hand against his chest. *Please, I don't want to kill anyone.*

"You'll come to work for me from this moment forward, or I will send people to kill you for spying on my family," he said, leaning into her hand.

"Must be just like your daddy."

"I didn't hear no, assassin."

I'm only an assassin sometimes.

"You will find I'm pretty hard to kill, prince. Make me an offer I can't refuse, otherwise, I'll be sure to send your assassin's dead bodies to your doorstep," Kilgi spat back at the prince.

"Perhaps I'll kill you myself."

I somehow don't doubt that. You have the same expression as Oliver on your face.

Taking a step back, Kilgi began walking to the other end of the alley. The prince stood and watched with a frown on his face. throwing a glance back over her shoulder, Kilgi did the only sensible thing and flipped him off.

Anger flashed across the prince's face, and Kilgi all but smiled at his anger before disappearing. As she walked, all she could think about was how she was going to get away from being hunted down by a royal family. The prince probably wasn't lying to her about the duke meaning to kill her, he probably knew him better, so her solution to the problem would have to be found alone.

***

Returning to Duke Lummington's, Kilgi verified everything she knew after accepting her payment. Lummington had tried to hire her to assassinate his wife over the king because her price for a king's head was too high. After a discussion, Kilgi politely declined the offer, which enraged the duke.

"You sniveling, little beast," he hissed at her.

"Duke, you'll have to mind your manners, you and I both know what comes of killing a royal. I will be pinned for the kill and not you." Kilgi sighed.

"I have paid you quite a sum already! You will do as I say, I am your master."

"Watch yourself, duke, They won't blink an eye at your death either."

"Think you can stop me, little assassin. I'll drag you around the streets in chains to prove how much I own you now," he seethed.

Quickly, the duke lunged for the assassin, only for Kilgi to sidestep him, grab his wrist, and kick his knees from under him. Crashing to the ground, Lummington squirmed around, trying to right himself. During his flailing, Kilgi crossed the room and picked up one of his heirloom swords. She inspected it with a frown before meeting the duke's eyes.

"Call for your guards, duke," Kilgi said with a hard stare.

Fear laced his voice as he called for the guards. Kilgi was met with three Greoll guards, they had varied different yellow skin tones, eyes like sand, and swords that were bought for cheap. They all took fighting stances and warned Kilgi to back down.

"Help me make it seem like he killed himself, and we will split his valuables that won't be missed," Kilgi suggested.

Focusing on each other, one guard spoke, "No one knows what happens tonight?"

"My lips are sealed if yours are." Kilgi smiled.

"You're a Matuen, though; we can't trust your kind," the first guard said.

"Honestly, have you met another one outside of me, my life is more on the line than yours no matter what right now." Kilgi rolled her eyes.

"No, we haven't, if we trust you and you betray us—" He was cut off.

"I'll slit my own throat first, we help each other get by and go our ways, deal?" Kilgi said.

All while the conversation was happening, the duke had crawled his way to the balcony. Seeing the duke she followed him, grabbing him before he could call out for help. Shoving him over the railing, he hit the ground with a sickening *thwack*.

Disgust came over her face as she watched his body twitch and still as blood poured from his head. Turning around she saw the guards staring at her with shock on their faces.

"Go on, I got what I need, make it quick then report the body as a suicide," she said coldly.

Kilgi lifted herself to the rooftops and laid down, soaking in what was left of the setting sun. The festival was supposed to start tonight, and Kilgi was tired from working all day. She heard the bustle of people heading to the ball and the cries of guards trying to hide Duke Lummington's body from the public. She listened to them talk about waiting until the ball was over to say anything because of how snobbish the nobles and royals were. A heaviness overtook Kilgis eyes, letting them fall closed, her thoughts wandered back to Prince Gorkem. He was someone to watch out for. He seemed scarily intelligent and willing to be a monster, something Kilgi respected but feared. Though she wondered what curse he bore that his eyes were a deep golden color.

"Wake up," a voice said.

Kilgi's eyes snapped open; the sun had gone down, and lanterns lit the streets. Sitting up, Kilgi let her eyes adjust to the nighttime setting. Airships floated above the city, music floated up from the lower levels, and more came from the palace to her right.

"Get inside," the voice warned.

"What?" Kilgi said, getting to her feet, adrenaline kicking in.

"Get inside," it warned again.

"Who—" Kilgi was cut off as a roar echoed over the music.

The assassin's eyes widened as darkness crashed over the lower levels like a wave; what light was there was suddenly gone. Without a second of hesitation, Kilgi turned and ran for the palace ahead of her. The wave of darkness sounded more like hissing instead of waves as it came closer to the higher sectors. Dropping to the ground, she crawled toward the doors and watched as the guards readied themselves against her.

"Get inside! We're under attack," Kilgi all but yelled at them before turning off to scale one of the trellises up to the second floor of the palace.

Disregarding her, the guards instead raced after her in pursuit. Kilgi, however, didn't glance back; the roaring of the darkness was starting to make her head pound. Rolling over the balcony, she watched as the guards below her had been swallowed by the wave of darkness. Scrambling to her feet, Kilgi ran inside and slammed the glass doors behind her; as she did, the wave smashed against the glass.

She saw red, white, and yellow eyes staring back at her. The monsters moved as if they were trying to free themselves from something else, but Kilgi held the doors as tight as she could. Turning her back to the monsters, she continued to try her best to keep the doors shut; her focus bouncing all around her, the royals and nobles were staring at her.

"What are you doing?" a male voice asked, parting the crowd.

Addressing the king, Kilgi said, "We are under attack, Your Majesty, a wave of darkness came over the city, can't you see the monsters behind me?"

"No," he said, frowning at Kilgi.

Peeking over her shoulder, she saw the monsters were gone. A new fear came over her because she was a hated race standing in the epicenter of Eckris with the king of Colkirk staring her down. She stood up from holding the door and put her hands up in the air.

This is bad; everyone is in some kind of danger.

"I mean no harm. I promise I am not lying," she said, not lowering herself.

"I think you shifted into a monster to scare everyone," he said, raising a hand for guards to take her away.

Dropping her hands, Kilgi said, "Only full-bloods can shift; very rarely can half-bloods. I'm half, and I have the money to pay my debt."

"Too bad, you can pay it off again for causing a scene at my ball." He sneered.

As the king finished his sentence, a loud crash came from the other side of the ballroom. People were smashed or flung to the floor by a piece of rubble. Kilgi stumbled but managed to catch herself at the sudden quaking. Briskly making her way to the king, she dragged him to his feet and stared into his eyes.

"I told you, we got to get you out of here." Kilgi panicked.

"Take him somewhere safe. My life doesn't mean much to you, so I'll try to do what I can. If you're lucky, maybe I'll die." Kilgi laughed.

Unsure, the knight nodded but took the king. Making her way through the now panicked crowd, Kilgi stopped to pick up a girl with white-blond hair, a light blue dress, and icy eyes to match. She seemed a little rattled, but overall, all right.

"I'm okay, my brother," she said, fear rattling her voice.

"Your brother is fine," a familiar voice growled at the girl.

"Iathos?" Kilgi questioned, turning to face the knight.

His now scarred face and green eyes stared back at her in shock. "Kilgi?"

"We can catch up later, we have some problems right now," Kilgi rushed out.

"Yeah, no kidding, pass me the princess, I'll escort her to safety. You work on finding the prince, as much as I hate him. His magic is probably going to help us out of something like this," the knight stated calmly.

"You mean Gorkem? What about—" Kilgi said but was cut off.

"Yes, Gorkem, and they're fine, I just can't find Alton," he replied.

"Guys, I'm okay, go find Prince Alton," Mika said, moving off of Kilgi.

Nodding at each other in understanding, Kilgi and Iathos parted ways. Mika was hot on her trail as she picked through the crowd. Suddenly, a rush of darkness came at the girls, knocking them both back. Kilgi took the brunt of the attack, and as quickly as it came, it was gone again. Letting out a hum of frustration, she drew her double weapon, splitting it into two.

"Stay behind me," Kilgi stated.

"I think we need magic," Mika said back.

As another wave came, and this time, Kilgi lunged forward, slashing upward into the darkness. Multiple hisses rang out from the shadow, and suddenly, they were splitting off from the main shadow.

"I hope you can use magic princess," Kilgi stuttered.

"Hehe, yeah," Mika said nervously.

Another attack rushed them, Kilgi sidestepped the wolf-like monster and ran her blade through its neck before pulling it out and slashing up the belly of another with both blades. Kicking the monster back, Kilgi pushed forward through the squirming darkness.

"Stay close, call for your brother," Kilgi said calmly.

"CLOVIS!"

"This way!" The girls heard him call back.

Turning to the left, Kilgi began hacking her way through the monsters. Shortly, she was met with a radiant bubble surrounding the prince. His hair was slightly flowing, and his arms were stretched out in front of a purple spell book.

"Clovis let us in," Mika said, pressing her fingers against the magic.

Kilgi watched as his sister's fingers passed through, and without hesitation, she stepped through too. His gaze snapping in their direction, she watched as shock crossed Clovis's face.

"You have any idea what's happening or how to stop it?" Kilgi asked as Mika crashed into her brother's side, crying.

Wrapping one arm around her, Clovis answered, "No."

"Fuck," Kilgi whispered.

"Does the city not have any defense against attacks?" Kilgi said with frustration.

"Not anything for something like this."

"What about the Colkirk Historical Building? They should have something, right?"

"Stop asking me dumb questions," he growled.

"At least I am thinking!"

"Watch your words, I am protecting you right now," he said coolly.

"Tsk, I'll figure it out myself then. I have people to protect too, asshole."

"Have fun." He waved her off.

Turning to leave, Mika's voice rang out, "Don't your weapons work on the monsters, we can work together."

"Sorry, princess, but your brother would rather see my dead body at the edge of his baby bubble," Kilgi said with half a bow.

"Wait—" she called as she stepped out of the bubble.

As she did, a sudden flash of light burst across the room. Clovis's eyes widened at the familiarity of the blast, but Kilgi's body disappeared with it. Ringing filled Kilgi's ears, and white flooded her vision. Her back was on the ground, and she felt like a weight had been pressed down on her chest. Opening her eyes, she found herself staring at a girl crouched over her. She had light green hair, solid yellow eyes, dark skin, and gold flakes that seemed to sparkle all along her like freckles that glowed.

Leaning down, the woman spoke with enthusiasm, "Hello, Kilgi Mohlo, I am Nell, fate of light. I have come to ask you to join our trial."

Still coming too, Kilgi asked, "What?"

"Oh, right, big blast," Nell said, waving her hands above her head, mimicking an explosion. "I am the fate of light, and if you accept, you will gain access to my power and will face trials to take my place if you are worthy. If at any point you abuse my power, die, or betray me, these powers shall be revoked, and I will remove you from this world."

Fear pulsed through Kilgi, and she moved to sit up, only to be pushed back down by one of Nell's fingers.

"I don't understand. You're a fate; why would I replace you? Why me? What is happening?"

"Easy. I can only live for so long. Our lives are prolonged, but not forever. You are clever and will create balance with our other players. An ancient evil has begun to make its way back into the world. We need younger, more suited people to take over. Otherwise, we will lose," Nell said, still smiling.

"You are plenty young, and I won't. I was born unfortunate," Kilgi said, relaxing against the ground.

"I am almost six hundred; I am one of the oldest. Not all of us will be replaced at once, so those chosen will still have guidance even after those of us who are dying are gone.

Standing up, Nell reached down and pulled Kilgi to her feet. Reaching out her hand for a shake, Nell said, "Will you try, or die now?"

Reluctantly, Kilgi took her hand. "I don't think I'm ready to die, my brothers still need me."

"Good, welcome to the trials, my queen. To use my powers all you have to do is say, 'Nell, bring me light,' and my power will flow to you."

"How will it work?" Kilgi asked.

"However you need it to, use your imagination. I will be judging you. Oh! You can't tell the others everything yet, they're not ready." Nell winked.

Her vision turned white again, and when she blinked, she was in an empty room with two blond-haired royals staring at her. Inspecting her body, she saw her blades glowing with white flames.

"What just happened?" Kilgi asked, the royal siblings.

Taking a step forward, Clovis raised his hand in Kilgi's direction. "Stand down."

"What happened!" Kilgi yelled at him.

What is happening?

"Stand down, Kilgi," Iathos called out from behind her.

To her other side, she saw Iathos with his blade raised to her, Clovis in front of her. Monsters could be heard roaring in the distance, some from below on the castle grounds.

"Now's not the time, boys, our lives are at stake," Kilgi said, worried.

"You can't do magic, Kilgi. You just blew up a room of monsters and then stood still like a statue with white flames pouring out of every orifice on your face," Iathos replied, still holding his blade to her.

"For fate's sake, we can figure this all out later, maybe the fates are helping us!" Kilgi yelled.

"Do you have any ideas on how to stop this massacre?" she asked, raising her blades to both boys.

Staring Kilgi down, Iathos finally gave in. "I read about some runes that could do a mass protection ward, there is one in the historical building, the palace, and in the first bank."

"A myth?" Clovis scoffed.

"Shut it. We have a start," Kilgi said, coldly.

"Are we seriously going to bank-stopping magical monsters with a myth?" Clovis asked.

"Yes," Mika said, moving away from her brother.

"Okay, Iathos, you find the palace rune, I'll go for the bank, and Mika you take the historical building," Kilgi said, seething her swords.

"Okay," Iathos and Mika said in response.

"I'll provide support and protection." Clovis sighed. "I'm not useful in a close combat fight, so the best I can do is make sure no one dies yet," he continued.

"Good enough, prince," Kilgi said.

"Let's not waste any more time," Iathos replied.

Breaking apart, Kilgi stepped to the edge of the now gaping hole in the palace wall. Squatting down, Kilgi motioned for the princess to climb onto her back.

"I d-don't want to slow you down," Mika stuttered.

"You won't. It will be faster, and I doubt you are a fighter. I can protect you this way," Kilgi said.

Hesitantly, Mika climbed onto Kilgi's back. Glancing back at Iathos, Kilgi smiled. "Race you." She laughed.

"You're on." He smiled before turning to run.

Dropping off the second story, Mika's screams filled Kilgi's ears. Calling on Nell's power, Kilgi watched in amazement as little stepping stones of light made their way across the sky for her. The princess's pale fingers dug into her shoulders as she clung on for dear life; the smell of hazelnut filled her nose. Kilgi took a deep breath and let her light steps fade as she descended to the ground.

That wasn't so bad for a first magic use.

"Be ready, princess, we're about to hit the ground," Kilgi warned.

Mika's hands squeezed tighter as Kilgi landed, and suddenly, they were going much faster. The downhill run was painful on Kilgi's back, with the princess as her package to deliver.

"There are monsters ahead, can you hold on without me supporting you?" Kilgi asked softly.

Mika shook her head yes to the princess's neck. Letting go of her legs, Kilgi felt Mika wrap her legs around her tighter. Drawing her blades, Kilgi focused her new-found power on the blades. They flickered, letting her know it probably wouldn't last long. Holding each blade lined with her elbows, she ducked under the swing of the first shadow monster and narrowly missed the second one's kick. Crossing her sword's blade down in front of her, the monsters screeched at the contact with the white flames. The blow pushed her backward a few feet; they had a power like no other.

"Careful not to get hit, princess, one blow could break our bones," Kilgi said grimly.

"I can try to use my magic," she whimpered.

Preparing for the next attack, a sudden surge of lightning cracked down on the monsters. They sizzled and dissipated into the night air. Staring in the direction of the palace, Kilgi knew the prince had used his magic.

"Let's keep going. Gather your courage, princess, I'm dropping you. The historical building is at the end of the lane, literally."

"Okay." Mika nodded.

"You got this. Otherwise, more people will die." Kilgi nodded in return.

Taking off in the direction of the bank, Kilgi felt a weight sinking in her stomach. Something wasn't right. Regardless, she continued, trying her best to ignore the dead bodies littering the ground. The bank was on the first level. She had about two miles to get to her destination.

Five minutes at most if I sprint and have no obstacles, Kilgi thought to herself as she sprinted down the steep ramp used for merchant travel between levels. Flying around the ramp's bend, she noticed a huge gap where part of the road used to be. Breathing deeply, she kept on and leaped over the gap, barely making the jump. Her feet tripped up, and she ended up rolling down part of the ramp.

Letting out a few coughs of pain, Kilgi climbed to her feet, taking in her surroundings. The lower levels were burning, and people were running for the water. Going to take off running again, Kilgi heard a loud whistle of wind; glimpsing to her right, a giant hunk of rubble came hurtling toward her. Ducking, she was thrown off her feet again by its impact, shards of rock leaving a few cuts on her.

Get up, get up, get up, Kilgi chanted in her head as another rock crashed into the last one, rattling her body against the ground. This time, however, the rock shards didn't hit her, and when she opened her eyes, a white bubble surrounded her.

Clovis, she thought and crouched low to keep out of her attacker's sight.

"I need a distraction, read my mind and give me one, you stupid prince," Kilgi whispered.

As if reading her mind, another crack of lightning crashed down through the sky, and a screech echoed across the ruined city. Getting up, Kilgi took off running again, though this time, she leaped off the ramp and took a hard landing on the roofs below her. Scaling down the building, Kilgi was finally on the lower-level streets. Monsters were everywhere; some Krystrusian magic users barely held some of the monsters at bay.

She went over to them, and she joined their fight against the sickly-looking monsters. They stayed like that for a few minutes, giving what was left of the civilians a chance to run for some sort of safety.

"Listen, we need to move this fight to the bank on First Street. there is a rune there that will protect the city, the prince of Aeberuthey said so himself," Kilgi said, hoping using the prince's name would give her the help she needed.

"It's do or die," one of them spoke.

"It's a Matuen, it's probably on the monster's side," the second one accused.

"She helped us," said the woman.

"There is no time, either follow or don't," Kilgi grumbled and took off in the direction of the bank.

Two of the group followed behind her, slowing her pace slightly so they could keep pace, the makeshift group managed to work its way to the bank. The building sat with half the roof caved in and a giant ball of shadows with tentacles hovered above it. Flames licked the edges of the neighboring buildings; however, there were no monsters with this one.

"It's strong, it has no buddies, be careful," Kilgi whispered.

Both raised their hands, ready to provide her with a distraction. Letting their spells loose, Kilgi took off running in the building's direction. The monster, however, grabbed up one of the spell casters and flung them across the city, Kilgi's eyes widened with surprise at its lightning speed. Reaching the edge of the building, Kilgi was almost through an opening in the wall when a warm, wet tendril wrapped around her ankle and yanked. All the air in her lungs was sucked out as she flew up above the city. Her stomach dropped as she plummeted back down.

"*Use my power,*" Nell's voice whispered.

Kilgi turned her head to see a black tendril speeding toward her. Drawing her swords, she lit them with Nell's magic and sliced through the tendril. Straightening herself out, Kilgi threw her hands out to create slanted platforms for her to make a landing without shattering her bones. Bouncing back and forth between the footholds, Kilgi found herself dodging tendrils. As she reached the ground, one hit her side.

Air rushed from her lungs as she crashed and rolled against some of the rubble. Quiet surrounded her as her ears pulsed from the blood rush. Spitting some blood out, she sat up. Taking in her surroundings, she noticed the monster had been nice enough to throw her into the building she needed.

Standing, Kilgi winced. *Yup, broke my arm.*

Looking around, Kilgi saw the bank was surprisingly more intact than it presented from the outside. The massive vault door still held up on the far side of the building, and some of the lights were still on. However, the number of dead bodies on the ground was concerning. If Kilgi had to guess, no one made it out of this building alive.

The feeling in her stomach came rushing back as a tendril reached through the building and picked up a podium.

"*That's it,*" Nell whispered again.

"I don't like this, Nell," Kilgi muttered.

Making her way outside, Kilgi watched as the monster went to fling the rune when a streak of purple suddenly pierced the monster's body. Letting out a loud screech, its body disappeared. Watching the podium fall, Kilgi's instincts kicked in, and she used Nell's magic and ran into the sky after the falling item. Catching it, the heavyweight nearly dropped her. On instinct, with a thought, she blasted herself with a streak of light into the next building.

Coming to a stop, Kilgi slammed her hands down on the podium and said, "I don't have magic, but Nell, make it work, please."

A sudden blue flash shot up from the podium, that rapidly turned into a wave and rushed across the city. Monsters began to disappear by the dozens, and Kilgi found herself flopping down on her back.

"I'd be good never doing that again," Kilgi whispered as pain flared in her lungs.

Chapter Three

Ehiliana

"Ehiliana, you're late, again," Marcus said, drawing everyone's attention to the Irkafenian woman.

"Sorry, the wards took longer than normal to put up," Ehiliana said with a blush.

Taking her seat, the meeting had resumed. Marcus went over the security detail for the Colkirk Historical Foundation during the festival, new additions to the building, and work schedules for the next few weeks. Ehiliana, knowing her luck, already knew she was working the festival weekend.

"I told you we'd be working," Ehiliana said with half a laugh to Regina as they left the meeting.

"Seriously, what does Marcus have against us!" Regina said, throwing her hands in the air.

"Well, we're female and not Krystru, so if we're playing favorite's bingo, we'd have to be Peter to win."

Regina stopped and bent, laughing. "He probably has a bed under Marcus's desk to get away with everything he does."

Lightly shoving Regina Ellie said, "Come on, our shift starts tonight. We should get some rest."

"I'd make sure you're on time, ladies," Peter said, appearing in the doorway.

"Move it, Peter," Ehiliana said, glaring at the krystrian man.

"Marcus has been trying to fire you. If you show up late, it could be your job," he said, tussling his hair.

"Since when do you care?" Ehiliana quipped.

"Oh, I don't, it's just an important weekend."

"Must be pretty cozy under Marcus's desk; too bad that's the farthest you'll ever get.

Grabbing her wrist, Peter turned to meet her wide eyes. "What do you mean, Ehiliana?"

"I mean, no matter how much you suck up to Marcus, you will never be anything else than his lackey," Ehiliana said, removing her hand from his grasp.

The man now stood over her, staring up into his dark slanted eyes, strands of his long dark locks hung framing his face. He wasn't the prettiest man to look at.

Smiling, he leaned in and said, "Marcus is just another obstacle, but no matter what, you are still under my supervision. Perhaps, in the future, you will regard me with more respect."

Feeling Peter's breath against her face, Ehiliana stood her ground.

"I have worked here for nearly ten years, worked my ass off, and you walked into this office and got the job I have been working for, simply because you are Krystru."

Taking a breath, she stepped closer to him and kept talking, "I understand that my race is supposed to atone for the betrayal they made back in the Anu era, but that was almost four hundred years ago. How much longer do we have to crawl on our hands and knees just to get by because no one will stand up for us despite all the dirty work we do for you now."

"Are you done?" Peter said, his lips almost brushing her.

"No, I am not. If you surpass Marcus, I think you will treat us worse, considering you are already making us work double shifts. I have little faith you will ever be something great because you can't even respect my personal space, Peter," Ehiliana said, never breaking eye contact.

"I couldn't care less about your race, I don't like you because you're my competition."

Surprise filtered across Ehiliana's face for a moment. "You're an asshole," she said before taking her leave, Regina in tow.

"Seriously, he just thinks he can come into my space and act like that," the bookkeeper huffed.

"I thought he was gonna kiss you." Regina laughed out.

"Yeah right, like I'd let him."

"What, tall, lean, and a bit of an asshole isn't your type?"

"Think more brown, curly hair, two sets of solid green eyes, green fingertips to match, and named Regina," Ehiliana said, raising her eyebrows before taking her girlfriend's hand.

"I see, it seems Peter has some competition."

"Not even a little," Ellie said, kissing Regina's cheek. "I'll see you tonight, get some good sleep," Ellie said, this time giving Regina a quick peck on the lips.

***

As nightfall hit, the city came to life, and the festival finally reached full swing. Ehiliana reached her destination just a couple of seconds short of Regina. Both girls sighed, walking up the stairs, they put their hands up to unlock the doors. However, as they waited, Ehiliana saw a crack in the door.

"Regina, be on your guard, something isn't right. The door is open," Ellie whispered to her girlfriend.

Pulling out her pocketknife, Ellie slowly toed the door open. Regina followed close behind, a trembling hand on Ellie's back. The building was dark, and the only lighting was from the glass dome. Moonlight poured through, dimly lighting the destroyed structure.

"The building seemed just fine from the outside, how has no one noticed this?" Ellie said quietly.

"We should leave, something doesn't feel right," Regina said.

"You can wait outside."

"No, I can't let you go alone," Regina said, unsure of herself.

The two Irkafens carefully made their way through the building, reaching the stairs to the lower levels. They could hear water running, electricity buzzing, and things falling. Steading her breath, Ehiliana picked up the pace and descended the stairs. As the light shifted, she closed her main eyes and opened her smaller set. These eyes set right below her main pair, though slightly farther apart; these eyes gave her the ability to see in the dark.

"We need to watch out for Jack and Lena. They had watch before us," she whispered.

She only got a confirmation squeeze on her arm from Regina. Pressing forward, Ellie heard noises coming from the third sublevel stairwell; it sounded like someone shouting while running from a monster.

Coming into view, Ehiliana saw a tall, lanky man moving out of the doorway. He was missing an arm, and two of his six eyes were hanging from his head.

"Fucking run," he shouted.

Turning around, Ellie pushed Regina. "Go, he said to fucking run, go!"

Roaring and clattering echoed as they ran toward the first level. Jack's labored breathing slowed Ellie down as she tried to grab around his waist to help him run.

"Regina, go get help, Jack is dying," Ellie said, panic quivering in her voice.

Nodding, Regina sprinted for the exit, leaving the two on the second sublevel. Slowing Jack down, she turned toward the armory, hoping there was a first-aid kit inside.

"Jack, what do you mean there are monsters?"

Searching for something to use as a tourniquet for Jack's arm, she heard a loud crash come from outside the room. Seconds later, the door flung open, and a short blond girl ran in, closing the door behind her.

"Everyone, shut up if you want to live," the girl whispered loudly.

Surprised, she said, "You're the princess of Aeberuthey."

Sputtering came from Jack as the girls glanced at one another, and they made their way over to him. Lifting his good arm to Ehiliana, he sat a pair of keys in her hands.

"They lied," Jack said aloud.

His hand fell, and his body stilled. With no time to think, both girls jumped when they heard a scream.

"Regina." Ehiliana gasped. "We need to save her."

Picking up one of the bows from the armory, Ehiliana addressed the princess. "I'm not sure why you're here, but you will help fix this, or so help me; there will be no law or magic to save you from me if she dies.

Swallowing and nodding, the princess turned to face the door. "My name is Mika. Let's save your friend, then talk," she said as she opened the door.

Together, they took off in the direction of Regina's screaming. The brunette Irkafen clung to the stairwell railing, kicking at what looked like an inky octopus.

"It's magic, we can't fight it without a magic item," Mika said.

That's just great.

"We don't have one, so do some magic, or something," she quipped coldly, making her way to the monster.

Swiping her bow at the shadow monster, it turned to face her, letting go of her girlfriend. Taking some steps back to give Regina space to run, Ehiliana aimed her walk toward the princess.

"My magic isn't stable!" Mika yelled. "You need to run away from it now!"

Without any delay, Ehiliana turned and ran away from Regina and the princess. Howling loudly, the monster gave chase, taking everything with it. Books and shelves slammed to the ground as she ducked and weaved away from the monster.

Aiming her spell at the monster, Mika threw her hand forward, drawing a sigil.

She yelled in a language she didn't know. An explosion of blue light came from her hand, and the shadow screamed at its brightness. As the light died down, both girls stared at the monster, now trapped in a giant bubble. Huge bubbles floated around, and all three girls looked at one another.

"There is a rune somewhere in your building, it's meant to protect the city if something like this happens," Mika said, waving her arms, "That's why I am here."

Helping Regina up, Ellie said, "Let's go then, princess I don't want to stick around."

"It's worse outside,"

Making their way up the stairs, Regina finally spoke, "How come we didn't notice beforehand? On the way here, I mean."

"Someone is probably using skilled illusion magic if I had to guess," the princess replied.

Silence fell over the group as they made their way to the top level. They could hear the screaming and howling of monsters as they neared the surface. Helping Regina sit down behind a flipped table, Ellie made quick work of wrapping her wounds with scraps of her shirt.

"Thank you, dear, I'll wait here. To help Princess Mika," Regina said, pulling her in for a hug.

"Stay safe." Ehiliana hugged back.

"Okay, princess, I'm sure the rune you're searching for is the one under our spell book stand for building security," The bookkeeper said.

"Following your lead Ehiliana," the princess replied.

Ready for business, both girls took off running for their main destination. While running, Mika gave Ehiliana instructions on how the rune works. However, things got messy fast, as if knowing what the girls were doing, more shadow monsters appeared.

"Keep going, I'll try not to spell you," the princess yelled.

Running side by side now, Mika spread both her hands, calling out the spell from before. Bubbles came pouring from her hand, eating up every shadow thing in their path. Closing in on the bookstand, both girls came to a halting stop. Slamming her hands down on the book, Ehiliana shoved it to the side, letting it fall to the floor. Still holding the stand, she watched as Mika put her hands down on the rune and said a spell in the same language as before.

"I hope that my magic works this time." Mika breathed out.

This time?

Peering over at the bookkeeper, Mika smiled at her.

"You're very pretty," the princess said.

"Thank you—" Ehiliana's reply was cut off.

Blinding light surrounded both girls, tingles ran up their bodies, and buzzing filled their ears. In the chaos enveloping them, Mika and Ehiliana managed to grab each other's hands. When the light died down, they opened their eyes. Ehiliana found herself in a big wildflower field, with white rook and bishop chess pieces sitting before them.

"I think I messed up again," Mika squeaked out.

"Okay, what is wrong with your magic?" Ehiliana said, throwing her hands up.

"I wish I knew. It's always been this way." Plopping down to the ground, Mika said, "You're the only person I've met who's been rude to me."

"If things were different, perhaps I would be nicer, but something bad happened. We have no idea what is going on. My friend Jack is dead, Lena is missing and now Regina is all alone."

Pausing,"

She narrowed all four of her solid pink eyes at the princess. "Perhaps if you could use your magic, we'd be better off, but I guess being a princess means being lazy in every aspect."

Tears pricked at the princess's eyes as she stood and muttered to herself. Ehiliana watched as she walked over to the rook piece and said, "Please take me back to my brother."

Bending down, the princess grabbed the rook and vanished.

"No, no, no!" Ehiliana's hands flew to her hair, panic setting in. Tears flowed down her eyes, and she fell to her knees. She cried for what seemed like ages, common sense said to grab the bishop, but fear kept her from the action.

That bitch just left me here.

Suddenly, the wind picked up around her, and a voice that carried in the wind spoke, "Make your choice now, Ehiliana Pinkali, for your life, is on the line."

Snapping her head up to the bishop's piece, Ellie scrambled to her feet and ran for the bishop. Grabbing the piece, a rush of warmth overtook her, and the world spun. When the spinning came to a stop, Ehiliana found herself back at the stand in the historical building, Regina screaming her name as a thick black tendril slammed into her side. Ehiliana flew across the room, slamming into some of the flipped tables and rolling until she came to an agonizing stop.

Pain blurred her vision, and everything sounded fuzzy. Slowly, she tried to stand, and as she did, a heavy weight slammed down onto her back. Blood spilled from her mouth and dripped as the tendril hoisted her up by her leg. Hanging upside down, she made out a blurry black blob. Silence fell over the room as she regained focus, and she could feel the monster lifting her higher. Letting out a loud screech, the monster whipped Ehiliana backward and then threw her forward.

"WAKE UP!" a strong feminine voice screamed in her head as her body hurtled toward the other side of the city.

"WAKE UP, USE MY MAGIC NOW," the voice screamed again.

Ehiliana's eyes snapped open. "How?"

"The wind, tell it to catch you." The voice echoed around her now.

Focusing, Ehiliana noticed she could see colorful streams of wind surrounding her. As her body got dangerously close to the monster's chosen destination for her, Ellie realized it was the palace. There was a giant gaping hole in the side of it, and someone was standing on its edge.

Having no time to tell them to move, Ehiliana closed her eyes for a second and said, "Help me, land."

When she opened her eyes, the colorful wind had steadied into a pink color. The wind swirled around her body and turned her sideways. Her body flew over the person in the palace, and suddenly, she was rolling on the carpet.

Pain overtook her body as she tried to lift herself, and she immediately fell to the ground again. Lying on her back now, she let out a sigh and cursed.

"She's alive," a female voice said above her.

"Get her out of the way then," a cold male voice rang out.

Coughing, Ehiliana pushed the hands away from her. "No, I can still help, just get me a bow and something to wipe my eyes with."

"How far can your main eyes see, Irkafen?" the male voice asked as she stood.

"Up to a mile, but I think that just changed, plus, I can see in the dark with my second set," Ehiliana said, wiping blood from her mouth.

Taking a moment to dust herself off and gather her thoughts, Ehiliana studied the man ordering everyone around. He had white-blond hair, a heart-shaped face, and golden eyes. The man looked like a slightly older male version of the princess she had met, though he seemed more sure of himself. He had on a white shirt, now slightly tattered; on top of the shirt, he wore a sleek vest with gold buttons, it had a very narrow V-line and pants to match. Grabbing the bow from the soldier in front of her, Ehiliana limped to stand beside the man.

"I'm ready, but I will need medical attention after this."

"The monster that threw you is the one now blocking the rune we need to secure the city," the man she assumed was the prince stated.

"Okay," she said, lifting the bow.

Slowing her breath, she aimed at the monster. It was hovering over one of the local banks, now throwing rubble. The air swirled around her, and she thought to herself, *Take this arrow where I aim.*

Letting her breath out, she heard the prince say a spell at the same time she released her arrow. Purple swirled and flickered around the arrow as it soared toward the monster, and it took seconds for it to hit its mark. A loud, piercing scream came from its body as it disintegrated.

She watched as the rune fell. Fear froze her at the thought of their hope shattering on the ground, but her fears ceased when a figure, quick as lightning, caught it midair before vanishing again. Seconds after, a blinding blue light flashed across the sky, and all the monsters began to vanish.

Ehiliana stood beside the prince as the chaos died down. A tiredness took over her body, worrying for Regina still driving her adrenaline. Looking over to the prince, she caught his gaze staring down at her arm.

Following his gaze, she peered down to see an elegant bishop tattooed on her left arm.

"Where did you get that?" he asked, meeting her eyes.

Before answering, a dizziness overtook her, and the world turned black.

Chapter Four

Iathos

After the heated discussion between Clovis, Kilgi, and himself, Iathos took off for the upper levels of the palace in search of the rune and Prince Alton. A sense of relief passed over the knight's face as he noticed the palace hadn't sustained any further damage from the initial blast. He could hear the roaring of monsters in the distance, and an uneasy feeling settled in his stomach.

"Why is it quiet?" he asked himself.

Making note of the empty halls, there were no voices or noise of any kind to be heard. Cold settled over his skin, raising goose bumps along his arms. Drawing his sword, he pressed onto the upper throne room. As he drew near, the lights flickered rapidly before going out.

Pushing open the immense oak doors, he strode into the grandeur of the throne room. Enormous braziers swung from the limestone pillars, casting an eerie, pulsating azure glow. The gem-encrusted runes etched into the sloped ceiling seemed to shimmer with a malevolent energy. Across the expanse of the room, Iathos discerned Alton's diminutive form, nestled within the embrace of the imposing throne. Adjacent, the lectern cradled the sacred rune.

"Alton," Iathos called out.

"Don't come near it's a trap," Alton cried out.

"It's okay, Alton, just stay calm for me, okay?"

"Yes, do as the knight says child," Echo said.

Stepping out from behind a column, the shadowy figure, Echo, turned to face Iathos. Glowing blue eyes pierced him, and a shiver ran down his spine as he smiled at him.

"Welcome, Iathos, to your first trial. While others fight for their lives, you will fight for young Alton's. Cut me once, and you pass. Should you fail to pass before the others are all chosen, then every breathing thing in this room dies with you, "Echo stated with a wave of a hand.

Silence filled the room for a few seconds before the ring of the sword sang as it was drawn. The long sword was silver made, with black leather wrappings and neatly lined writing along the edge of the blade. Surprise filled Iathos as he took notice that the runes weren't runes but the names of people. Taking a step forward, Iathos readied himself for the battle.

Easy enough, I'm a high-class swordsman, I can do this.

The sudden image of Echo was upon him, bringing his sword down vertically on him. Iathos barely dodged the attack as he went to right himself. Returning a blow, he met the strike of Echo's sword. Sliding back a few feet, the knight felt a sense of fear at the realization Echo meant it when he said he'd kill him. Iathos met another hardening blow, and this time, it shattered his sword.

Blood trickled down his face from where the shards of his sword cut him. Having no time to think, Iathos continuously dodged Echo's attacks. His opponent's haunting laugh swept the room as the knight backed up toward the throne room's door and did his best to stay calm despite the relentlessness of, the fate's attacks. A slash met the edge of his arm, a sharp pain shooting through him as blood splattered on the ground.

As the next swing came, Iathos took a page out of Kilgi's book. Ducking under the swing, he rose and punched Echo in the throat as hard as he could. Echo took a few steps back, and Iathos used his chance to run. Grabbing the basin of water at the edge of the room, he splashed the liquid over the first brazier, dashing its light. Racing up the column, he threw water over every light.

"How do you know I can't see in the dark?" Echo taunted him.

"I don't."

The loud crash was enough to turn Echo in his direction, but Iathos made his run for the podium and Alton during the commotion. Grabbing Alton, he pulled him to the podium and gave him whispered instructions for what to say. With what little magic the boy had, it was enough to light the rune and send waves of light across the room. Across the throne room, he spotted Echo holding an arm out, blocking the light from his eyes, yet still marching forward at a fast pace.

Picking Alton up, Iathos ran for the servant's door, now making a run for their lives. Silence filled the air as Iathos made the run toward the ballroom. The young prince's hands dug into his shoulder blades, crying softly into the older man's chest.

"Don't worry, prince, I've got you, we are almost to our allies," Iathos whispered harshly from running.

A few minutes later, Iathos was kicking open the door to the ballroom. Stepping inside, he set the young prince on his feet. A redheaded Irkafen woman was passed out on the floor by the prince. Many nobles and a few royals were on the far side of the room being treated by Vulocri, and the prince himself was close to passing out.

"I'd ask what happened but we may have another problem," Iathos informed the prince.

"What?" he barked out harshly.

"Echo is here, wants to kill me if I can't land one cut on him before something."

"Just you?"

"Anyone in the room, and now that's you too."

"Bastard."

"Let's go somewhere where we won't get everyone killed then," Clovis said, walking toward the door Iathos arrived in. "Just one cut?" Clovis questioned.

"He said one."

"What's different about him?"

"He's very fast and strong. He shattered my sword with two swings of his own."

"So, he has a magical weapon? Anything else?" Clovis asked.

"Yes, the sword has names, not runes, carved into it, and he's slightly impaired by bright lights," Iathos said more confidently.

"Okay, then this is what's going to happen. I'm going to stay in the hall and provide what little support I can. I don't have a lot of magic left, and it's starting to not work again, so you'll get what I can give." he continued, "I will not be entering the room because of the terms of this fight. I don't feel like dying today, so I suggest you figure out how to beat him fast."

Making his way past Clovis, Iathos stepped back into the icy throne room. Moving into the room, he could only make out the glow of Echo's sword. Behind him, Clovis whispered a spell and a blur of light orbs came streaming into the room. Now he made out the fate crouched on the floor, using the sword to hold himself in a kneeling position. What appeared to be rotting hands turning into ash were grabbing at his ankles, and as he stepped closer, fate's eye snapped up to his.

"Stand back, something isn't right," Echo said harshly.

Eyes widening, Iathos turned back to Clovis, who seemed just as confused. Taking another step forward, Iathos felt as if he were suddenly plunged into the coldest depths of the ocean.

"Let me help you," Iathos said sternly.

"You cannot."

"You chose me for something, maybe I can help."

"Fine, I won't kill you, but listen carefully. Help me lift the sword, and once we do, we will have to deliver these souls to the other side.

"All right," Iathos said as he bravely stepped into Echo's space.

"You will need to slash the air vertically."

The cold hands were pulling on his legs, fear filling his senses. Voices whispering, sobbing, and yelling, overwhelming him. Pushing through, he wrapped his hand around the sword's hilt and lifted it above his head.

"Now, focus on giving them peace, only then will the sword work," Echo said calmly.

Inhaling, Iathos lifted the sword and brought it down.

Swinging it through the air, he felt resistance, like cutting thick fabric. Before him, a shadowy rip in the realms floated, and the hands grabbing at his feet let go, rushing into the portal, the air warming as they went.

"How do I close the portal?" Iathos questioned.

"Cut it horizontally," Echo instructed.

Lifting the sword, he made one last slash. Lowering it, he went to hand it back to its rightful owner, only to find that he was alone. He took some steps back toward the servant door to find Clovis staring at him, perplexed.

"Did you see any of that?" Iathos asked.

"I saw you talking to a magic sword standing by itself in the middle of a throne hall."

"You couldn't see Echo?" The knight's brows furrowed.

"No, you were talking to the air, then picked up a sword and did magic. If I recall correctly, you hate magic, so I'm going to chalk it up to you being a hypocrite. Now that this is over, we have other work to attend to, like helping people who are hurt," Clovis said sternly.

Watching as the prince turned and walked away, Iathos ran a hand through his hair, letting out a heavy sigh.

Alton.

Alton's terrified face came rushing into his mind, pushing Iathos to make his way back to the ballroom. When he reached the room, the young prince's face lit up with joy. Brown curly hair hung over his lean, friendly face. He had lidded gray eyes, set far within their sockets, rimmed red from crying. Despite the young prince's disheveled appearance, relief washed over Iathos.

Slamming his body into Iathos, Alton declared, "You saved me!"

"Well, your magic saved everyone," he said.

"You said magic was harmful though."

"Yeah, I did." Iathos sighed. *It is.*

"So, it's not bad if it's being used for good?"

"I'm not sure, that's up to you." *I can't stop you.*

"I will show you how good magic is! Just watch me!"

"I will, prince, it's always a pleasure to serve you," Iathos said, bowing to the little prince.

"Then I have a request," Alton said shyly.

"I'm at your service."

"I'll search here for my family, you go bring Kilgi back," Alton ordered.

Bowing and walking away from the young prince, he passed royals and nobles on his way out of the building. He locked eyes with Clovis, who studied him with curiosity. Iathos gladly returned the look before continuing. *Somehow, I wouldn't be surprised if this was his fault. Could I even stop him if it is?*

The change of scenery was disturbing. What once was a lovely mix of limestone and greenery was now chunks of rubble mixed with the acrid scent of smoke and blood soaking into the ground below. Some of the bodies littered about were torn to shreds, while others appeared as if they were drained of all life. Iathos, having seen battle before, wasn't prepared to see so many people in tortured states. An urge to vomit overwhelmed him; steadying his breath, he tilted his head to the sky.

Taking a few minutes to calm himself, he walked in the last known direction of his cousin. Making his way through the rubble proved difficult, trying his best to ignore the cries of injured people and the arguing of those trying to save them. Making his way further down the city levels, the chaos only seemed to increase. Numbly, he watched as fires spreading across the city were desperately trying to be put out, children cried for their parents, and blood ran down the streets like runoff on a rainy day. *It would be a good day for rain.*

"My family first though." He sighed aloud.

Half an hour later, Iathos found himself in front of the bank. What once was a beautiful, domed building now sat completely caved in. Seeing no sign of Kilgi, Iathos began to worry. Looking around, he saw a few people sitting. Wanting to ask them questions, he changed his mind, seeing their hateful stares from across the road. His entire body stiffened as a hand touched his shoulder.

"Come to save me?" Kilgi asked from behind the man.

"On orders from Alton, I would have left you for dead otherwise," he said jokingly. *Thank goodness you are alive.*

"I'm pretty sure I won."

A frown appeared on his face, her long purple hair hung disheveled around her defined jawline, her gray eyes were sunken in from no sleep, and her green shirt left her no modesty now that it hung in rags. Turning his head away from his cousin's mostly bare chest, he removed his jacket and held it out to her.

"Please put this on," Iathos said.

Kilgi let out a loud laugh and said, "I'll need help, my arm's broken. It hurts like a lot, to be honest."

"Oh, I'll be gentle."

Laying the jacket over her shoulder, he held it still while she put her good arm into the sleeve. She stood still, only wincing once as he buttoned up the jacket, her arm cradled against her chest.

"Thanks, I was cold."

Carefully, he picked his cousin up, making sure her right arm faced him, giving her broken one more room. Careful with his pace, he walked back to the palace. He wanted to ask her every question that came to mind regarding the events of the night, but now she needed rest. So he let her head fall against his chest and walked back to the palace.

The stars across the night sky gave Iathos a calm he hadn't realized he needed. Breathing, he counted his blessings and reminded himself that everyone would recover in time from this tragedy. To take his mind off the situation and focus on getting Kilgi to safety, he listed the constellations in the sky above him.

"Bunda, Vandris, Phera, Eliqis, Vander, Thuro—" Iathos was cut off.

"Hey, that's me."

"What?"

"Thuro, my star sign."

"You're still on about that stuff?" he mused.

"My ancestors knew their stuff."

"How are you feeling?" he asked.

"Like shit, but I should stay awake until I can be treated properly. If the healers will even see me."

"Well, you can tell me about your star knowledge. Maybe it will make this walk easier." *I'll make sure you're seen.*

"Sure," she replied.

Continuing, he listened as Kilgi explained how the stars were connected to how people were born and that it could even tell if someone was born with magic or not. He found himself amused at his cousin's ramblings, but hesitancy settled over him.

He found himself wondering exactly why his cousin's race was considered evil. There was never a conclusive reason for the initial call for the hunt of the Matuen. The more he thought about it, the more he realized there was no answer for how any race was treated during and after the war of Anu. Shaking his wandering thoughts, they had found themselves back at the castle.

Once inside, he set Kilgi on her feet but kept a hand on her back for support. Seeming dazed, he steered her toward the grand staircase so she could sit. Vulocri nurses were rushing around, one finally stopping before the pair.

"I'll take her. I'm assuming you are all right for now?" the dark-skinned woman asked.

"Yes, I'm fine. I have other things to attend to, but please update me if anything happens with her," he said calmly.

"Will do," the woman said with a bow.

"Wait, what is your name?" Iathos asked.

"Oh my name is Nilan." She blushed.

"Thank you, Nilan, you're doing a good job."

"You're welcome, general." She smiled before returning to her task at hand.

Walking up the grand marble staircase, Iathos was careful to avoid the wet blood that had made its way onto the stairs. The once elegant family portrait of King Hawkore now hung crooked and torn on the wall, blood dripping off the corner. *This is too much like Luella's death*, he thought to himself.

Reaching the halls of the third floor, he saw many noble families standing and sitting in the open corridor. They all wore grim expressions but continued their gossip. Listening, many of them blamed the Gorkem family for the incident, mainly using the family's strong magic as an excuse. *It crossed my mind as well, but Clovis doesn't seem the type to get himself cursed. Maybe he meant to curse only you.*

"You'll have to wait at the end of the line, to see the kings," a noble woman said, interrupting his thoughts.

"Are you new to the noble families?" he asked.

"I'm recently married, yes," she said confidently.

Taking her hand and bowing, he said, "You'll have to pardon me, lady?"

"Cromsel," she answered.

"Lady Cromsel, I am the general of the Kamouraska Kingdom. You'll have to excuse me, but my business is on the other side of those doors."

"Oh, my apologies," she said, a blush covering her face.

"You're forgiven." He smiled.

Turning on his heels, he made his way to the oak doors he had encountered not too long ago. The familiar throne hall was now more lit than it had been; the three major families sat in a semi-circle around the throne. On the left were King Gorkem, his wife, and his son. Iathos put it in the back of his mind that the princess hadn't yet returned. To the right was King Quade, his wife, and their five sons.

"Sorry for the late arrival, your majesties," Iathos said, bowing.

"Take your place," King Hawkore said, waving his hand.

"Yes, your majesty," Iathos said, rising from the bow.

Iathos stood by one of the pillars behind the Quade family and listened as the kings heatedly discussed the events of the night. The queens were annoyed, and the sons wore expressions that were concerned and confused. From the way things sounded, the kings had a suspect in mind and planned to take immediate action.

"If I may interject, your majesties?" Clovis inquired.

"Go ahead, prince," Hawkore responded.

"Your suspect, the girl who entered the ballroom when the attack took place, she is one of the few who helped with the city-wide protection spell. I am not usually one to come to a stranger's aid, but during those events, she also protected Mika and, if I recall right, made sure that you got out of the room during the attack," Clovis continued.

Pausing in contemplation, King Hawkore finally spoke, "You trust that woman despite her race? She could be trying to gain our trust."

"I doubt it, she had stated she wants nothing to do with the royal families because she knows how dangerous we can be. So I'll make a proposition on her behalf."

"You will negotiate for her life?" King Quade asked.

"Yes, I promised through these events, I'd protect the lives of everyone who helped. I don't fully trust her, but she gained just a little today," Clovis answered.

Taking a breath, he continued, "I will pay for her race debt with my funds, and she shall be hired as my bodyguard, considering her fighting skills."

"You would make someone you don't trust your bodyguard?" Clovis's father interjected, standing from his chair.

"Yes, because she has everything to lose. That woman is the perfect pawn." Clovis smiled at his father.

Who is he talking about?

"What if we object?" his father said, coolly taking his seat.

"You won't," Clovis said, now seemingly amused.

He's very confident.

"Who are we discussing? I haven't heard a name brought up once," Iathos asked.

"The purple haired woman who helped us earlier tonight," Clovis interjected.

Shock washed over Iathos, but he spoke again, "Then I agree with the prince. She should be given a chance to prove herself despite her race. Tonight, she showed she is at least willing to fight for life as a whole." Taking a breath, he said, "I am sorry for interjecting, but I was sent to retrieve her on behalf of the prince. She is downstairs if you would like to speak to her."

Locking eyes with the knight, Clovis smiled, "That won't be necessary, I made up my mind. She will work for me and should she betray me, I will kill her without question."

"It seems that matter is settled for now. Should this Matuen prove herself worthy, she will live under your watch until her dying days. She, however, will have a few rules outside of your instructions," King Hawkore interjected.

"What are your demands?" Clovis questioned.

"She is to report here biannually for questioning, and she must take on a brand representing the Gorkem family. Should she cause any trouble, it will fall back on you," King Hawkore listed.

"Does this sound fair to my kings?" he asked his fellow royals.

"Yes," they said in unison.

"Then it's decided, I suggest you keep a close eye on her," King Hawkore said, narrowing his eyes at the Gorkem prince.

He could see the tension in the faces of everyone present. King Quade, however, was unusually quiet through the conversion. Normally, he demands the heads of any person of interest before proven guilty. Iathos knew long ago he would have left working for the family, if he didn't have a sense of loyalty to the Quade Prince's.

Iathos thought about how King Quade looked many years older than the other kings. He had a narrow, sunken face with bright green eyes. His curly brown hair hung neatly, framing his face, and his beard was speckled with gray but neatly trimmed to give him a clean apperance.

Upon first glance, someone would think he doesn't sleep enough, not that he regularly does sacrificial magic to "stay young."

"If I may interject once more, where is Princess Mika?" Iathos asked, changing the subject.

Chapter Five

<u>Mika</u>

Mika felt a rush of warm air around her; when she felt the air stop, the princess opened her eyes. The feeling of tall grass brushed against her legs, the moon's bright light detailing her surroundings. Wildflowers bloomed over the long stretch of field, and pine trees littered the open space. The feeling of dew dampened her shoes and tattered skirt but had a calm, earthy smell with a mix of campfire.

Knowing someone must be nearby, Mika walked in the direction of the campfire smell. The princess walked for a few miles, listening to late-night critters' ambient noises. Feeling a little calmer than before, she replayed the events of the night in her head, from arguing with her family about Clovis's curse, gossiping with some of the younger noble girls, to the woman with purple hair, and the Irkafen woman.

A sense of uselessness came over Mika, having to get help from others. Tears spilled down her face as she fell to her knees. She thought about the dead bodies all over the city and how her shaking legs struggled to move forward to help anyone. Wrapping her arms around her head, she sobbed and replayed the events of the historical building.

***

The doors to the building had already been opened, but she shut them behind her. There were people inside hiding, and an Irkafen man was moving people to the lower levels of the building. If she had to guess, it was to protect people if the building collapsed.

"E-excuse me," Mika stuttered out.

Turning to face her, the black-haired man grabbed her wrist and led her down the stairs, while shushing her.

"P-Please, I am here to help," Mika said, trying to wiggle from his grasp.

"Sorry, miss, but you can help by hiding and staying alive." His deep voice echoed.

Crashes were echoing down the stairs behind the pair. Then suddenly, it was quiet. Jack didn't hesitate to throw Mika out of the way as a large squid-like monster smacked him across the room. The monster had matted down fur and was dripping black, inky liquid. It had no visible eyes and sharp tentacles that reeked of rotting flesh.

The lights flickered, making it hard to see. What Mika did see was the monster lift its heavy tendril from the Irkafen man. A scream pierced her ears as two of his eyes audibly popped from his eye sockets. The monster smacked him again, and this time, he flew through the doorway the pair had come through. Out of fear, she ran after the only hope she had. There were loud crashes from ahead of her, and she could hear him shouting something in his people's language, then it was quiet.

She crawled past the monster as it made its way back to where she had previously been. Taking her chance, she bolted for the first room she could find, only to find Jack and another Irkafen before her. She had long, curly red hair that framed her face; she had two sets of solid pink eyes and freckles scattered across her face like stars. She wore a loose white blouse and black slacks that fit her hourglass frame.

They had a rushed conversation about getting to the podium with the rune, which the woman seemed to know what Mika spoke about. Jack died in those moments and left the girl with a key and a cryptic message. Fear laced the princess as she used her unruly magic to help save the irked woman's friend, then again when they were both teleported to a field with a rook and bishop in front of them.

"Perhaps, if you could use your magic, we'd be better off, but I guess being a princess means being lazy in every aspect," the woman spat at her.

***

A feeling of exhaustion washed over Mika, now sporting a headache from crying. Pushing forward, she got to her feet and continued her march toward the campfire smell, with the moon lighting her way. Before long, she came to a stop at the top of a steep hill, now staring down at an encampment at the base of the hill.

"Be prepared for anything." Her brother's advice echoed through her head.

Taking a deep breath and puffing her chest, the princess went down the hill, only to lose her footing on the damp grass. Slipping and tumbling down the hill, she bounced off a few rocks and scraped her knees along the ground. Landing hard on her side, she stayed like that, letting herself recover her breath from taking the fall. As she did, she made eye contact with a pair of brown leather boots. Turning her head to peer at the person before her, she could only see the silhouette of a man. Bending down, his strong hands grabbed her arms, hauled her to her feet, and then let her go. *Ouch.*

"Are you all right?" the man asked.

"Yes, no. Not, sir," Mika stuttered out.

"Come with me," he replied before walking off toward the camp.

Mika followed the unnamed man. Entering the base of the camp, she stared at their beautiful tents, wood-carved furniture, and cast-iron cookware. She noticed everyone around was a Vulocri or Jesatyl. At the end of the row, Mika was led into one of the tents and told to wait.

After a few minutes, a Jesatyl man walked in. His shaggy, dirty-blond hair hung around his tanned, oval face. He had red almond-shaped eyes that matched the red freckles scattered across his face and slightly pointed ears. He wore a loose-fitting black shirt and pants. The man who followed in was broadly built. He had his snowy hair in a long, pulled-back braid. He had a triangular-shaped face and big gray eyes, with a septum piercing bringing attention to his plump lips. He dressed fine compared to the Jesatyl, with a light blue shirt and black slacks to match the metal blue band around his throat.

"What's your name?" the first man asked, taking a seat in front of her.

"M-Mina," she lied.

"Mina, how did you get here?" he asked.

Glancing at the man behind her and then back at the one in front of her, she gave them a half-truth. "I'm not sure. I was in Colkirk, then somehow got teleported here."

"There was a festival going on, right?"

"Um, yes, it's the Auros Festival, when we celebrate the late King Auros Hawkore for ending the Anu war," the princess stumbled out.

"You got teleported here?"

"Yes, the city was attacked. I'm not sure how I ended up here," she said nervously.

"What a peculiar set of circumstances," he said, leaning forward toward the princess.

"I know it sounds crazy."

"Colkirk is a well-defended city. How do I know you're not lying?"

Stepping forward, the taller man interjected, "Back off, James, she's already scared enough."

"Stop being such a bleeding heart, she's lying about some things," James said.

"She's not obligated to tell us everything," the man replied.

"She found our camp; she is if she wants protection. Otherwise, I have no problem throwing her to the wolves," the man said angrily.

"She has no reason to lie about an attack on Colkirk, it's too absurd to lie about."

Mika said, "I'm right here, I'm not lying. I just don't have any answers for what's going on."

"Were you going to mention you're a noble?" James asked, leaning back. "Your clothes, they're a dead giveaway," James continued.

"That's not really important, right now," Mika stuttered out.

"Oh, but it is. A noble woman fetches a good ransom price."

"What?" Mika said, now panicked. "This is not the time to talk about that. People are in danger," Mika said.

"Why would I care about that? it doesn't affect me." James laughed.

The man raised his hand, and a wave of exhaustion hit her. Standing up, James came and leaned over her, grabbing her chin to meet his gaze.

"H-Help," she breathed out.

"No one is coming to help, sweetheart," James said, his breath hitting her face.

Mika's body felt weak as if she were moving in slow motion. She watched as something heavy was smashed over James' head, and he stumbled backward and swung on the other man. James staggered around during their fight, and Mika took the chance to try and run away. When she stood, her legs collapsed beneath her, and her world spun as she hit the floor hard.

The world spun again as someone lifted her bridal style. She could smell campfire and pine needles coming off of the person carrying her. She felt a rush of cold in her lungs as the person took off at a suddenly fast past. Mika's body was weak, but her mind was racing a hundred miles an hour. *It has to be the Vulocri carrying me.*

"We're not out of the woods yet, Mina," the man spoke as he landed.

"My body feels weak," Mika said, exhausted.

"Yes, it's one of four types of magic the Jesatyl can wield. James is one of the strongest around, he can drain someone's stamina, you'll know them by their freckles. The distance between us and them should help for now."

"Oh. What should we do?" Mika asked, still holding his arm for support.

"I'm not sure. Normally, I would just let James do what he's got to do. This time was different, though. He isn't normally hostile with hostages of any kind."

"We should keep moving then. I'm sorry I caused trouble for you and your friend."

"Please, it's not your fault, I don't think you asked to be forcefully teleported. I'm sure James will come around." The man waved.

Hesitating, Mika spoke, "We should keep moving. I'm not sure where we are, though."

"We're on the West Coast of Three Crows Mountains."

"Then we should head for your people's temple. My brother is supposed to be headed there sometime soon," Mika said, more hopeful.

"We will head for Pero, it's where they would stop for supplies if he's smart," he replied.

"I might as well catch a ship back to Colkirk if we go there," Mika said, letting out a breath and feeling a little better.

"Even though it's being attacked?"

"He won't come until everyone is safe. So, if possible, yes."

"I see. My name is Zeppo."

"Nice to meet you, Zeppo," Mika said.

Picking Mika up again, Zeppo spread his wings. Watching white and blue wings sprout from his back, she examined their beauty. Holding on tight, she tucked her face into his neck as he took off. *I think I can trust him.*

"We have pursuers, so hold on tight," he said over the rush of wind.

Tightening her grip, Mika found herself upset that she had to be carried for the second time in one night. The sense of uselessness hit her again, then anger. Not wanting to be useless, Mika peered over the man's shoulder. She saw other Vulocri silhouettes not too far behind the pair.

Lifting one of her hands, she recited a spell and waved her hand. She felt a rush of energy up her arms as a bolt of lightning scattered like broken glass across the sky, piercing three of their adversaries. Mika watched as they fell from the sky like dead flies. Thunder boomed loudly above them from the magic's aftermath.

"Yes! My magic worked this time," Mika shouted excitedly.

Her smile left her face as storm clouds rapidly formed above them, covering the star-filled sky. Rain began to come down, and thunder boomed loudly. She felt Zeppo make a hasty downward track, landing hard. He slipped on the wet grass, and they both tumbled across the ground, rain now pouring down. They got up as lightning scattered across the sky and toward the ground.

"We need to get off the hills!" Mika yelled at Zeppo.

"What the hell was that!" he yelled back.

Grabbing one of his large hands, Mika pulled him down one of the hills. Both of them stumbled against the wind of the wild magic storm. Slipping, they both went down and held on to each other as they slid down the hill.

"We need to get low, but not completely," Mika yelled over the thunder.

"What?"

"We won't get hit this way," Mika said, pulling him down with her. "Follow my lead," she shouted.

He watched as she crouched into a ball, leaving only her feet touching the ground, then covered her head and ears with her arms. Following suit, the two stayed like that for what seemed an eternity. They could hear thunder booming all around them, rattling their bones, and the cool rain froze them. Eventually, they could feel the heat of lightning striking near them and hear the screams of those who got hit by it.

The storm died down, and the only thing the two could hear was the rain. Lifting her head, Mika stared at Zeppo, his clothes clinging to his broad frame. She touched Zeppo's shoulder to gain his attention.

"Hey, we should move now."

Zeppo stood up, his eyes meeting Mika's. Feeling nervous at the man's hard stare, Mika rocked on the heels of her feet. He didn't say anything and, instead, took off walking. Having little choice, Mika took off after him, the events of the day catching up with her. The princess wanted to speak but found she couldn't. Instead, she trudged behind the man, letting her tears mix with the rain's gentle downpour.

They walked along the grassy hills for hours, carefully watching their footing on the slippery ground. The smell of wet dirt mixed with the breeze as the rain stopped. Without saying anything, the pair walked side by side, trying to save some semblance of warmth during their trek through the dark landscape. As the sun began to rise, the pair set their eyes on Pero, a coastal city in the eastern nation.

"How far have we walked?" Mika asked, tired.

"We flew around half an hour total, and have been on foot since, so around eighty-one miles we've traveled from the mountain's edge."

"You did the math that fast!" Mika said, slightly more awake.

"It's a normal part of my job, and yes, I can fly that fast. However, let's focus on getting in town, then figuring out what to do next." Zeppo smiled.

Compared to other places in the eastern kingdom, Pero was relatively little and lacking. Many of the houses along the waterfront were made of weathered wood and broken windows. the cobblestone streets had filth littered everywhere, the scent of the ocean mixed with the smell of grime. However, the unusual part of the normally quiet town was the amount of people on the streets. Women, children, and injured people were sitting around crying or arguing with authority figures.

The Vulocri man stiffened at the unusual number of people in the town, Reaching behind himself and grabbing Mika's hand.

"Stay close."

"It's okay, Zeppo, they're refugees more than likely," Mika whispered.

Mika stepped in front of Zeppo and lead the way. Surprise filled his features at the girl's sudden confidence. She led him over to an airship guard, and confusion replaced his surprise.

"Excuse me, sir, but I need an airship back to Colkirk please," she said with authority.

"Sorry, miss, but we are dealing with a crisis," the man said.

"I am Princess Mika Gorkem of Aeberuthey. You will take my personal healer and me back where we are needed."

Laughing, the man said, "Yeah, and I'm the King of Colkirk."

She pulled a pendant from under her tattered blue dress and presented it to the guard. It was a golden circle with three crow's feathers and runes carved around its edges. Stepping back, the man bowed and apologizing, before rushing the pair onto the airship. Mika and Zeppo took seats next to each other in the cramped space, drowning out the rage of the citizens behind them.

"It's a couple hours until we land, princess, so please get comfortable," the guard said from the airship's door before closing it.

"You're a princess," Zeppo stuttered out.

"I'm sorry I lied." She paused. "We have a lot to discuss," Mika continued.

"I need some time first," Zeppo found himself saying.

"That's okay. I'm sure you're mad, and you're allowed to be," Mika said, leaning her head against the window.

"Are you mad?" he asked.

"I'm tired." She sighed. *I am exhausted.*

Closing her eyes, she continued, "Thank you, Zeppo, I promise to protect you and repay you for your kindness."

Focusing on the princess, he frowned at her appearance. She was petite, with wet, long, white-blond hair clinging to her diamond-shaped face. Her eyes sported dark circles from exhaustion, and her cheeks were puffed red as if she were crying. The princess had cuts across her face, along her arms, and legs. Her damp light blue dress that clung to her was now splotched red from where it soaked up some blood.

He took the princess' hand, her icy blue eyes opening to meet his gray ones. Mika felt a gentle wave of warmth pulse over her body, and the aches she felt began to ease. Closing her eyes, Mika smiled at the Vulocri man.

"Thank you." She yawned before letting sleep overtake her as the airship lifted to the sky.

Chapter Six

<u>Clovis</u>

Sitting in his room, trying his best to not let his mind get the better of him, Clovis studied the worn leather of the couch he sat on. Old bookcases held multitudes of books, ranging from romance to history. Glancing down to the dark coffee table that held his now blackened spell book, Clovis let out a long sigh, running his fingers through his hair. Sitting there disheveled for a while, still wearing his torn clothes from the night prior, the prince closed his eyes.

Eventually rising from the leather couch, he went to the bathroom to clean up. Turning the handle to the shower, he stepped in and let the hot water wash away the evidence that such a tragedy had ever happened. During his shower, a hard knock pulled the prince from his heavy thoughts. Turning the water off, Clovis stepped from the shower, wrapping a towel around his waist. Opening the door, one of his hall guards stood before him.

"What is it?" he said, annoyed.

"A Matuen woman said that she is supposed to see you," the guard replied.

Rolling his eyes, Clovis said, "Let her in."

"Yes, sire," the guard replied with a half bow.

Walking out of the bathroom and back into his suite, the prince gave the woman a side eye as she entered the room. She was half a head shorter than him, with long purple hair braided neatly and dressed in high-waisted black slacks tucked into black leather boots, with a red blouse and studded earrings to match.

Crossing her tanned arms over her chest, her gray eyes met his gold ones. "Morning."

"What do you want?"

"Well, obviously, I came to watch you get dressed."

Glaring at Kilgi, he let out a *tsk*. "You and I are not friends. You work for me. You do not get to joke with me."

"I'll grow on you," she said with a smile, plopping down on the couch.

I doubt it. "Get out, I have better things to do than deal with you."

"I think not. You'll find I'm much more interesting." She smiled.

"If you have nothing to offer, get out. I am tired." He sighed.

"I'm sure you are."

Finally snapping, the prince, still clad in a towel, stormed over to her and grabbed the front of her shirt. Dragging her forward into his personal space, he felt her hand press against his chest to keep space between the two.

"Let me go," her voice whispered in his thoughts.

"We are not going to play this game, you don't get to walk in here and pretend you run this place or me. You forget that your life hangs in my hands now, so please, go ahead and show me how much you want to die," Clovis said, letting go of her shirt.

Kilgi rose to her feet, entering the prince's space, pressing her hand against his chest again, she harshly shoved him. Watching as he fell over the table, she walked around the edge of the table, squatting over him. His eyes widened in fear as Kilgi grabbed his book from the table and threw it across the room.

She touched the book, and it didn't hurt her. Is she going to kill me?

"Listen here, you entitled prick. You don't control me, and without your magic, you're useless without others' help, my help," she hissed out. Continuing, Kilgi said, "Not everyone gets to be born as privileged as you, yet here I am trying to get along with the man who holds my strings. You may not like how I am, but it is what it is. I will not change or bow to you, prince."

Taking a breath, she said, "I will do what I have to do, but since we are stuck with each other, I came to negotiate this situation. We can talk once you've cooled off, though until then, I'm going to be in the library."

"I don't want to die," her voice whispered again.

Standing, she walked away, never once glancing down, leaving him bewildered on the floor. Scrambling to his feet, he crossed the room to the now discarded spell book. Picking it up, his eye widened at the handprint wrapped around the spine of the book, where Kilgi had grabbed it. The rest of the book was black, and where the handprint sat was purple, as if she had burned off some of the curse. Peeking over at his discarded towel, Clovis huffed, walking over to the table and sat the book down while picking up the towel.

He threw the damp towel into a hamper, and went to the dark wooded armoire. Sliding on a pair of brown pants and black leather boots, he glanced at the book, making sure the handprint was still there. Continuing to dress, he grabbed a long-sleeved silk shirt that showed off his chest. Walking over to the mirror, he fixed his hair only letting a few strands of it fall into his face. Grabbing the book off the table and hooking it into its proper spot on his belt, he left the room.

"Clovis!" Vivian shouted from down the hall.

Why must you always show up to annoy me?

"Wait up, I was coming to speak with you!" she yelled.

Ignoring her, he turned in the other direction and walked at a brisk pace. A hand grabbed his elbow as he went to take the flight of stairs leading to the first floor. Turning, he saw Lady Vivian; her dark hair had been neatly put into a bun, and her gold embroidered green dress looked as if it were choking her.

"Clovis, please stop running from me."

"I have other things to attend to, Miss Vivian." He tried to say politely.

"Then let me come with you."

Turning to face her completely, Clovis stared down at the woman. "No. If you do not recall, we just faced some mysterious attack, I have work to do that doesn't involve indulging your fantasy."

"Yet you have time for a Matuen to visit your chambers so early in the morning."

"It would appear that way."

"I'll be upfront then. Your parents and I discussed a marriage proposal yesterday before the attack," she said smugly.

"Good for you," he said, turning his back to her.

"She's just a phase for you, I know that somewhere inside, you want me too."

Turning his head to glance at Vivian over his shoulder, he said, "You'll find pretty things wilt when not properly cared for. I don't like you enough to try and take care of you should my hand be forced. If it would destroy what hope you and my parents have at this, then that Matuen woman will have everything you wish you could."

"You don't mean that," she said, voice quaking.

"When have I lied to you, Vivian," he said, coolly descending the stairs, leaving Vivian alone.

"I'll have her dead before our announcement," she yelled down the stairs, only to meet silence.

Making his way to the library, he started planning his next steps.

If I talk Kilgi into a fake engagement, it should provoke Father enough to negotiate with me on my freedom to at least choose who I am forced to marry. Obviously, I won't keep the engagement. It would cause too many problems in the long run. Vivian will be a wild card, which means if she takes some extremes, Father will be forced to listen to me. On the other hand, I can keep Kilgi close and find a cure for my curse before it kills me. Then there is the attack and the fact none of the kings seem bothered by it.

"I need more time, why do I never get a break?" he muttered.

Stepping into the library, he leisurely surveyed the expanse. The room seemed to unfurl in front of him, adorned with pristine white shelves that embraced a treasure trove of books. Their pages whispered the tales of ages past, and the comforting scent of well-worn paper danced in the air.

A series of plush sofas formed a welcoming semi-circle around a stately stone fireplace, where a handful of patrons reclined, engrossed in their chosen tomes. Above, elegant glass chandeliers hung from the lofty ceiling, their brilliance muted by the generous stream of natural light cascading through the colossal glass wall at the library's far end.

And there, in the corner by the window, he spotted Kilgi, engrossed in her world of words, the soft glow of daylight illuminating her reading nook.

Walking over to her, Clovis awkwardly sat down next to where her feet ended on the sofa. Clearing his throat, her gray eyes snapped up to meet his. She held up a finger to indicate she was going to finish her page. Waiting patiently, Clovis found himself twiddling his thumbs.

"Cooled off that quickly?" she asked.

"Let's negotiate."

"I'll provide my services if you help end the killing law on my people, even if it's just in your lands. I also want the race debt to officially be abolished and made illegal. No one should live like this because of how they were born. The Irkafen deserve their freedom too."

"Those are not promises I can make until I am king."

"But you will be king," Kilgi said, raising her eyebrows.

"How do I know you will give me your devoted service," Clovis asked.

"Good avoidance," she said, laughing. "I don't want to die, and I want bigger things than myself. I don't get to be reckless about this in particular, that's how you know I'll be loyal. I just make no promises to be respectful all the time.

Running a hand through his hair, he replied, "Can you wait until I am king for this?"

"If that's what it takes, what do you want in return?"

"You're not just offering your loyalty?" he questioned, raising an eyebrow.

"Feels too easy that way."

"Start by telling me how you can touch my book, but nobody else can," he said, pulling the book from its holster.

Taking it from his pale hands, Kilgi studied the book. Dragging her fingers across the worn, black leather, she noticed it turned purple as she did, then faded back to black. A cold, prickling feeling tickled her fingertips the longer she held the book. She handed it back to the prince.

"It's cold and tingles, but I don't have an answer," she said with a shrug.

"I don't like the idea, but I think you should hold on to it until it's purple again," he said, rubbing his chin.

"You touch your face a lot when you think," Kilgi said, taking the book.

"Yeah, I should probably stop doing that."

"Anything else, my lord?"

"Not for now, I'll have a holster made for you. Though you will need to remain close when you have the book," he said, standing.

"Why?" Kilgi asked.

Side-eyeing her, he said, "Do you have a tattoo of a chess piece on your forearm?"

"No," she said, raising an eyebrow.

"Does he know I have one?" her voice whispered in his head.

"Nothing, just a theory I had, concerning yesterday's events." He waved. *Why am I hearing her voice in my head?* he thought.

"We should continue this later, we have a stalker," Kilgi said, pointing with her eyes.

Following her gaze he saw Vivian sitting not too far off from the pair. Scowling, he motioned for Kilgi to follow him. Walking in silence, the pair made their way toward the training grounds. Their footsteps echoed off the limestone walls, empty suits of armor lined the walls, and swords clashing could be heard off in the distance. Clovis watched as Kilgi ran her fingers along the tanned walls, her slim hands seemingly graceful.

Opening the doors, the pair entered the sun-filled training ground. A group of fifteen knights were sparring on a giant patch of moss. The smell of sweat, metal, and morning dew filled the air. staring at Kilgi, her eyes were already on him, gesturing for her to join the training.

"You're testing me?" she asked.

"Yes," he said shamelessly.

"Knights!" Clovis's voice boomed out.

All of the Krystrusian knights stopped sparring and bowed to the prince.

"Which one of you is the best swordsman?"

"Me, sire," one knight said, stepping forward.

"Your name?"

"Malcom Granis, fourth squadron leader of Colkirk, sire," he said, standing straight.

"Malcom, you will be testing my new bodyguard's skills for me today. Please, try your best to kill her."

"Yes, sire," Malcom replied, meeting Kilgi's eyes.

Appearing to be bored, she walked over to the weapon rack and browsed the weaponry. Leaning against the castle wall, he watched as Kilgi ultimately chose no weapon. Standing now in front of the guard, she put her fist up and slid a foot behind her to steady her stance. Malcom seemed off-put, and the two had a quick conversation he couldn't hear.

Malcom made the first attack, swinging vertically at the assassin. She dodged and brought her foot to the side of his head, throwing the guard off balance. He went to swing sideways at her, only for her to drop low and swipe her leg under his, causing him to fall. Before he could shift into an upright position, Kilgi stepped on his wrist and stared down at him. The fight was over; Malcom had lost to a weaponless foe. Clapping, Clovis stood from the wall and walked toward the pair.

"How amusing, one of Colkirk's best defeated by a weaponless Matuen." He smiled.

Stammering, Malcom failed to give a reply.

"Come, Kilgi, I have other things to attend to today," Clovis said, motioning for her to follow.

"How long have you had this stalker?" Kilgi said, motioning to Vivian.

"Since I was nine. Why, are you jealous?"

"Thought we weren't allowed to joke with one another?"

"My interests have changed," he said curtly, the smile falling from his face.

"Does it involve your stalker?"

"Well, you're not an idiot, it would seem."

"Yeah, yeah, let's get on with your day."

"Maybe you'll die of boredom," he replied, voice still cold.

"Already am," she mumbled.

Glancing at a clock, Clovis checked the time, only to find he had a few minutes before he met with the kings. Turning his walk into a light jog, he and Kilgi made their way to the throne hall. Leaving her outside the room, he entered, taking his seat among the royal families. Meeting Iathos eyes across the room, he gave him a curt nod, accepting his existence. His father's hand tightly grasped his shoulder, letting Clovis know of his disapproval of almost being late.

The meeting began and went like any other. They discussed how to clean up the damage and re-home citizens, how to keep civility in these times, and how to go about dealing with the present danger. All the kings decided that more than likely, a reckless magic user tried to attack the city and killed themselves, or at least that's what they planned to tell the public. Rolling his eyes, Clovis bounced his knee up and down, waiting for such a charade to be put to rest.

"Clovis? What do you think?" King Hawkore asked.

"I think it won't change anything," he said, meeting the king's bored eyes.

"How so?" the king mused.

"A threat remains. Lying to the people will keep them calm until it happens again. They will lose trust in us for lying," he said pointedly at Iathos.

"How do we know the threat isn't you? You are a prodigal magic user, recently cursed," the king said.

"You dare accuse my son!" King Gorkem stood.

"Father, I can handle my own," Clovis said, putting a hand on his father's arm.

"It's plausible, if the curse didn't take away my ability to do magic, and Mika is out of the question because she has trouble controlling hers," Clovis responded calmly.

"Yet she isn't here," King Quade answered.

"No, she isn't, which worries me. She could have gotten hurt while trying to take care of the rune in the historical building. But there are no reports on her, so something else is going on," the prince said, sweeping his gaze over the crowd. *Why are none of them concerned?*

"What about the Matuen, now in your care?" King Hawkore asked.

"We will wait and see."

"If you'll excuse me, your majesties, but these are all things we already discussed and I can't be productive on your behalf within these walls," Clovis said with a bow.

"I'll accompany you," his father replied.

Standing to leave, the Gorkem family made their exit into the hall. Making eye contact with Kilgi, he made a discreet motion for her to follow as his father grabbed his elbow, steering him toward an empty room. He motioned for Kilgi to stay outside the door and he almost smiled at her eye roll. Opening the door, his father shoved him into the room, and his mother closed the door behind the trio.

The room was quaint, with bright walls, cream-colored furniture, and an antique tea set sitting on the glass table accenting the furniture. A set of large glass doors led to a balcony overlooking the courtyard. Sitting Clovis down, his parents sat on the other side of the table, fixing him with a stern gaze.

"Clovis, we need to have a serious talk." his mother said, clasping her hands.

"If it's about Vivian I already know," he said, leaning back.

"Did she speak with you this morning?" his father asked.

"Yup."

"Well, when should we announce it?" his mother asked.

"Never."

"Clovis!" his father yelled, standing to meet his gaze.

"No." Clovis cut his father off. Continuing, he said, "I will not marry Vivian, Mika is missing, and you're sitting here asking me to marry a woman I despise."

"We already have guards searching for your sister."

"That's not good enough. Obviously, I will have to take care of it like everything else," Clovis said, walking toward the door.

"You are an heir to my kingdom and you willingly disrespect me?" King Gorkem yelled.

"If either of you truly cared about your children, you'd clean your own house first before bringing a homewrecker into it," Clovis said, meeting his gaze.

Leaving his parents' mouths agape, Clovis opened the door to find Kilgi stumbling backward, presumably from eavesdropping. Quirking a brow at the woman, he motioned for her to follow.

"Well, that was awkward," Kilgi said embarrassed.

"Perhaps for you, now be silent, I haven't had any all day," Clovis said, clasping his hand behind his back.

"Hmm, well, can I be done for the day?"

"Where do you plan to go?" Clovis asked in return.

"I have no idea." Kilgi shrugged.

"I don't trust you."

"Prince."

"Fine, go, but if you get in trouble, I'm not helping you." He waved.

Just a few minutes to calm my mind, then I need to find Mika.

Finally alone, Clovis headed toward his room. Entering the room, he took a deep breath, smelling old paper and sage. Walking over to the leather couch, he flopped down, grabbing one of the history books he'd be researching. Opening the book on Matuens, he continued where he left off.

The Matuen's shapeshifting abilities depend heavily on whether they are half-blood or full. If they are a half-bred, there is a fifty percent chance of having this ability. If they can, their shifting abilities are limited. They cannot change their hair or eye color, unlike fullbreeds, who can change everything down to color at will.

"Hmm so, if she can shift, then she won't be able to change her colors," he muttered.

When hunting a Matuen, one major sign of their shift is if the animal seems conscious and more intelligent than a normal animal.

"Now the writer just sounds like a mouth breather."

The easiest way to track a Matuen is by using blood magic. Typically, being paired with a Jesatyl mercenary, for they are experts in physically draining strength, stamina, focus, and dexterity.

"Well, now he sounds like he doesn't do any of the work. What a useless book, this isn't even history." Clovis huffed and threw the book down.

Kilgi has my spell book, he thought suddenly.

"Where would someone like her run off to," he mumbled as he walked down the hall. "I can't find Mika without it."

"Guard," Clovis called to the man standing watch at the end of the hall.

"Yes, sire?" the knight said.

"Where is my bodyguard's room?" he asked.

"In the servant's quarters," he said, nodding.

"Thank you," Clovis said, walking away.

Making his way toward the servant's quarters on the first sublevel of the palace, he got caught in a sudden rush of maids hurrying toward the palace entrance. Grabbing one of their arms, he met the green eyes of a dark-skinned Irkafen woman.

"What is going on?" he asked, letting her go.

"Princess Mika has returned," she said, half bowing.

"Where?"

"The infirmary, she brought a guest," she said, taking a step back.

"Thank you," he said, turning to leave. *Thank the fates she's been found.*

Breaking away from the rush, Clovis took off, running for the infirmary. When he got there, the bright walls were almost blinding with how the lights bounced off them. Beds lined the walls, and nurses were diligently at work, with guests being brought in from the disaster the night prior. Mika's bright blond hair stuck out compared to the others in the room, quickly he rushed to her.

"Mika."

Turning her head, Mika's puffy red eyes met his. "Clovis!"

Wrapping Mika in a tight hug, Clovis said, "I was worried about you, I was planning a recuse."

"You didn't know where I was." Mika laughs.

"You're my sister, with or without magic, I would hunt you down to make sure you are safe," Clovis said, letting her out of the hug.

"Thank you," Mika said, Smiling sadly.

staring at the man Mika was sitting by, Clovis asked, "You made a friend?"

"He saved my life, betrayed his friends to help me get back."

"Then we should make sure he receives the best care, and compensation," Clovis said.

"He didn't know I was a princess, what if he's mad."

Putting a hand on her shoulder, Clovis replied, "Let things play out how they play out. For now, let's get you cleaned up and rested; you seem like you need it." *I will keep an eye on him.*

"Will you stay near?"

"Will it make you feel better?"

"Yeah, Mom and Dad will leave me alone if you're around."

"Something else is on your mind?" He asked, leading her out of the room.

"Yeah, but we can talk about it after I sleep," Mika said, letting Clovis support her weight.

"All right, once I drop you at your room, I'll be on my own until you wake. After that though, I have to go find someone," Clovis said.

"Oh, who?" Mika asked.

"Well, you'll meet her soon, but she is my new bodyguard." Clovis laughed.

"You've never had a personal guard before," Mika said, suspicious.

"She's a person of interest."

"Quit being coy, I'm tired," Mika said, pushing him.

"Well, I think she also somehow got marked yesterday, but it's just a theory," he said.

"Marked?" Mika asked.

"Yeah, the king piece appeared on me during the day before the attack. A girl who helped me kill a monster had a bishop, so I think Kilgi and Iathos may also have one. Kilgi, however, said no to the forearm tattoo.

"Bishop? I picked up a rook before I got teleported, but there isn't a tattoo on my arm. Could it be somewhere else?" Mika said, lifting her arms to check. "A-Actually there is something, look," she said, presenting her arms.

There, almost completely blended with her pale skin, was a rook on her left arm.

"Well, I guess that answers that. Now I need to ask what happened?"

"A story for after I rest."

"Yes, sorry," Clovis said, letting his sister step into her room.

"I'll send for you once I'm up."

"Okay," Clovis said, taking his leave.

Walking away, Clovis found himself standing out on one of the hallway balconies. His eyes roamed over the courtyard, many noble women were walking around or sitting gossiping with one another. Surprise caught him as he noticed Iathos and Kilgi seated in a back corner, talking to one another. Recalling briefly, they seemed to know one another; Clovis suddenly felt like he was their subject of conversation.

As if sensing his stare, Kilgi turned in his direction, Iatho's gaze following. Meeting both of their eyes, Kilgi gave Clovis a nod; Iathos narrowed his eyes at him. Raising an eyebrow, he made himself comfortable sitting on the thick stone railing, leaning his back on the wall connecting to the balcony. Closing his eyes, the prince let the sound of running water and bird calls calm his nerves, finally letting himself relax a little before being jolted back into reality by Vivian's loud voice.

"Clovis!" she called from down in the garden.

"For fate's sake." He seethed.

Chapter Seven

<u>Ehiliana</u>

Soft hands gently touched Ehiliana's forehead, brushing strands of her dried, bloody hair. She could hear murmuring voices and soft clanking noises as she struggled to open her eyes.

"Ehiliana, wake up please," Regina begged, soothing the redhead's forehead.

"I'm up," Ehiliana's voice cracked.

"You've been out for three days, you were on the brink of death. They had four different Vulocri healers working on you. I don't know how you managed to make yourself worthy of royal healers, but gosh, I had to pretend to be your wife just to get in here," Regina said, taking a breath.

"Slow down, Gina, what?"

"I'm glad you're all right."

"Me too, how long have I been out, and where am I?"

"You are in the palace infirmary. You have been for three days, and you have a meeting with the royals after you're discharged," she told her. "I'll go let the healer know you're awake," Regina said, placing a kiss on her head.

Letting out a breath, Ehiliana plopped back on the bed. Lifting her arms and inspecting them, she noticed gold and red sigils drawn on her.

"Must be two different Vulocri," she said to herself.

"Well, you must be more well-versed on our race then?" a younger boy said.

Ehiliana noticed his round face and almond-shaped eyes; one was yellow, and the other was red. He wore a white shirt and a long light blue coat that stopped at the back of his knees with a silver Quade kingdom crest attached to his jacket. His wild, black, fluffy hair bounced on top of his head as he walked.

"Yes, I do."

"Pop quiz," he said, sitting next to Ehiliana.

"What's your full name, birthday, age, place of residence, and work?" he asked, holding up his fingers as he asked.

"Ehiliana Stari Pinkali, Odhem fourteenth, twenty-eight, Colkirk, Colkirk Historical Building," Ehiliana said, putting her fingers up in response.

"What do you last remember?"

"Getting thrown across the city, talking to a blond man, then nothing."

"Well, Miss Pinkali, you had multiple broken bones, organs, nerve, and brain damage. Four of us ended up working on you. The fates must have blessed you because you should be dead."

"I see. Thank the fates, then."

"You should be good to go but try not to strain yourself for the rest of the week. If you need anything else, my name is Ethan," he said, smiling politely.

"Ethan, how old are you?"

Turning to face her, he said, "I'm twenty-two."

"You look a couple of years younger."

"I get that a lot, have a good day, Miss Pinkali." Ethan waved.

Regina helped Ehiliana to her feet with care, the blanket cocooning the taller woman in its warm embrace. She draped it securely, making sure every inch of her was shielded from the lingering chill. A gentle hand rested on Ehiliana's lower back, offering both support and comfort as they made their way from the infirmary.

Sunlight streamed through the expansive windows, casting a golden glow that painted the room in a soft, warm radiance. It illuminated the sterile surroundings, revealing the stark, utilitarian nature of the infirmary. The air bore the faint scent of antiseptic, a reminder of the care that had been administered to those in need. The beds, many in number, stood in neat rows, each with a patient from the recent attack.

As they stepped into the hallway, the buzz of activity enveloped them. Palace workers hurried to and fro, their purposeful movements creating a lively hum that seemed to pulse through the very walls. The details of the grandeur of the building were almost obscured by the constant bustle.

Regina's hand remained a reassuring presence on Ehiliana's back, guiding her with a steady and determined touch. Turning into a narrow corridor, Regina led them to their quarters. Pushing open the door with a soft creak, they entered. The room exuded a sense of modest comfort despite its humble size. Two neatly made beds stood against opposite walls, their frames worn but sturdy. A trunk nestled in the corner held their meager belongings that Regina moved to open. Crinkling her nose at the light smell of mildew, she watched as Regina picked out an outfit for her and then led her out of the door.

"I think you'll appreciate a shower," Regina whispered as she walked.

"Yes, perhaps a bath, though; my body hurts."

"We could probably manage that."

As the women pushed open the heavy wooden doors, Ehiliana's breath caught in her throat at the sight that unfolded before her. The floor, a mosaic of polished marble, gleamed with an almost ethereal luminescence as it caught the gentle radiance emitted by the delicate orbs that floated above, casting a warm, golden glow that danced playfully across the surface.

The walls embraced a rich, velvety, red hue, like the heart of a ruby, adorned with delicate etchings in sterling silver. Each door bore an intricately wrought tapestry of nature's handiwork, silvered boughs, and leaves reaching out to cradle those who entered. The craftsmanship was exquisite, capturing the essence of the forest in every delicate stroke.

The air was alive with the sweet, intoxicating perfume of honeysuckle. Its fragrance mingled with the steam that rose in sinuous tendrils from the ornate baths, creating a heady, almost dreamlike atmosphere. Ehiliana couldn't help but let a delighted smile grace her lips as she took in the luxurious sanctuary before her, a haven of respite in the heart of the bustling estate.

"Just choose a door?" Ehiliana asked.

"Pretty much."

"We should work here." Ehiliana laughed.

"I considered."

Entering one of the bath stalls, Regina set Ehiliana's clothes down and turned on the hot water for the bath. Running her pale hands along the white porcelain tub, Ehiliana stopped and gripped the edge. Her black hair was pulled back, and her cream-colored dress hugged her curvy frame. Letting her smile fall, Ehiliana took her clothes off and stepped into the bath.

Sighing, Ehiliana said, "This is nice."

"Mmm," Regina hummed.

Ehiliana let her eyes slip closed as Regina ran water over her head and massaged soap into her hair.

"I thought you were dead," Regina said.

"Me too, love, but I'm not," Ellie said, opening her eyes.

"I wasn't there to help you; I couldn't help you. You just went and did what we were all too scared to do! You're always so brave and bold, but this time, I could've lost you." *I wasn't willing to lose you.*

Sitting up, Ehiliana turned to face Regina. "You did help me, you give me courage every day to do things I don't want to, this time included. None of this is our fault, and I still have catching up to do."

"I have so many questions," Regina said, tears stinging her eyes.

"Me too, love, I don't have many answers of my own, but I don't think it's getting any better."

"What do you mean?"

"Look at my arm, the bishop. It wasn't there until after the princess and I disappeared."

"You mean something, put it there?" Regina asked.

"Yeah, but I'm not sure what yet, not really," Ehiliana said.

"Okay, we'll figure it out, researching has always been my strong suit."

"You're not mad?"

"I am, but not at you. at this situation. I don't know what's to come, but I'm here for you. For us," Regina continued.

"You're cute," Ehiliana said, turning to slide back into the hot bath water.

"Shut it, let me wash your hair." Regina giggled.

Silence fell over the couple, leaving them with a content feeling in each other's company.

***

Ehiliana wore a simple yellow dress, and a white head wrap to keep her curls healthy as they dried. Straightening herself. she gave Regina a quick peck on the lips.

"I have no idea where I'm supposed to go." She laughs. "Guess I'll just get lost, I promise to fill you in on what they say," Ellie continued.

"Third floor, can't miss it, biggest set of doors on the floor."

"Mmm, thanks." Ehiliana smiled as she walked out into the hall.

The third-floor halls had Krystru men carved into the pillars to appear as if they were holding them up. Big semi-round windows lined the walls on one side in between the pillars, and red carpet ran down the length of the hall. Guards were posted at almost every door. As she passed royals in the hall, she opted for keeping her head straight as they all turned their heads following her with their eyes. *"You can't be weak around them,"* she thought to herself.

As she reached the large set of doors, a purple-haired woman appeared in front of her, half-smiling.

"Ehiliana?" the woman asked.

"Yes."

"Follow me," she said and turned to lead her into a hallway.

"Where are we going?" Ehiliana asked.

"I'm Kilgi, and I am escorting you to the conference,"

"Oh," Ehiliana said.

"Be warned, though, the prince is an asshole," Kilgi said coolly.

"He is a royal," Ehiliana stated.

Smiling, Kilgi opened the door for Ehiliana and led her inside of a study. The walls were completely lined with books, and a dark desk sat in the middle of the room with a set of dark red chairs on one side. Sitting in one chair was Prince Clovis, and off to the side was his sister, Mika. Surprise etched its way onto her face. peering to the right, she met the hard gray eyes. The man was a little taller than her, with longer salt-and-pepper-colored hair. A scar lined his face, stubble trying to hide the slight sink in his cheeks.

Must be a crowded conference.

"Ehiliana," Clovis said. "This is Princess Mika Gorkem, Kilgi Mohlo, and Iathos Casxes. I am Prince Clovis Gorkem," he continued, using his hand to gesture to each person in the room.

"H-Hello, it's a pleasure to meet all of you, and you again, princess," Ehiliana said, bowing.

"You met my sister?" he asked.

"Yes, during the attack, sire, we helped each other," Ehiliana said.

"I see. Well, I'm here to discuss the nature of the tattoos that appeared on all of us," he stated.

Ehiliana surveyed the room as a sense of shock washed over everyone, relief filling her at not being the only one.

"You mean we all suddenly have tattoos?" she asked.

"The tattoos, it's a hunch, but I'm going to put it to rest today," he said.

"You called all of us here, for some hunch," Iathos said, standing from where he leaned on the wall.

"Yes, I had a king chess piece appear on my arm, Mika has a rook on her left arm, and Miss Pinkali has a bishop on her forearm," Clovis said, now staring Iathos down.

"You think the tattoos are connected?" Mika asked.

"Yes, I think it has to do with our situation," Clovis said, raising his eyebrows at Iathos.

"Fine, fine. Yes, I have a knight on my wrist," Iathos grumbled.

"How could we possibly help one of the best wizards in Eckris, based on a tattoo?" Ehiliana interjected.

"I think we are all tied together as a repercussion of the attack the other day. However, I think it could also help break the curse on Iathos and me," he said.

"You're cursed?" Ehiliana asked. "Wait, never mind, I see your eyes," Ehiliana stated.

"Yes, I can't use my magic, and Iathos doesn't have magic to use. I'm not sure how it's affecting him, but I'm sure he could fill in," Clovis said, leaning forward on the desk.

"Ah, yes, well, It was eating me up until I got the magic sword. My hands were pretty much black up until a little after I used the sword," Iathos said, pulling the collar of his shirt.

"Sorry to interrupt, but should you be trusting a stranger with this information?" Ehiliana asked.

"Well, I do have a personal bodyguard, if you squeak," Clovis said.

"Oh," Ehiliana said, rocking on her heels.

"Do you know how the sword works?" Kilgi asked.

"Not yet, but it had names on it, now it doesn't," he said.

"So we study the sword," Clovis insisted.

"If we are going off the theory that we are connected somehow, then the pieces should play a role right. The prince is a kingpiece, meaning he is a leader of some kind, probably a strategist. Iathos is a knight, meaning he is a defender. Mika is a rook, meaning she is a blatant threat," Ehiliana ranted. "I'm a bishop so I'm probably something along the lines of a defender also, and Kilgi—" Ehiliana said, meeting her eyes.

"I'm a queen piece," she said.

"But it means we all are meant to protect the king," Mika said.

"What a mess," Iathos said.

"Ehiliana has a point. For now, Ehiliana will be doing research on runes and such while she rests, Mika will work on her magic, Kilgi will be near me, and, Iathos, you can figure out what you'd like to do."

"Prince, I have a life outside of this, I can't just abandon that," Ehiliana said.

"I will give you a salary and housing if your home is destroyed, and your wife will be accommodated as well. She's a feisty woman, demanding my head if you get hurt in my care," he said, raising his brow.

"You'd do that for us?" Ehiliana asked.

"Yes, all I demand in return is hard, honest work, and that my space be respected," he responded.

"Thank you, I thought—"

"That I wouldn't because of your race. Well, if you turn to your left, Kilgi is Matuen. You have nothing to worry about unless you cross me," he said coolly.

"Sorry, sire," she whispered.

"I'll see all of you after breakfast on the training grounds, I want to see what I am working with," he said, walking out of the room.

"Do you want me to take you to your room, or do you want to wander?" Kilgi asked Ehiliana.

"I'll wander," Ehiliana responded.

"All right see ya," she said, waving.

Exhaling, Ehiliana collapsed into one of the red chairs and put her hands on the side of her head. The world felt like it had plunged her into the deepest depths of the sea. Goose bumps ran up her arms, and a bad feeling dug its way into her gut.

"Ehiliana?" Mika said.

Surprised, Ehiliana said, "Yes, princess?"

"I'm going to show you I'm not worthless." She huffed and walked from the room.

Ehiliana's stomach dropped at the memory of yelling at the princess during the attack. The way her tiny frame dropped to the ground, exhausted after also fighting against the monsters.

Ehiliana sighed.

Replaying the conversation in her head, Ehiliana felt like many loose ends had not been resolved or thoroughly talked about. Standing up, Ehiliana left the study to follow the prince. With fire in her eyes and a new sense of motivation, she ran to catch the prince.

"I am sorry to keep interrupting you, but we had less than half a conversation and I need some more details before starting anything," Ehiliana said, catching up to the prince.

"Ask them quickly."

"The curse affects your magic use, how?"

"Can't use it for certain intervals of time, there is no pattern," he said, voice low.

"Iathos said he didn't go away until he used a sword, I'm guessing a magic one. If that's the case, then you both are backward. To quell the curse and keep it at bay, you can't use magic and Iathos must?"

A frown appeared on his face. "That could be the case."

"I'm still certain the pieces are meant to mark our roles, but I doubt a curse would do this to strangers, something weird is going on."

"Did you not meet anyone upon getting that mark?" Clovis asked, stopping.

"No, we didn't see anyone, just chess pieces. However, a voice spoke to me when I was flung across the city."

"There may be more going on, but I still think you all can help break this curse. It makes sense with the timing of everything going on."

"I'll start my research now, but I do have one other concern, prince," Ehiliana said, clasping her hands together.

"What?"

"Assuming that you're right and these marks connected us and that's why we met. Where is the pawn?"

Ehiliana watched as concern appeared on his face, clenching his hands and letting them go. She watched as a million thoughts ran through his eyes, and a smile appeared on her face.

Please don't be mad if I upset you. "I don't like what's going on, prince, and I know we don't have answers, but we will get through this. I'm sure the pawn will make their appearance sooner than later if your hunch is right," Ehiliana said.

"I'm hardly wrong," he said, leveling his gaze to hers.

Feeling cold suddenly, Ehiliana stepped back and said, "Yes, sir."

"Go now, I have other things to attend to." Clovis waved and took off walking.

"Guess I'll go study," Ehiliana muttered under her breath.

Chapter Eight

<u>Zeppo</u>

Zeppo finds himself searching the palace library while waiting for the princess to get back from her meeting. A frown had made a home on his face over the last couple of days of being forced to stay in the palace at the demand of the princess. He grabbed a book titled *Magical Herbs For Advanced Healers* and sat on one of the sofas by the fire, he cracked the book open and read.

"Drumaglin: When crushed, and mixed into salve, can numb cuts."

Oppilium is a better substitute, he thought.

"Red Firelum: When mixed with water, acts as a migraine relief."

"That's interesting to know, I'll have to write this one down," He said.

"Greenleaf-Dreadful: When used, can act as an antidote to most poisons."

"Hey, Zeppo, sorry for being late," Mika said, from behind the book.

Peering up from his book, he caught the faint smell of cinnamon coming from the princess. She wore a turquoise long-sleeved dress that had white edges, and her hair was loose with a few braids holding her bangs out of her face.

How was the meeting?" he asked, from behind the book.

"It was fine, how is your book?"

"It's fine, I'm reading about Greenleaf-Dreadful," he said, closing the book.

"What's that?" she said, sitting down beside him.

"Well, if you ask this book, a good antidote for poisons when in reality, it has more versatile uses. For example, you can use it as a powder to clot cuts," he said, setting the book on the table.

"You know a lot about that plant."

"Yeah, it's a hard plant to come across though, it mainly grows in Violet Cove."

"Oh, because of the Feydevor? They're cursed, right? Or that's what the history books say," Mika continued.

"They were once a peaceful race until they were stricken with an infectious blood curse, which caused their race to lose their minds and crave violence when in contact with another race. They speak of an ancestor named Vandulif who cursed his people so they could never be harmed by other races for egregious use again," Zeppo ranted.

"That's messed up," Mika interjected.

Taking a breath, Zeppo continued, "Yeah, before they were cursed the Feydevor were all born with nature magic, they brought good harvest and weather wherever they went. Other races took notice and kidnapped them. Most newborns and children were sacrificed for 'natural power enhancement.'"

"Yeah, I knew about them being kidnapped, I never heard that they were used for dark magic."

Smiling, Zeppo kept going, "Amazing what they hide from us in history books. Anyway, when Vandulif placed the curse upon his people, he sacrificed a child from every race outside of his own and created a powerful blood curse with the intent to infect his kin. Placing the curse upon himself Vandulif traveled all of Eckris spreading this new magic disease and telling his people to find their way home. The only exception to the curse is us Vulocri, because we didn't yet exist when he placed the curse on his people."

"That's intense, where did you learn that, it's slightly different from what I learned," Mika said.

"The fyedevor told me when I was younger and still learning medicine," he stated proudly.

"That's interesting."

"Yeah, it's sad though, they don't know how to cure themselves of the curse. I hope that I can find a cure for them. On another note though, we were supposed to have a meeting with you and me," he said, gesturing between the two of them.

"Oh, yes, I just wanted to ask how you're doing, and if there is any way I can repay you for helping me."

"I'm not sure."

"Are you mad I lied?" asked the princess.

"No, I was, but if I was a princess in your situation, I would have too," he said leaning back into the sofa.

"I was mad too."

"Yeah?" he said, raising his eyebrows.

"Yeah, I don't want to keep getting help from every one, no offense," Mika said, flopping back into the sofa beside Zeppo.

"Why do you feel like you're constantly getting help?"

"Well, it just seems like every time I try to do something on my own, someone comes and fixes my mistakes for me."

"Be more specific." Zeppo tilted his head to the side.

Huffing, Mika said, "Well, for instance, I tried to banish a monster yesterday, and instead I trapped it in a bubble! It's like my magic works against me, it's infuriating, and I shouldn't even be telling you, because my parents would kill me if they knew someone outside of our family knew."

"Did it stop the monster?" he asked.

"Well, yeah, but that's not the point."

"Sure it is, you weren't helpless, your magic did something. That's better than most, and you saved some lives by trapping them in bubbles."

"You're being way too optimistic for my liking right now."

"Oh, right, I'm supposed to be the broody one," Zeppo said sarcastically.

"Shut up." Mika rolled her eyes.

"As you wish, princess."

After a while of sitting in comfortable silence, Zeppo stood, stretching his arms above his head. Flashing Mika a smile, he pointed toward the door and gave her a wave. Smiling, Mika gave the healer a wave of her own. Turning his back to the petite princess, he furrowed his brows in frustration and left the library. He clenched his fist as he walked, letting himself get lost in the winding halls. Eventually, he found an arched wooden door at the end of a narrow pass and entered the room, ducking through the doorway.

The room was made entirely out of marquina marble, the only light flowing into the room was that from the domed sunroof. On the far wall, there was a statue of the life fate Umbri carved from moonstone, with water running from her outstretched hands. Taking off his shoes, Zeppo walked further into the room, letting the cool marble chill his feet. He went to the pool that Umbri's still hands filled, and let himself kneel before it.

"How is it that you always seem to find me when I'm feeling lost?"

Peering into the pool before him, a shiver ran down his spine. He rippled his reflection on the surface.

"Where do I go from here? I betrayed my only friend on a whim for this girl, James has never been violent with any hostage in this manner. Why do I never trust him?" Zeppo questioned Umbri's statue.

Cold filled the room, as the words fell from his lips, the light vanishing above him. Feeling his stomach drop, he stood.

"Who is standing behind me?" he questioned.

Zeppo closed his eyes in the silence that followed his question. Following his instincts, he stepped into the pool of water, a surge of warmth rushing through his skin. Opening his eyes at the sensation, fear laced his body as an overwhelming darkness swirled around the room, covering what little light was there before.

"I am impressed you felt my presence so quickly," a heavy voice echoed. "I am your fear, I am your end, I am all that consumes."

The darkness brushed against his skin, chilling the warmth of the pool at his feet, the air felt sharp and ridged. The cold that fell over him was like being hit by an avalanche.

"You couldn't save your family, you couldn't save your friend. You are the biggest failure of your divine race, a blue-collar, locked in chains, never able to do more. Let me and I will end it for you, just step from the pool," the voice soothed.

Images of his family, yelling for him to run as they were being slaughtered flashed through his mind, their blood spilling on the cobbled road. His friend burned at the stake, while he was held back by James, the smell of burnt flesh filled his nostrils. Tears formed at the edges of his eyes, but he held firm in the water. He instead focused on his family's smiles, his friends' encouragement, and Mika's kind apology.

"No," he answered.

"Then I will give you the knowledge of your next failure." The voice laughed.

Another wave of cold hit Zeppo, making him stumble and kneel in the water. The world spun, and he was watching through shrouded vision, as a version of himself ran across a room. As he ran through a wave of darkness, a purple-haired woman was running toward them with bloodied blades. The vision skipped forward to Mika lying on the ground in a pool of blood, blood was splattered across her face, and her eyes were glazed.

"This is what is in store for you, her life will end in your hands, but if you let me end your life, I can stop this tragedy."

"You're lying." Zeppo breathed harshly. "I will not let your horror come to pass," Zeppo said, as held his eyes closed.

"This is only the beginning, little bug."

Once the voice faded from the walls, Zeppo opened his eyes, to find the room as it had been when he walked in. Letting the breath he was holding out, he collapsed in the pool, staring hard at the reflection staring back at him. His lips parted, as he noticed his reflection had white eyes and was smiling at him, though he wasn't smiling himself. Trying to scramble to his feet he fell from the pool, scooting backward making room between him and the water. He watched in horror as the water suddenly turned and rose from the pool then suddenly dropping, leaving him in silence.

"You have not been told lies this day, leave and change the results, should you succeed, I will reward you my child," a feminine voice whispered.

Clamping his hands over his ears, Zeppo stood up abruptly, turned, and ran from the room, only to crash into Mika. Stumbling backward, his hands grabbed the princess's arm to steady her. He stared at her shocked face and felt his heart slow a little at the sight of her being alive.

"What happened to you, are you all right? I had something I forgot to tell you, but the door vanished after you closed it," Mika said, eyes wide.

"Uh, I-I'm not sure." Zeppo deflated.

"Maybe we should get you changed and speak to my brother. Weird things are going on now, and he's investigating it.

"What do you mean weird?" Zeppo questioned.

"Well, I can't say, I've been sworn to secrecy, but Clovis can help."

"Princess, something just attacked me, I'm soaking wet, and want some answers," he said, taking a step back from her.

"I know, but I can't break my brother's trust, and we've only just met,"

"I am leaving, I heard the rumors of your family being involved with dark magic. I don't want to be dragged into your messes, people I care about get killed because of families like yours."

"I am not my parents," Mika whispered, tears stinging her eyes.

"What about your brother, prodigal magic user? No Krystru has done magic that well, without using dark magic!"

"Don't you dare speak out of turn about my brother!" Mika yelled, tears spilling down her face. "You haven't got a clue about us, so shut your mouth and leave if you are going to be mean."

Shocked, Zeppo watched as the princess stood before him, trembling with tears streaming down her face. Mika telling him about her magic not working right crossed his mind, and he took a step back got to his knees, and bowed his head before the princess.

"I am sorry, I spoke out of turn and assumed things that I, myself haven't witnessed. I am stressed out, I just betrayed the only friend I had left to ensure your safety, and don't know what to do."

"Be my friend."

"What?" Zeppo asked, shocked.

"Be my friend, if you felt like you couldn't trust him then he isn't a real friend, and he sent people after you. I don't think he thought the same as you."

"Why would you want me as a friend? I just yelled at you."

"It's because you are honest, I will be honest as well. I planned to tell you what's going on, but it is my brother's business and I can't break his trust, so we have to do things the right way."

"We just met," he stated Mika's words from earlier.

"We did, but you have shown your worth to me, so let's be friends."

"You are confusing, princess."

"Mika."

"Mika," he corrected himself.

"Let's get you cleaned up and start sorting this mess," Mika said, standing straight.

I have a feeling it's going to be a long day, he thought.

As the duo walked from the room, a gentle chill crawled up Zeppo's spine; from the corner of his eye, the shadows seemed to move. Shutting the door, he quickened his pace to stay close to Mika, letting her presence calm him.

Chapter Nine

<u>Kilgi</u>

Sitting on the soft moss on the training ground, Kilgi bent forward wrapping her hands around her toes. She took a deep breath in, smelling the salty ocean breeze, mixing with the morning fires upon the breeze. Exhaling, she let go of her feet, letting herself fall back on the moss to stretch her back, her hands curling in fists. Watching the clouds drift by, Kilgi found her thoughts wandering back to the prince. *A servant to the prince without my consent, shall I forever remain without freedom?* Kilgi thought. *What must I do, to have a life of my own?*

Anger coursed through Kilgi, leading her to stand and draw one of her swords on a straw practice dummy. Heavy blows landed against the dummy's sides, clumps of straw falling to the ground with each swing.

Have I not already done enough? I have seen some of the deepest sorrows of the land, I've been spit on, degraded, a puppet for others to use, yet I haven't raised my hand in selfishness.

Breathing, she lunged forth on the dummy. *Yet fate would choose me, and still have me be a puppet.*

"Should I be worried the dummy offended you?" Iathos laughed.

Startled, Kilgi turned her sword in the knight's direction. Letting out a sigh, she lowered the sword, "You startled me."

"That would be a first," he mused.

"Want to spar?"

"Are you going to treat me the same as the dummy?"

"Maybe, did you steal my first-born child and take my family heirloom?" Kilgi smirked.

"Must be quite the straw man, to do all that." Iathos laughed, drawing his sword.

"Maybe not that sword," Kilgi said, pointing to the magical sword in his hand.

"Fair, perhaps wooden swords?"

"Sounds good."

Picking up the sparring swords, the two took their places in front of one another holding their swords in front guard. Dropping their stances, Kilgi tightened her grip and advanced on Iathos. Bringing her sword down vertically, Iathos deflected the blow. Lunging forward with a strike of his own, Kilgi had no choice but to fade, avoiding the attack. Iathos advanced, keeping Kilgi engaged. Smiling, Kilgi ducked the next blow, switching the sword to her left hand to parry Iathos' attack. Moving forward into his space, Kilgi slid her sword along the edge of his sword, while doing so she suddenly stopped and shoved the pommel forward hitting Iathos in the face.

Taking a few steps back, Iathos was forced to retreat and parry her rapid blows. As she brought down a heavy strike, Iathos dodged sideways, lunged forward, and grabbed her wrist. Surprise filled her face as he threw her to the ground. Rolling backward, Kilgi positioned herself into a crouched window guard position.

"I think we have sparred enough," Iathos called out.

"Don't wanna lose," Kilgi teased, from her stance.

"No, our companions have arrived," he responded, sweeping his arm to where the others stood.

"Oh."

Standing from her crouched position, Kilgi turned to face the group and waved awkwardly. Everyone made their way onto the mossy grounds, forming a circle.

"Well, it would seem some of us got an early start to the day, but now that everyone's here we will get started," Clovis stated.

"How exactly are we going to go about training today?" Ehiliana asked.

"One by one, you will attempt to call forth a display of power in what way feels natural to you. Magic doesn't work the same for everyone, it will call to you," Clovis said, meeting Ehiliana's pink eyes.

"I will go first, then."

"Let us clear the area," Clovis said, motioning for the others to move.

Walking to the side of the open ground, Kilgi watched as Ehiliana equipped herself with a bow, and took aim at a target about four hundred feet away. Closing her eyes she drew the string back, the arrow still aimed at the ground. Silence filled the air, everyone intently watching as they waited for her to do something. Kilgi felt a hand snap the button on her belt, holding Clovis's magic book. Grabbing the hand at her hip, she side-eyed the prince now staring back at her, then she let go. Taking the book, Clovis settled down beside her, watching as Ehiliana raised the bow, opened her eyes, and took the shot.

Everyone watched as the arrow took flight turning a deep red as it flew, Ehiliana's bow did the same seconds later. When the arrow hit the target a large rush of wind came over the field, tearing the target to shreds, and Ehiliana got knocked off her feet by the magic. Immediately, she got up and turned to face the group. Ehiliana gave an awkward smile and rubbed the back of her head before making her way to them.

"Sorry, I thought I would have better control."

"Control comes with practice, it was a good display." Clovis waved.

"Iathos, you're next."

"Sure," he said, making his way over to one of the straw dummies.

"I'll try not to hack it to pieces." Iathos smiled.

Kilgi snorted but said nothing in return. Watching Iathos, as he also tried to meditate and focus on his power. Lifting his new sword, he brought it down upon the dummy, only for it to be a normal slash. Frustration appeared on his face, and he attacked a few more times.

"Why am I even trying to do magic, I am not a fan of it," he said, turning to the group.

"It's all right, Iathos, we will figure it out," Kilgi spoke before Clovis could.

"Yeah, yeah, all right," he grumbled, making his way back to the sideline.

"Mika, take your turn," Clovis said, a hint of anger in his voice.

"What if I have performance anxiety?" Mika said, fidgeting.

"Just do it," Clovis snapped.

"Hey! Watch how you're talking to us," Kilgi said, grabbing the prince's shoulder.

"Do not touch me," he said, ripping himself from her grip.

"Then do not disrespect your sister and her wishes, she is just as much an authority here as you," Kilgi argued. *Are you going to hurt me for defending your sister?*

Meeting Clovis's golden eyes, she watched as his shoulders dropped and his eyes lowered from hers. She reached out and took the book from his grasp, his eyes snapping back to hers.

"Call it a hunch," she said.

"If practicing in private is better for you, then please do what you feel is best. We will not stop you, princess, we are here to work together," Kilgi said, returning her gaze to the prince as she spoke.

"Thank you," Mika said.

"I think we have practiced enough today, we should maybe instead compare similarities to our experiences with these tattoos. Perhaps it will give us better insight on how to use these new powers, without hurting ourselves or others," Kilgi said, addressing the group.

"I agree with that."

Kilgi watched as the group nodded and made their way off the training grounds. Leaving her and the royal siblings, she watched as Mika reached out for Clovis only to draw her hand back and turn to walk away. A long silence passed as the group walked away, Clovis running his fingers through his hair, lifting his head to face the sky. Kilgi watching as a frown appeared on his face, damping his handsome features.

"You have only been in my service four days and you keep showing you do not care for my status," he said, lowering his gaze to Kilgi.

"I think this curse is making you sick."

"You don't know a damn thing about this curse."

"I know you took the book, and immediately lost your cool, or are you always so short tempered?"

"Stop talking."

"You owe your sister an apology."

"I said, stop talking."

"Why?"

"Because I can't stand you," he said, leaning toward her.

"Well, that's original." Kilgi snorted.

"Give me the book."

"Not until it's purple."

"I am ordering you," he said, taking a step closer to her.

"As the person helping curb your curse, I say no," Kilgi said, standing her ground.

Clovis lunged at her, in an attempt for the book, however, Kilgi grabbed his arm and pulled him against her. He stilled at the sudden closeness, and Kilgi held firm, never breaking eye contact as he struggled to free himself from her grasp.

"Calm your nerves," Kilgi said, void of emotion.

"I am calm."

"You are far from it."

"What do you know?"

"Let it rest, prince, we do not need to rush."

Hopelessness crossed the prince's face at Kilgis's words, his body surrendering the fight from her grasp. He stood still eyes focused on Kilgi, as the morning sun lightened the shadows that previously darkened the castle walls.

"My parents are trying to force me into a marriage with Vivian," Clovis stated.

"Is that why you are having an outburst?"

"I'm not sure, I have no privacy or much time to myself," he whispered.

Letting go of the prince, Kilgi said, "That is part of your responsibility."

"I know."

"Then what is bothering you?"

"Why would you care?"

"I'm not sure yet, maybe I hope you will give me my freedom one day."

Running a hand through his hair, he whispered, "I can't protect Mika while I'm cursed like this, and every day something feels more wrong.

"Then I will help you protect her."

"It is not something you can help with."

"Why?"

"Because my parents would have you dead first, they do not try anything because of my magic."

"Your parents are a threat to your sister?" Kilgi said, with disbelief.

"Yes," he whispered. "Why am I even telling you?" he asked, confusion filling his face.

"I don't know, here I thought you couldn't stand me." *He needs some serious help.*

"I can't," he said, standing tall.

"Go, meet me in front of the palace at noon, that should give us both some time to cool off."

"As you wish, prince," Kilgi said, raising an eyebrow.

Kilgi watched as the prince walked away, as he did so she felt relief at the loss of his dangerous presence. Placing the book back on her belt, Kilgi climbed up to the rooftops with a new sense of determination. Once there, she studied the worn tiles before plopping down and grabbing the book from her side.

"This is either a good or a really bad idea," she murmured to herself.

Running her fingers over the worn black and purple leather, she opened the book. The first page had his name and birthday. A sense of fear and excitement filled Kilgi as she turned the next few pages only to find drawings. The first one she studied was of a pair of glasses, they were rounded with a metal frame. The next drawing was a bunch of little orbs with the words.

Cautiously trailing her hand over the drawing, Kilgi felt the pages calling to her. Knowing she shouldn't be going through the book, she went to close its pages.

"*Imagine it,*" Nell's voice whispered to her.

Jumping, Kilgi took in her surroundings, finding no one.

"Imagine it, call it forth."

"Okay, okay." Kilgi sighed.

Feeling sudden warmth as she imagined lights; she watched as little orbs of light came pouring from her fingertips. Suddenly, feeling freaked out, she dropped the book and shook her hands to make the magic stop, only for the orbs to follow the trail of her shaking hands. Peeking down at Clovis's book, she grabbed it and frantically searched for something to stop the spell. After a few pages, she came across a drawing of a closed book.

Slamming the book shut and blanking her mind, she watched as the spell died. Leaning back, she let out a heavy breath and tried to calm down, only to feel warm blood spilling from her nose.

"Damn," Kilgi said, pinching her nose and tilting her head back.

Standing, she walked to the edge of the roof and jumped down onto the balcony she climbed to get there in the first place. Making her way inside, she pretended not to notice the stares of people staring at her as she walked by. Holding her nose with one hand, she kept the other on the book and walked at a brisk pace toward her room. Once she neared, Vivian came from the shadows to interrupt Kilgi.

"You must be free for sport," Vivian smirked.

She is a stalker.

Sidestepping Vivian, Kilgi continued, only to feel the weight of something heavy hit her in the back. Forced to let go of her nose and catch herself, Kilgi watched as her blood spilled on the palace floors.

"Let me go," Kilgi said, never moving from her place on the floor.

"Stand up," Vivian demanded.

"No."

"Stand up."

"No."

Kilgi gritted her teeth as Vivian smacked her with the heavy weapon again.

"Stand."

"No, I know my rights, if I stand you can kill me for attempting to defend myself. You could kill me anyway."

"But I can't because you are the prince's pet, so stand."

"No."

"Fine."

Kilgi, this time, was repeatedly hit with the weapon, eventually losing balance and slipping on her blood. Once completely flat on the floor, Vivian dropped the weapon and kicked Kilgi. White blurred her vision, her breathing felt like fire, and everything smelled like copper. After enduring the nobles' beating, she felt Vivian grab her hair and lift her face to hers.

"Understand this, you will not live long enough to get what belongs to me." Vivian sneered, dropping Kilgi's head.

Listening to Vivian's retreating footsteps, Kilgi lay on the floor, unmoving from pain. Slowly, though, she reached to make sure the book remained at her side, more scared of the prince's wrath. Closing her eyes, she tried her best to breathe and calm down, tears pricked her eyes as she recalled the last time she was forced to endure a beating like this.

"You thought I would ever really love you?" Oliver laughed.

"I hoped."

"How daft of you, all you are good for is beating. No one is dumb enough to love your kind."

A tear slipped down her face, as the image of his tanned skin, green eyes, and curly brown hair bounced laughing at her pain with his friends. Kilgi suddenly felt like a heavy chain had tied itself to her and was dragging her further into the bad memories, until loud footsteps pierced her ears.

"Miss? Can you hear me?"

Blinking hard, she saw white hair and gray eyes staring at her.

"Yeah," she croaked out.

"We are close to the infirmary, I'm going to pick you up," he said.

"Don't, they won't help me," she whispered.

"I will do what I can then."

"Thanks."

"I'm Zeppo."

"Kilgi."

Hot, searing pain flared through her body, as the Vulocri used magic to pull her injuries back together. Breathing hard, she could hardly make out his encouraging words. After a few minutes, he picked up an exhausted Kilgi and walked her away from the infirmary.

"Where are we going?" she whispered.

"I'm taking you to Ethan, he's more skilled than me and can reset your broken bones," Zeppo stated.

"Oh."

"Who did this?"

"I can't say without risking my life." Kilgi hissed in pain.

"I see, well, go ahead and rest. I will take care of you from here."

"I don't know you," Kilgi said, starting to panic.

"*Calm yourself, he will help you*," Nell's voice soothed.

"Rest," Zeppo demanded.

"*Let him help you*," Nell whispered, as Kilgi relaxed.

Closing her eyes, Kilgi said, "Thank you."

***

Opening her eyes, Kilgi stood before a teal-colored building sitting at the edge of cobbled paths, splitting on each side of the place. The entire inside of the place was lit up, and she could hear voices inside, from where she stood. A cold shiver ran down her spine at the familiarity of the place she stood in front of, taking a few steps forward she read the sign hanging above the door. Clenching her fist she read, "Mare Pub and Inn."

This is a dream, it has to be.

Pushing open the door, she surveyed the bar, people filled almost every seat and many stood around the tables talking. Walking further into the building, she made note of how no one seemed to notice her.

"Nell, what is this, why am I here of all places?" she whispered.

Getting no response, Kilgi suddenly felt she was experiencing something she shouldn't be. Hugging herself close to one of the pub's pillars, she watched as an all too familiar face approached the stage on the far side of the building. Seeing Oliver's smiling face turned her stomach, and her fingers dug a little tighter into the pillar.

"Hello, ladies and gentlemen! As many of you know my name is Oliver, and tonight I have a real treat for all of you."

The crowd cheered loudly before Oliver motioned for their silence.

"Tonight, I would like to introduce you to my master—"

What? Why can't I hear his name? Kilgi thought.

Walking onto the stage, Kilgi watched as an unusually tall man stood before everyone. He had snow-white skin, with hands the color of black ink that seemed to blend into a gray farther up on his forearms. He wore a deep blue silk shirt unbuttoned, leaving nothing to the imagination, and black pants paired with blue boots. Kilgi stood speechless as his pretty face and smokey-colored locks scanned over the crowd, only stopping once his golden eyes met hers. *His eyes were like the prince's.*

Smiling, he said, "Hello, everyone, I am glad that I can grace you with my presence today. All of you know, that recently I have taken young Oliver in as my apprentice and will be making some changes to Eckris over the next few years. My goal is to unite everyone under one banner—my banner."

Frowning, he continued, "However these changes do not come without a price. There will be kingdoms that don't agree. Some blood will be shed, but for your undying loyalty this land will be greatly rewarded."

Stepping forward, Oliver quieted the crowd and said, "Any questions?"

"What about the disagreeable races, will they be a part of this unity?" an older man asked.

"Everyone I deem fit will be a part of this unity."

"When will it happen?" Kilgi asked, glaring at the man.

"It already has." He smiled.

"Where?"

"Now, now, little one, no need to be so eager."

Kilgi took a few steps forward, only hesitating at Oliver's presence.

"A brave one you are." He laughed.

Leaning in, Oliver whispered something to the man, before he suddenly frowned. Kilgi stood still at the exchange.

"My apologies, folks, it would seem we have a guest you cannot see in the crowd."

The crowd erupted into a loud buzz of voices, some yelling questions at the man, and some searching for Kilgi. After a few minutes, the crowd was silenced again, and the man gestured for Kilgi to follow him outside.

Hesitantly, she did, leaving Oliver with the crowd. Darkness surrounded the pair, barely illuminated by the soft glow of lanterns.

"Who are you?" Kilgi asked.

"Names of those you do not know cannot be heard in the realm you are in, little fate," he said, towering over her.

"Then how do you know me?"

"I do not know your name, only your face and pieces of your life that reside in the dark."

"How?"

"You're asking the wrong questions, little one, but it's because that's what I am."

"You chose Oliver on purpose then?"

"Yes."

"Why him?"

"Because he can give me what I want."

"What is it that you want?"

"You."

"That makes no sense, what do you really want?"

Laughing, he reached out and tilted Kilgi's chin up. "That is for my allies only. I want you because you provide me value, just not yet."

"You make little sense," Kilgi said, stepping back.

"It will make more sense with time, you will see that your fates are the true evil in this world. Though I suggest waiting until Nell gives you her full power before turning on them."

"What makes you think I would betray them?"

"Because you are like me."

"What a lie, I'd never attack a city the way you did in Colkirk."

"Give it time, my dear, you can only give so much with nothing in return before something has to give."

"You don't know a damn thing about me."

Stepping forward his dark hands pulled Kilgi to him. "The light is nothing more than a different type of darkness." His lips brushed her ear as he whispered, "The only difference is you don't get burned in the dark." Letting her go he took a step back, "You will not get what you want, the life you strive for is in vain."

Shaking, Kilgi took a few steps back. "N-No, it's not."

"My dear, you are one of three Matuen left in this world."

Now, wake up.

Chapter Ten

<u>Clovis</u>

Sitting at the top of the palace stairs, Clovis peered at the clear sky, while waiting for Kilgi. Peering out into the courtyard, he watched as a few of the nobles who'd been wandering around stopped to stare at him.

"I don't have anything to offer your gossiping lips," he mused to himself.

"What about mine?" Vivian asked, sitting next to him.

"I have none for you either."

"Hmm, what a shame, I feel like your romantic moment on the training grounds this morning was pretty juicy."

"I'd hardly call that romantic." He waved.

"Yet you never walk away from her."

"I have known her for four days, not everyone is a hopeless romantic, Vivian."

"You've known me for over a decade, and yet I am still not enough."

"Perhaps you should re-evaluate your character then."

"I can be whatever you want me to be."

Smiling Clovis said, "That's why I don't like you."

"Because I'm adaptable."

"Because you're fake."

"Let me show you how real I am."

"No, I have other things to do."

"I'll make it clear to you then, you will spend time with me or more of your friends get hurt."

"What do you mean? You are implying someone has gotten hurt."

"I mean, the friends you have been running around with these last few days won't get hurt."

Now standing over the sitting woman Clovis said, "What do you mean, *more of my friends?*"

"I mean, more of your friends, it would seem the poor Matuen girl got pretty hurt a little while ago."

Pinching the bridge of his nose, Clovis walked up the stairs away from Vivian. His brows furrowed as he heard her scrambling up the stairs after him.

"Your father already gave me permission to do as I please to get you to comply."

"I'm sure he did."

"Then what will it be?"

"Follow me," he said coolly.

"Guess I lost that bet with myself, I thought you'd let them die."

"Shut up."

"Aw, come on, you don't care about anyone but Mika, and now, suddenly, you care about a few more people."

"For fate's sake, Vivian shut up."

Making his way down the palace halls toward his room at a quick pace, Vivian hurried to chase after him. Making it to his room in record time, he dismissed his guards from their spot and opened the door for Vivian. Shutting the door behind him, he watched Vivian stroll around his room with an unusual ease.

She ran her fingers over the books on the wall, then walked to his bed taking a seat on the edge of his dark sheets. Choosing to ignore her, he took a seat on the leather couch leaning his head back.

"Finally dropping your calm act?" Vivian teased.

"I told you to shut up."

"Shut me up," she said, moving to stand in front of him.

"I'm pretty sure this is coercion."

"You are pretty when you're compliant."

Groaning, Clovis closed his eyes and ran his fingers through his hair as Vivian straddled him. He let his hands fall to Vivian's hips and pushed her back while sitting up straight.

"I'm not sleeping with you, Vivian."

"I'm just testing my boundaries, though rumors suggest you have quite the sexual appetite."

"Vivian, This is your only warning to get off me."

"I think I like sitting here."

As the words left Vivian's mouth, Clovis shoved her from his lap and watched as she hit the table and then the floor. Trying her best to gain her composure, Clovis leaned forward and grabbed her throat before she could. Making a gargled choking noise at the force of the prince's attack Vivian began panicking, clawing at Clovis's surprisingly strong hands.

"I didn't invite you into my chambers to give you what you want. My father's blessing will not protect you, this I can guarantee." Taking a breath, he hissed out, "Harm my company again and you will find I am not so courteous the second time around."

Letting Vivian go, he watched void of emotion as she sat on the floor catching her breath with her hand on her throat. As she went to stand,

Clovis lifted his foot, dropping it on the hand she had steadied on the floor.

"I didn't give you permission to stand."

"C-Clovis."

"I didn't give you permission to speak."

He is going to kill me, her voice whispered, through his mind.

Choking back her words Vivian peered at Clovis with a new sense of fear, his golden eyes pierced hers with a ferocity that left her feeling cold. His gaze only left hers when the chamber doors opened and he saw Kilgi standing in the doorway surprised.

"Sorry, it would seem I am interrupting something," she said.

"Stay, come in," Clovis said.

Never letting Vivan up, he watched as Kilgi closed the door and gave the prince a half bow.

"I am sorry for being late, I ran into some trouble and had to visit the healers."

"You are forgiven, are you okay?"

"I think so?" she said, confused.

"Kilgi, this is Vivan."

"Yeah, we met," Kilgi said coldly.

"I'm assuming before you went to the healers?"

"Y-Yeah, why?"

"Is she the one who hurt you?"

"Clovis," Vivian whispered.

"Kilgi, did she hurt you?"

"Yes."

"Thank you for being honest."

Letting his foot off Vivian's hand, he stood and walked over to Kilgi. Vivian kept her head down and stayed where she was on the floor.

"Vivian, look at us," Clovis demanded.

"Yes, sire," she said, letting her glossy eyes meet his.

"From this day forward, Kilgi will be my fiancée, the announcement will be made by the end of the day and she will receive all it is that you wished to have."

"W-What!" Kilgi and Vivian both sputtered.

"You can't do that!" Vivian cried, standing from the floor.

"There is no law against marrying a Matuen, it will provide Kilgi with immunity from the crimes that can be committed against her race, and you won't get what you want."

Smiling, he continued, "Besides, I did promise you that she would have everything you've ever desired."

"Clovis, it's a bad idea. If anything, your dad may just outright disown you," Kilgi interjected.

"I agree with the Matuen." Vivian sneered.

"You and I both know he won't," he said, giving Kilgi a pointed stare."

Understanding, she nodded her head, then said, "We will for now do what you see fit, if that means gifting me a social boost then so be it, however, we have some more pressing matters at the moment."

"I despise you," Vivian spat out, tears rolling down her face.

"Okay," Clovis and Kilgi responded.

Staring at Vivian, Kilgi said, "Vivian, I don't like you either, but I will give you some advice. Don't fuck with royalty, you won't win."

Sneering, Vivian went to the door and slammed it on her way out, leaving an awkward silence in the air. Cracking a half smile, Clovis put his hand on Kilgi's back and led her to the couch.

"I'm pretty sure this is the most messed-up four days I have ever had in my life," Kilgi said, falling back onto the couch.

"Yeah, I can agree with that."

"You're making me your fiancée?"

"Yes."

"We are gonna be here for a while then because things are going to get complicated."

"We will loop back around another time, for now, we will talk about this pressing matter."

"Ah, yeah. I think while unconscious I met our enemy."

"You astral projected?"

"Uh, yes, I'm not quite sure what happened."

"Tell me what you do know, our plans for today can wait."

"Well, I was in a pub called the Mare Pub and Inn. This place is in Nearon. There was an unnatural man with pale, white skin, and pitch-black hands who gave a speech about uniting Eckris under his banner."

"Is that all?"

"No, he could see me, but no one else could. He told me the fates are liars and are the true evil."

"I've never seen the fates attack an entire city."

"He also said that I am one of three Matuen left in the world."

Silence filled the air, as Clovis and Kilgi stared at one another.

"Did you know?" she asked.

"I knew there weren't many of you left, but I didn't know there were only three."

"Everything I've ever done has been in vain."

"Then let's stop these bastards, cure my curse, and overthrow my father. What do we have to lose?"

"You make it sound easy."

"Well, worst-case scenario, I get disowned and maybe killed and you keep living your life like you always have. You just may have some unwanted company. I've never been on the run before."

"You'd be the worst company."

"I'm offended."

"You should be, I saw how you had Vivian on the floor, I'm not trying to take her place."

"Well, you're not Vivian, I don't entirely dislike you, but you definitely annoy me. Besides, if you just received bad news from our enemy, you can be upset."

Pulling a pillow over her face Kilgi muttered, "There is going to be another attack soon, I don't know when he didn't give a date but, things are stacking up in the worst way possible."

"Yeah, we should probably get the ball rolling on our end. I'm sending Ehiliana and Iathos to dig around in the historical building, Mika is going to special training with her new friend, and we are going to stir up trouble for my father.

"Sounds like we are going to have a busy day. Also, why are we harassing your father?"

"So he leaves us alone. At this rate with his political games, I won't get much done, so I need to shut him up before this curse kills me from doing nothing."

"Fair point."

"Yeah."

"Are we going to pretend that this slightly friendly conversation never happened?"

"No, so long as we both keep up our ends of the bargain, then I will treat you right, I just don't believe in love at first sight, but I could come to stand you."

Laughing lightly, Kilgi said, "At least you are honest. When are we letting them know this is happening?" Kilgi asked.

"Right now. I'm gonna go send word, why don't you rest, you seem exhausted."

"In the prince's chambers?"

"Might as well get used to it, you're my fiancée now."

"Gross."

"You weren't grossed out when you pushed me over my table naked."

"I didn't look but was thinking gross."

"Sure," he said, walking out the door.

Chapter Eleven

<u>Iathos</u>

A few weeks had passed since Clovis handed out missions for each pair within the group. Ehiliana and Iathos were finally granted permission to enter the historical building, now with safeguards in place, in the event another collapse happens during rebuilding. Both seeming unsure of what kind of conversation to have, opted for silence as they walked the trashed streets of Colkirk. Many civilians were working to clear debris from the streets, while others made temporary living quarters for those left without housing.

"Don't gaze too much, the people aren't too fond of palace folk," Ehiliana warned.

"Does that include you?"

"Depends on what type of palace folk you are."

"Guess you will have to figure it out then."

"Would seem that way." She smiled.

Approaching the historical building, the pair glanced at one another before entering the busted building. The inside was destroyed, papers were laid all over the floors, tables were broken and flipped, and the bookshelves were knocked over. The only item that seemed to still be standing was the podium Ehiliana had mentioned earlier in the week. Walking over to the stand, both of them were filled with surprise at the bright blue runes glowing all over its surface.

"You think the spell is still active?" Iathos asked.

"Has to be if it's glowing like this."

"We should keep moving."

"Yeah, something feels wrong," Ehiliana stated.

"We will keep alert then."

Ehiliana nodded as she took the lead. Making their way to the back of the room, they were hit with the potent smell of mildew wafting up from the lower levels. Dim lighting flickered at the bottom of the stairs, and dripping water echoed off the walls. Exchanging an unsure glance, they made their way down to the second level.

"What's on this level?" Iathos asked.

"It's more like a museum, the upper level holds each country's historical books and documents. The second level is for artifacts, paintings, and office space for bookkeepers."

"What about the levels after that?"

"Well, the third level only has partial access, we can inspect the magic items that no longer have magic. The other half are items forbidden to the public."

"Who can go into the restricted areas?"

"The king, of course, and those who are considered archivists."

"I've never heard of these archivists."

"They are very secretive; us bookkeepers don't know what they do on the lower levels."

"Well, today, may be the day we find out."

"They didn't give us access though," Ehiliana said, with a worried tone.

"No, but I doubt many people are lingering around right now, there was only one guard at the door when we entered."

"I don't like this."

"Yeah, but we have to do it." Smiling, Iathos dropped his hand on her shoulder and gave a light squeeze. Making his way past her, he walked down the stairs to the third level. Reaching the bottom of the stairs, Iathos moved Ehiliana against the wall and put a finger to his lips, indicating to be quiet. Closing his eyes, Iathos listened as he let his eyes adjust to the dark.

"Hurry up, they will be down here soon," a male voice whispered.

"Shut up, Ehiliana is a stickler for rules, she would never dare come down here without permission," said the other.

"We don't know about the palace knight though."

"Marcus isn't going to be happy if we don't get this box moved."

"Shut up."

Opening his eyes, Iathos quietly drew his sword and snuck into the barely lit room. The pair of men were standing over a box with a torch in between them, seeming to be adjusting their grip on the box. Crouching low, Iathos made a wide sweep along the wall to keep out of their vision. Ehiliana, stared at Iathos in concern, furrowing her brow before deciding to take a few steps into the room.

"Hello?" she asked, taking a few steps in their direction.

"Ehiliana is that you?" the torch wielder asked.

"Yeah, I know I'm not supposed to be down here, but I need some help," she said panicked.

"We are busy right now."

"The knight I'm with is upstairs right now picking a fight with Peter because of a book, I can't break it up."

Focusing on one another. They set the box down and motioned for Ehiliana to lead the way.

"Come on, let's make it quick," he said.

Turning to lead the men from the room, Iathos reached out and grabbed the man at the back of the group. Putting a hand over his mouth, and his sword to his neck, he dragged him back into the darkness. A few minutes later Ehilian"s head popped around the corner scanning the room for the pair.

"We're over here," Iathos said, quietly.

"Good to see you're all right," she said, smiling.

"Guess we better get some answers from this guy then."

"His name is Allen, he is one of the higher-ranking bookkeepers and has been trying to become an archivist for years."

"Good to know." Iathos smiled.

Walking past his hostage he opened the box they had previously been moving. Inside was an obsidian slab of rock with a bunch of runes drawn in a circle with lines crossing through its middle. Glancing over at the man on the floor, Iathos came and crouched before him.

"What is this?" he asked.

"I don't know, they told us to move it before you two came."

"You're a bad liar, Allen."

"I swear, I don't know!"

Rocking back on his heels, Iathos stood and returned to the rune slab. Studying it, he frowned but then motioned for Ehiliana to follow.

"Go upstairs and get some paper charcoal, we are gonna copy this down and keep going," he whispered.

"Are you sure?" she asked back.

"Yes."

Watching Ehiliana leave the room, Iathos returned to Allen and kicked him in the side of the head. Allen's body slumped against the ground and a cry left his lips; crouching down, Iathos grabbed his hair and lifted his head.

"Listen, Allen, I know neither one of us wants to be doing what we are doing right now, so, for your sake and mine, I suggest you keep your mouth shut about everything that's transpired here today." Taking a breath he continued, "That means, not telling them we know about your slab of rock, or that we aren't leaving for a little while. I suggest you get this rock to Marcus and let him know everything is fine."

With wide eyes, a few tears slipped down his face as he shook his head.

"Good boy," Iathos said, patting his head.

Sitting beside Allen's slumped body, he waited for Ehiliana to come back. The darkness of the room seemed to calm and unsettle him all at once, making no move to investigate the feeling.

"Iathos?" Ehiliana whispered into the room.

"I didn't go anywhere," he said, standing.

"Let's make this quick."

Standing guard in the dark, Iathos watched as Ehiliana laid out the papers along the tablet's pieces and scribbled over the papers with charcoal. He smiled at Ehiliana's face of determination as she scribbled like her life depended on it, and laughed.

"Shh," she responded to the laugh.

"Ah, my apologies, I didn't realize art was so serious," he whispered and rocked on his heels.

"I'm telling my girlfriend you're flirting."

"I would never flirt with a taken lady or man."

"Oh?"

"Shut it."

"Am I the first to know?"

"No, hurry up, our time seems to be running short."

"I am done, just rolling up the papers."

Finishing rolling the papers, Ehiliana walked over to Allen and helped him to his feet.

"I am sorry, Allen, but there is some bad stuff going on, please don't say anything."

"Let's go, you lead the way," Iathos interjected.

Making their way down the next set of stairs a cold breeze rolled over the pair, sending shivers down their spines. Their footsteps echoed down the stairs loud enough to wake an army, but it couldn't be helped with the uneven footing the stone stairs had to offer. Staring at the woman ahead of him, Iathos slowed, leaving room to draw his sword as the temperature dropped suddenly.

Sensing the change in the air, he grabbed Ehiliana and pulled her behind him as their torched light was dashed. The familiar feeling of the heavy tentacles grabbed his ankles and swept him off his feet, cracking his head with a sickening thump. He heard Ehiliana's cry for him, as he was pulled down the stairs. Acting quickly, he tightened his core to hold his head high enough to keep from hitting each stair and lurched himself forward to swing at the thing grabbing his ankles. A loud cry came from the thing that had grabbed him, scrambling to his feet as it let him go.

"Elly!" he shouted up the stairs.

"I'm here, I'm coming!" she shouted back, her footsteps echoing down the stairs.

Reaching Iathos, her hand darted to his shoulder. "I'm here, I can see."

"They have to be hiding something if we are being attacked."

"We need to come back with the group Iathos," Ehiliana pressured.

"No."

"Iathos, please, I am scared."

Turning to face Ehiliana in the dark, he grabbed her wrist and said, "I am here, you don't have to be scared."

Letting her go, he descended the stairs into the darkness, ignoring her murmurs as she silently followed. Approaching the bottom of the stairs, the darkness ebbed away as green flames began lighting the path up the stairs.

"It would seem we lost the element of surprise," Iathos said, irritated.

"We should turn around," Ehiliana whispered.

"Stop being a baby, we can't stop evil if we run from it."

He pushed open the weathered, wooden door and stepped onto a balcony paved with ancient stones. Twin staircases descended on either side. At the heart of the colossal cavern stood a towering stone pillar, encircled by wooden walkways spanning various tiers, each branching out to diverse destinations. Scattered across the expanse were scores of graceful balconies, some connected by those same pathways.

"This place is too big to explore without the group," Ellie said.

Walking forward, Iathos faced the group of guards making their way up both sides of the stairs and archers lining up across the cavern.

"We have company, be ready," Iathos warned.

"Iathos, I'm being serious, we need to leave," Ehiliana said, taking steps backward.

"There are only a few guards." Iathos waved.

As if on cue, five guards stepped onto the landing, two on the left and three on the right.

"Stand down, general," the leading guard warned.

"I can't do that," he replied.

Taking a few steps forward, one of the guards rushed forward to attack. Raising his sword to meet the blow, Iathos lifted his leg and sent a heavy kick to the guard, making him stagger backward. Adjusting his grip he rushed forward and shoved his sword through his attacker's belly, pulled it free, then swung at the nearest guard.

The clashing of swords began as the guards joined the fight against Iathos, some making their way toward Ehiliana. Fending off the guards, he took notice of his partner keeping some of the men back, leaving room for him to fight. Moving backward, he managed to merge the fight so he and Ehiliana were back-to-back.

"You okay?" he asked, strained.

"No," she said with gritted teeth.

While the fighting continued, Iathos took notice that the more enemies he took down, the heavier his sword felt. Adjusting his grip he lifted the sword to match the last guard's block and cut right through his sword as he stepped into the swing, splitting the guard's skull. Dusting himself off, Iathos glanced over at Ehiliana who was staring at him with wide eyes. Pointing at his sword, Iathos lifted his hand glancing at the object before him. Different colors were pouring into the sword, all connected to a different fallen guard, etching their names into its blade. The feeling of gravity came over Iathos, forcing him to take a knee as he was flooded with the guard's voice.

"Arthur Stranhon, captain of the imperial archivist, age thirty-five, father of three. I did dishonest work for the country's betterment. My wife Emily doesn't know the depth of my work, but I think she would forgive me for what I have done."

"What did you do?" Iathos's voice stuttered.

"I killed her parents for conspiring against the royal family. They were going to publish the Brailin's Tome of Eckris. The information in that tome would have started a revolution."

"What's in it?"

"I don't know."

"Why tell me this?"

"I want to be free of my sins, you are death, are you not?"

"No, I am not."

Gripping his head, as multiple voices overwhelmed him, Ehiliana's firm grip anchored Iathos and quieted the voices.

"Stand up, Iathos, we need to go, now."

Lifting his head, Iathos looked across the cavern where Ehiliana's gaze fixated. Perched on one of the balconies was a giant fox-like creature with human hands and feet. Its skin was bright red as if dipped in blood with black sunken eyes, and razor-sharp teeth smiling at them.

"Yeah, we should run," he said, shaking off the daze.

Turning to run, Iathos led the way up the stairs as the demonic creature let out a piercing scream. The sound of it running up the stairs pushed the pair to run faster, fear making their hearts pump hard enough that their chests felt full. Before long, Iathos heard a crack as Ehiliana was slammed into him causing both of them to fall up the stairs. The creature's large sharp hands pressed down on Iathos pushing out what air was left in his lungs. The smell of blood filled the air as its claws dug into flesh.

Unable to see the creature, Iathos struggled against the monster, until a bright flash of red lit up the stairway. Letting out an ear-piercing screech, the monster backed off, falling down the stairs. Scrambling to his feet, Iathos ran up the stairs.

"Iath-os, my-my leg is broken," Ehiliana sobbed in pain.

Hearing the creature move, Iathos turned around and hesitantly picked Ehiliana up, starting up the stairs.

"Don't focus on the pain, we have to survive for now, you are going to have to keep it back, can you do that?" he asked breathily.

"I'll try," she half-sobbed.

Adjusting herself, with quiet whimpers of pain, she leaned over Iatho's shoulder and summoned her bow, aiming for the stairs. Iathos focused on moving up the stairs, only feeling the shake of Ehiliana's shots, and the creature cried every time she landed a hit. Climbing the stairs was harder than anticipated, but the pair managed to make it into the open room.

"Don't stop, please get us out of here," Ehiliana whimpered.

"That's the plan, but we have no way of warning the public what's following us out."

"How are you so calm?" she whispered.

"Practice." He grunted.

After a few minutes, Iathos stood in the main hall of the historical building, a group of guards blocking the door and an unfamiliar man.

"What is going on?" the man asked.

"There is a monster following us," Iathos said, curtly.

"I wasn't speaking to you, knight."

"Peter is telling the truth," Ellie said, never turning to face him.

As Peter went to speak, the monster's loud cry echoed as it crashed into the room; Ehiliana released another shot. Some of the guards ran for their lives, while others stood ready to fight the creature. Iathos moved across the room, not glancing back, and dropped Ehiliana into Peter's arms.

"Keep her safe, I will handle the creature now," he said, pulling his sword.

Rushing forward, Iathos slammed into the creature knocking it backward, then brought his sword down into its matted fur. Screeching, the monster swung its hand back slamming into Iathos knocking him off his feet. Pulling the sword from its body, the monster flung it to the ground and ran for Iathos as he struggled to his feet. Taking a leap to hop on top of the knight, it was knocked sideways by one of Ehiliana arrows.

Making a run for his sword, he heard Ehiliana release a few more shots. Grabbing his sword, he turned to see the monster running at Ellie and the guards. Making a quick decision he threw the sword like a spear at the monster.

"Echo, kill it, please," he demanded.

"As you wish," Echo said, sarcastically.

Materializing beside Iathos, Echo placed a cold hand on his shoulder and gave him a smile before taking off at an unnatural speed, his long locks flowing behind him. Grabbing the sword midair, Echo ducked as the monster swung for him and lunged forward stabbing the creature.

"Watch closely, boy, I will not help you like this again," Echo called out.

Ripping his sword from its flesh, Echo maneuvered around its swings like a ballroom dancer. Adjusting the grip on his sword, he side stepped another blow from the monster and jumped up, landing on its large clawed hand. Echo jammed the sword through its throat with ease, and pulled out before jumping down from its falling body. With a heavy thud the monster's carcass hit the ground, black liquid pouring from its body. Echo walked toward Iathos, an eerie calm over him as he cleaned the blade. Iathos took in the fate before him, his long, wavy black hair clung slightly to his jawline, and a smile graced his face Making his glowing blue eyes and slightly sunken cheeks appear intimidating and crazed.

Standing before Iathos, Echo placed a hand on his head. "You seem eager to get yourself and your friends killed, Perhaps I should judge you now."

Lifting the sword and running Iathos through, Echo said, "It is time for your trial."

Chapter Twelve

<u>Mika</u>

Okay, Mika, you've been in training for a few weeks now, things are not going well for any of us. Iathos is magically dead right now thanks to his fate, and we have new clues to something bad going on. Your dad is suddenly being nice to you and trying to get you to talk about your brother because he got engaged, and your new friend is being weird and won't talk about it.

So if we're going to survive today, we need to first clean up and dress how we want to feel, and maybe things will take a turn for the better.

Turning the faucet to her bath, she walked away to let the tub fill while she did her hair. Sitting down in front of her bathroom vanity, Mika picked up her brush and detangled her hair. Making quick work of it, she sectioned off strands and braided her hair from the top of her head back, tying the bottom off with a pale green ribbon. Grabbing a pin to put the braid up until after her bath, Mika lowered herself into the hot water, closing her eyes with a sigh.

"Are you in the water yet?" a higher-pitched male voice asked.

Startled, Mika sat up and looked across the room to find a short, skinny man with gray skin and white fluffy hair leaning against her vanity.

"Who are you!" she yelled out.

"Calm yourself; I am your fate, ya know the one who put that cute little rook on your arm."

"I-I'm not sure I believe you," Mika said, sinking back into the tub.

"My name is Ellis, the fate of the ethereal, the same fate who put you and the bishop in my realm to save you from being eaten alive by ancient magic."

"How did the place look?"

Sighing, Ellis said, "It was a giant field with a rook and bishop, you chose mine, while the other girl chose the bishop."

"Maybe you are my fate then, but why must you invade my privacy?" Mika said, calming down.

"You spend too much time around others, and this is the perfect place to help train you," he said, waving his hand casually.

"No offense, but I am naked, and don't know your motives."

"No motive, just trying to train you, I'm not a sexual being if that's what you're worried about. If you would feel more comfortable, I could invite my best friend Ora."

"Your best friend is the fate of prophecy?" Mika asked.

"Yeah, she's cool."

"You promise nothing bad?"

"Promise, nothing bad within my control, but your bath has been the only moment you are alone aside from sleeping these days."

"Okay, but one thing goes wrong and you're done."

"That's all I needed to hear," Ellis said, walking over to Mika and gently poking her forehead.

Feeling warmth, the world spun, and suddenly, she was standing in the same field from a couple of weeks prior. Flowers bloomed, and off in the distance, a narrow creek ran through the field.

"I figured a familiar place would make you more comfortable, and some clothes," Ellis said, smiling.

Mika saw a white blouse and skirt sitting against her skin, blowing with the breeze. Letting out a sigh, she turned to face Ellis and put a hand on her hip, in an attempt to seem brave.

"What now?" she asked.

"Show me what I am working with, cast the most powerful spell you can muster," he instructed.

Mika let the cool breeze steel her nerves as she drew the feeling of magic to her. Lifting her arm she could feel the breeze pick up, pulling from her feet, wrapping up her body and down the outstretched arm."

Snapping her fingers she said, "*Luvoreia ex nox lufrix.*"

Together, Ellis and Mika watched as the ground below her caved in and the flowers began growing at a frightening rate, as the sky turned from day to night. Feeling fear course through her veins, she turned to face Ellis with the intent to run, only to find him smiling like a madman. With the flick of his wrist, the world reset itself as if Mika's spell had never happened.

"Ho-How did you do that?" Mika stuttered out.

"With magic."

"B-But."

"Ah, none of that now, let's get my questions answered. I'm sure mine are more important. Because this is my realm, I can reset it when I so please, and in terms of practice, I have a lot more experience than you.

"Are you reading my mind?" Mika said, sitting down.

"No, it was just written all over your face. Anyway, first question, why are you saying spell in Auromic and not your tongue?"

"Oh, um, my spells were worse in my language, and my brother said, it's harder for people to counter spells if they don't know what you are casting," Mika said, picking at the grass by her legs.

"Next question, how do you picture your magic when you use it?"

"I picture what I think the spell would manifest as after I cast it. So if I want it to be dark, I picture the sun going down."

"Well, then, perhaps the next step will be easier for you. Your problem may be that everything you're doing to cast is too overwhelming. So, for your next spell simply clear your mind, conjure your magic, and instead of saying the spell, picture it in your head with intentions of making it tangible."

"That's it?"

"Yes, now let's see a simple light spell." He clapped and walked a few steps away.

Inhaling, Mika again let the breeze calm her nerves and let her mind fall blank. Feeling less anxious than before, she lifted her hand, picturing lights floating. Feeling a warmth she watched as little lights manifested in the field before her. Smiling she couldn't help but run to hug him.

"That's the first time since I was nine that a spell worked for me!" she said, pulling back from the hug.

"Don't get too ahead of yourself though, kiddo, there is a big difference between doing it in a controlled space with more magic than in your reality." Continuing he said, "For now, only practice that spell, the way we just did, everything else will come with time, there is a big chance your magic is connected to your emotions so it will take quite a lot of work on your part."

"I will try my best, Ellis, thank you for helping boost my confidence, can we do this again soon?"

"When I find another moment, I will come to find you, for now, though I will leave you with something important to do."

"Oh, okay."

"Tell your father, should he try to harm you or your brother, that the little loophole he has been using to avoid the fates for years, will finally meet his end."

"I don't understand."

"Your father is not a good man, Mika. Due to the nature of his magic and our ability to interfere in some world affairs, I cannot tell you everything, but you can ask Clovis about Isla Gorkem and get some answers."

"However, when you have a chance, you can find a useful spell book in the library. Just investigate your surroundings and you'll find it. The book may give us an upper hand in what's to come," Ellis said, standing by her. Pressing a finger to her forehead, Ellis said, "Until next time little one."

Feeling the rush of warmth and the spin of the world, Mika was sitting on her bed lacing up her outdoor shoes.

"I need to find Clovis now," Mika muttered, as she finished lacing her shoes.

Briskly walking down the corridor, Mika felt as if the world around her was rushing with the beat of her heart. Feeling the onset of anxiety, she stopped at the top of the marbled stairs, trying to ground herself, before a few tears slid down her cheek. *There is no way our father is a bad guy, right? I know he has been fighting with Clovis, but family fights sometimes,* she thought, as she sank next to the stairs.

Feeling a strangling weight settle on her chest, Mika closed her eyes, trying her best to regulate her breathing. Leaning her head against the stair post, she suddenly felt another's shoulder lean against hers.

"My brother's senses were tingling and felt like you needed me," Clovis said, resting against her.

"I don't have brother tingles, but I can kill whoever makes you cry," Kilgi offered up from behind the two.

Laughing loudly and wiping at her tears, she said, "I needed to ask you a question, alone?"

"Yeah, you can," he said, helping her up and leading her back to his room.

Leaving Kilgi outside the door, he brought Mika to sit on the dark leather couch.

"What's on your mind that's heavy enough to give you a panic attack?" he asked.

"My fate came to train me this morning, and after he told me some things."

"What did he say?"

"That if our father harms me or you, he will have ended a loophole he has been using to avoid the fates," Mika said, shrinking back. "Our dad is a good man, right?" she asked, grabbing his arm.

"I don't have a clear answer for you, Mika. He has, over the years, done some things I don't agree with, but I never thought him evil. I always thought of him as controlling and selfish, so I am a little concerned about your fate saying this. How do we know your fate is trustworthy?"

"I don't know, but he did help me today, and that wasn't all he said. He also asked me to bring up Isla."

Sucking in his breath, Clovis shot to his feet, and walked across the room leaning a hand against the wall before turning to face his sister. Walking over to her, he knelt and took her hands into his own. "Mika, that is a dangerous thing to pursue."

"You know about this Isla? Who is she and how is she related to all of this?" Mika said, her hands now shaking in her brother's hands.

Sighing, he said, "Isla was our older sister, she died before you were born, and I was forbidden from ever speaking about her."

"You kept it from me?"

"Father pretty much made it clear that I was to forget she existed or I wouldn't like the consequences. I was too little to fight back."

"How did she die?"

Letting go of Mika's hands he ran a hand through his hair and said, "She was kidnapped and used for some blood ritual. When they brought her body in it was as if it had aged a whole lifetime. Her dark blond hair hung in white patchy strands on her head, her skin was wrinkled and stretched against her skeleton, and her eyes were glazed over as if she lost her sight. It was horrific to see."

"That's so awful, why would you go see her?"

"I refused to believe she was dead, so I had to see for myself. Our father caught me while I was in there, that's when he told me to forget her."

"That makes Dad seem like not the best person if he told you to forget our sister," Mika whispered.

"I am sorry for not telling you, Mika."

Pulling Clovis into a hug she said, "It's okay, Clovis, I didn't get to meet her, but I'm sure you loved her as much as you love me."

"Yeah, but your fate made an implication with his statement," he said, pulling from the hug.

"What do you mean?"

"This fate knew Isla and makes me think there is more to investigate after stating our father is going to mess up if he hurts us. More than likely, your fate is implying that our father hurt Isla."

"Of course, I missed it, I didn't know who she was until now."

"Mika, if I find out Dad hurt Isla and may hurt you or me, especially you, I will kill him before he can speak another sentence," Clovis said, now pacing around the room.

"Clovis, maybe it's not what it seems, he is our dad shouldn't we give him some trust?"

"No."

"Clovis, how could you say that!"

"Because I am not losing another sister. I want to believe despite how unbearable he is, that he is a good man, but recently there have been things that have changed my mind on this matter," Clovis stated with the wave of a hand.

"Maybe you are overthinking things, Clovis," Mika pleaded.

"Mika, he cheated on Mom, with a Flemington! And has been trying to marry you off for months, and me for years. Honestly, I only engaged myself to Kilgi because he was trying to force a marriage with Vivian, despite my protest. Now, it is being implied that he had something to do with my older sister's death, I can't keep letting him do whatever it is he is doing," Clovis said.

"Clovis, Dad just wants what is best for us, he may be stern about it, and I know you two have been fighting but he can't be a bad guy. Maybe it was someone who resembled Dad, you know how gossip is," Mika said, now nervous.

"I saw it myself, Mika, the only reason Dad isn't fighting my engagement anymore is because I blackmailed him, or he has gone silent to find a way to fight me on this."

"No," Mika said in a hushed voice.

"Yes, Mika, Dad isn't trustworthy, he hasn't been for some time, really ever, he has always been cold to us. We have a lot on our plates, so I will delve into this matter. Just keep it quiet. I don't want you to get hurt if you slip up. If nothing comes of it then we will address your fate for causing this stir up," he said.

"Okay, Clovis, I trust you to be honest with me, you have to keep me in the loop," she said, tears now streaming down her face.

Coming to hug his sister, he said, "I promise to keep you in the loop, and keep you safe. I do have some things to take care of, but if you need me let me know, okay?" Clovis asked.

"Yeah, I will, now get out of here, try not to annoy your fiancée too much."

"Watch it," he quipped,

"I figured that only a woman who could beat you up would be the one to catch your interest." Mika laughed while wiping at her tears.

"Should I tell Zeppo you're in need of a fiancé?"

"No! We don't have that kind of relationship," Mika said, now embarrassed.

"Your face says otherwise."

"Shut up, we are only going to be friends, now get out," she said, practically pushing him out the door. *Honestly, he's not into women,* she thought, shaking her head.

Shutting the door, Mika walked over to the mirror to make sure she managed to dress herself well enough before facing the public. Smoothing down her green coat, and fluffed the white dress underneath. Grabbing her matching sunhat, she unpinned her braid letting it fall down her back and left the room. Putting on a brave face, she decided to make her way into the garden to walk off the morning stress.

***

The fresh ocean breeze caressed Mika's pale skin as she walked outside. Taking a deep breath she suddenly felt more refreshed than she had in a few days. Studying the hedges and willow trees neatly lined down the middle of the garden space, Mika headed toward the first tree. Letting her fingers run against the rough branchy texture of the bushes, she smiled a little at the way it tickled her. Ducking between the willow's hanging leaves, Mika sat near its trunk and closed her eyes letting the ambient noises calm her down. The pressure she felt lifted from her chest as the birds sang their song and the wind rustled the leaves and wafted the smell of lilies through the air.

After a few minutes, she opened her eyes and pulled a pocket-sized red leather-bound notebook from her bag. Letting her fingers touch its smooth surface, she opened it, flipping through the pages of her past sketches. Pulling a charcoal pencil from her bag, she drew clothing ideas for her new friends. Feeling the itch for her sewing machine, Mika made a mental note to take some time to actually sit down and enjoy her hobby later that night. After drawing for a little while, Mika slipped the notebook back into her bag.

Leaning her head back against the willow's trunk, Mika stretched her hand before her, picturing little lights floating everywhere.

Before her, a spark of light flickered in front of her fingertips. Smiling just a little bit, she watched as it flickered in an attempt to stay lit. Instead of letting it die, Mika focused on steadying her breathing and feeding the light a little more magic. The gentle breeze had now picked up a little, and the bird songs seemed to quiet as more magic pooled around her.

"Just a little bit," Mika whispered to herself.

Closing her hand into a fist, she opened and then closed her palm in an attempt to act as a physical stopper for her magic. Suddenly, the flickering light burst before returning to a little flickering orb. Scared of causing something bad to happen, Mika let the spell end after that and stood up. Smoothing out her skirt, she smiled and danced around.

"I did it! I controlled my magic for a few seconds! I have to tell Clovis and Zeppo."

"I'm sure it could wait," an unfamiliar voice came from behind her.

Spinning to face this person Mika said, "Who are you and were you spying?"

"It's not spying if you're in public," he answered.

"Who are you?"

"Ah, yes, I am Noa."

"Well, Noa, I am Mika Gorkem, princess of Aeberuthey."

"A pleasure, princess. I was hoping to hold your company for a while."

"You'll have to forgive me, but I am otherwise occupied."

"You mean, meeting your brother, or the Vulocri you keep in your company?" he asked, smiling.

"Yes, now I know you are spying on me," Mika argued.

"I am merely inquiring after what you said, just a moment ago."

"I never said Zeppo was a Vulocri," Mika said, taking a step back.

"Just have a conversation with me, princess?" Noa asked.

"No, now leave."

Sighing, Noa responded, "I could have at any time drained your focus, yet I have not. I come bearing news for Zeppo."

"Make it quick," Mika said, taking a step back.

"James made a contract with some man touring around the eastern country and has made orders for James to come after Zeppo. I wanted to warn him before something bad happens," Noa said.

"Are you planning to stay?"

"No, I am going back, I was sent to spy on Zeppo."

"Then why tell me at all?"

"Because Zeppo still has some people on his side, that's all."

"You are going to tell James what you found?"

"Yes, princess."

"Then I am sorry, I can't let you leave."

Pushing her hands forward, she conjured the image of Noa trapped. Noa took graceful steps backward as the roots from the willow tree came bursting from the ground in wild attempts to grab him. Making his way through the now crazed roots, Mika threw her hands up pushing the magic further. Suddenly, feeling unfocused, Mika made eye contact with the Jesatyl whose eyes and freckles glowed a brilliant blue. Trying to run away, she felt Noa's warm hand grab her wrist, and she flinched as the tree behind them slammed to the ground from being uprooted.

The smell of damp soil and clove filled her nose as Noa turned her to him. Feeling unfocused, she tried to regain her train of thought as she stared up at his glowing face. Bringing her close to him, he brought her to a sitting position and smoothed out the wild strands of her hair. Unable to think, Mika mindlessly reached out and touched Noa's green scarf.

"My apologies, princess, but that's some scary magic you got. I'll let you keep the scarf as an apology gift for using my abilities on you," Noa whispered as he wrapped the scarf around her.

"You're pretty." Mika giggled.

Untangling himself from the princess's grasp, Noa said, "No, princess, that would be you."

Hearing voices echo in the background, Mika watched as Noa disappeared, leaving her in the mess of the willow tree. As the world seemed to fade in and out, Mika felt a few pairs of hands haul her to her feet. As the guards escorted her, she couldn't help but giggle and reach to play with the tassels of their uniform's shoulder pads. Everything seemed to move fast, as she was sitting in the infirmary and the guards called for Ethan. Leaning back on the bed, Mika lazily pulled the scarf to her nose and closed her eyes to sleep.

Chapter Thirteen

<u>Ehiliana</u>

"You know, I thought I'd find you here," Regina said, coming through the study door.

"Mm-hmm, I'm pretty sure I live here now."

"Mind if I join you?"

"Only if you brought lunch."

"Lucky for you, I did bring lunch."

"You're the best girlfriend ever." Ellie smiled.

"How's your leg?"

"Mending, but it will be a few more days until I can receive another healing session."

Setting down a plate of sandwiches, Regina pulled the quill from Ehiliana's hand, setting it down beside her. Pushing the plate in her direction, Regina picked up her sandwich and motioned for her to eat as well.

"The palace has me running around like crazy, so I got to run, but you will have to fill me in once you make progress," Regina said, pecking Ellie's lips, and making a quick exit.

"Yet another day alone in this room," Ellie said, rolling her eyes.

Leaning back in her chair, sandwich in mouth, Ehiliana let out a groan, spinning in her chair before stopping at the messy desk in front of her. While eating her sandwich, Ehiliana stacked the note pages she had taken while reading through books on runes. peeking over at the smaller version of the rune she had drawn, she grabbed the paper and once again, decided to compare them to the runes in her notes.

"This is useless, I might as well be learning a new language," Ehiliana muttered.

Wait! maybe it is a language.

"That's it, maybe it's not actual runes!"

Grabbing the drawing, Ehiliana folded it up and placed it in her breast pocket. Leaving Clovis's study room, she made her way to the library. Upon arrival into the large room, she found Zeppo sitting on one of the couches by the fire reading. Hobbling up to the Vulocri, she gave a smile and waved.

"Hey, I'm pretty sure I told you not to walk around too much," Zeppo said, lightly.

"Heh, well, I need some new books, my research took a turn."

"You mean the secret research I'm not allowed to know about, because I'm not special like the rest of you," Zeppo teased.

"That would be the one, yes."

"I'll make a note of that, where can I help?"

"I need a translation book, for pretty much each known language."

"Well, I'll get to work on that, where does Clovis have you holed up?"

"In his study."

"Well, head back and I'll fetch what you need, have you had lunch?"

"Yes, Regina brought me some."

"Good, now get going," Zeppo instructed.

***

Sitting back in the study, Ehiliana decided to clean up the mountain of books that covered the desk, and surrounding floors. Laying the books in piles by the desk, she also bound her old notes before setting fresh paper out. The room had a strong smell of ink and burnt paper

150

from the previous days' writing and burning papers she thought useless. Hearing a soft knock on the door, Ehiliana took her seat.

"Come in."

"So, I found books on Auromic, Jesatyl, Old Speech, and Wayling. Between you and me we have Fenian, Kryish, Vulcan, and Devourian covered," Zeppo said, kicking the door closed behind him.

"I'm pretty sure, you aren't allowed to be a part of this."

"Well, I don't know how you're going to learn Devourian then."

"As you know it, the Feydevor are feral, nobody has been near them in centuries without injury or worse."

"That you know of. The Feydevor have a great trade relationship with us Vulocri, we have just kept it quiet all these years for their safety."

"There is no—wait what?"

"Yes, us Vulocri can interact with the Feydevor one of my best friends was one."

"How? The blood curse?"

"We didn't exist then, so I guess that makes us an exception to their curse, and potentially maybe a cure one day."

"That's incredible, though."

"But it will remain a secret like me helping you." Zeppo smiled.

"Fine, this all stays secret."

"My lips are sealed."

Falling into a comfortable silence, the only sounds that came from the two, were the turning of pages and quill against paper every so often. Both had the idea to make charts of each language's alphabet, they started laying the pages out around the drawing of the rune.

"So, if I can take a stab at what your guess is, you think the runes on this page are a combination of languages and not just simple runes?" Zeppo asked.

"Pretty much, now to see if we can figure it out."

"I'm going to come stand over your shoulder and look, if that's all right?"

"Yeah, just don't touch me, please."

"All right, I just didn't want to make you uncomfortable."

"Thank you."

"Now, let's see if we are good at puzzles."

***

Losing track of time, both Zeppo and Ehiliana took turns filling page after page with different combinations of letters until they found matching some runes. Feeling a rush of excitement, what had taken Ehiliana too long to figure out was starting to come together. Sitting back, Ehiliana picked up the paper and peered at Zeppo.

"Guess we can finally know what this rock says," Ehiliana said.

"Go on, what's it say?"

"It says, 'Twelve pillars to a prison we raise, twelve blood sacrifices must be made to unleash that which will end magic reign.'"

"That's it?" Zeppo asked.

"No, there is more. It continues, 'Blood of my blood, to reach what you want you must give to me what I desire. Bring me one of your offspring at the turn of the next five centuries and I shall grant you that which you wish and more upon my revival.' It is as if it was etched in by someone else, do you think whoever is in that prison can do such a thing?" Ehiliana said.

"I think maybe we need to fill in your friends."

"Yeah, I'll call a meeting."

As if being summoned, Clovis burst through the door slamming it behind him. Throwing a hand out, Ehiliana watched as Zeppo was thrown sideways, slamming against the study's dark walls.

"You," Clovis sneered, walking toward Zeppo's fallen form.

"Putting herself between the two, Ehiliana said, "What is going on?"

"Move aside," Clovis ordered.

"Prince—"

"I said, move." His voice was deadly calm.

Noting the shadowy ink lacing up his arms, all the hair raised on the back of Ehiliana's neck, and subconsciously she backed away. Watching, as Zeppo stood back up, blood now dripping down his forehead, she stared at the prince.

"If this is about me helping Ehiliana—"

Slamming Zeppo back against the wall, Clovis said, "No, this is about the man who attacked my sister and left a message for you, his name was Noa."

Grasping at his throat, he rasped, "Noa?"

"Said there is a man named James coming after you, and that he is going to be giving this James intel on us, so you're going to tell me why you're wanted."

Ehiliana interjected, "How can he respond if he can't breathe, prince?"

Letting up on the spell, Zeppo gave Ehiliana a look of gratitude.

"Noa is a friend of sorts, he is more than likely in a position where playing both sides is what's keeping him alive. James is after me because I saved your sister from being ransomed and worse."

"I'm not sure I believe you. I think you used my sister as a means to infiltrate and distract us from that which we are pursuing," Clovis sneered, tightening the spell's grip.

"Clovis, he helped me with the runes," Ehiliana said, pleading.

"Shut it, Pinkali."

"Just come to the desk Clovis."

"After I kill this traitor."

You are going to kill an innocent, don't make me do this, she thought.

Summoning her bow, Ehiliana hesitated but aimed at the prince. She moved into his peripheral vision as a silent warning. Rolling his neck, his cold gaze met hers, and fear raced through her, leaving her hands shaking. As if answering her prayer, Kilgi came through the door.

Chapter Fourteen

<u>**Kilgi**</u>

"Clovis Gorkem, what the hell do you think you are doing?" Kilgi asked, walking across the room.

"Killing a traitor."

Coming up behind him, kicking him hard in the back of his knee, she caught his shirt yanking him back as he fell, pulled a knife to his throat, and stared down at the prince with a frown plastered on her face.

"Give me your spell book now," she demanded.

"I'll kill them before I do." He almost sang to her.

"With your sister watching?" Kilgi whispered in his ear.

Letting his head fall back, his gold orbs met his sister's shocked gaze, a frown on his face. Quickly replaced by a shock of his own, Clovis hit the ground with a thud from Kilgi letting him go. Sitting down on top of the prince, Kilgi motioned for Mika to enter the room and grab the book from her brother. Standing over the prince, Kilgi met his cold gaze, as Mika darted for the book, grabbing it from her brother's grip.

"Sorry, Clovis," Mika whispered.

As Mika grabbed the book with a cloth, a sense of calm washed over the prince's face.

"How are you feeling?" Kilgi asked.

Groaning, Clovis placed a hand on the side of his head. "Like I've been possessed."

"Seems like you could've been. You didn't take the news of this Noa guy well," Kilgi mused, from atop the prince.

"I have to agree with Kilgi, you seemed like a madman the way you dashed for your book. How did you even know Zeppo was here?" Mika asked.

"I-I don't know," Clovis said, groggily.

"Great, more mysteries," Ehiliana murmured.

"Zeppo, are you all right?" Mika asked, coming up to him.

Placing a hand on her shoulder, he said, "I am okay."

"Kilgi, get off me, I am fine now," Clovis said, breathly.

"Not until you give me your word within the next week that we will be heading to the mountains for an answer to this curse plaguing you and Iathos."

"Fine, I promise, now get off of me."

Standing up, Kilgi offered her hand out to Clovis. Seeming annoyed, the prince took her hand, dusting himself off once he was standing. an awkward tension filled the silence. Walking over to the study door Kilgi shut and locked it.

"Let's get comfortable, it seems we have some things to discuss," Kilgi said after clearing her throat.

Once settled, Clovis spoke up, "Zeppo, who is Noa, exactly?"

"Noa is a Jesatyl spy, he works for a mercenary group that operates within the eastern continents. He joined the group a few months before I did, we became friends after that."

"Who is James to you?" Clovis probed.

Sighing, Zeppo responded, "James is the leader of this clan, I ended up being a close confident because of my ability to shut my mouth and patch a wound." Continuing he said, "It may be best for me to leave if James is after me. They are a dangerous group, I knew saving Mika would put me at risk, but you all have done a great job at making leaving hard."

"Sorry, Zeppo, but you don't get to leave now," Mika interjected.

"Mika," Clovis said glaring.

"No, Clovis! Zeppo saved me and is my friend. He stays with us or I go with him. I owe him my life and for that, we will protect him."

"I agree with the princess," Ehiliana chimed in.

"Seems like it's unanimous then," Kilgi said, standing.

"I have never met so many people who are disregarding royalty so willingly." Clovis sighed.

"We aren't, Mika is just as royal as you are," Kilgi smirked.

"Prove me wrong then, Zeppo, make me trust you," Clovis said, addressing the Vulocri.

"I'll try, but that would require filling me in on what the hell is happening."

"That would require us having more of an idea ourselves." Clovis sighed.

"We may," Ehiliana stated.

Raising a brow, Kilgi said, "Do tell me, what have you found?"

"Zeppo and I managed to figure out what the rune says."

"What does it say?" Clovis asked, now a little more alert.

"It says, '*Twelve pillars to a prison we raise, twelve blood sacrifices must be made to unleash that which will end magic reign.*'

"However, it has a second part that speaks about someone's kin needing to sacrifice their offspring to be granted their wishes upon this person's revival," Ehiliana continued.

"What a headache. We at least know now that the rune you found is some kind of prison with twelve keys," Kilgi said, pinching her brow.

"This is significant," Clovis stated.

"It states, twelve pillars. My guess is this is a prison the twelve fates raised to keep something or someone inside. Perhaps this relates to our marks."

"What do you mean?" Mika asked.

"Well, there are technically six different types of chess pieces: king, queen, bishop, knight, rook, and pawn. If I had to take a guess we are being marked for roles in some greater game and seven others have been marked."

"So, you think that we are being marked by significant pieces and not the entire board, because if not, then we are missing a lot of pieces," Ehilian said.

"Pretty much. In theory, we probably have a counterpart," Clovis explained.

"You think someone is pitting others against us? What if all the fates are trying to replace themselves?" Mika now asked.

"It makes sense. But white starts the game and our marks are black. It would also be unwise for all of the fates to replace themselves at once though. So, seven others are on our side, or we have six significant counterparts and a missing pawn on our side," Kilgi answered.

"That also means they knew this would happen, it said twelve sacrifices," Ehiliana said, with disbelief.

"Of course they did. Any magic done can be undone, it just may not be the same as it was before. They knew this day would come, and selected who they thought could prevent whatever is arising, seeing as it is us, I think we may be facing something serious," Clovis said, dejected.

"It says sacrifices Clovis," Mika pointed out.

"Why don't we just ask them? If we are connected to them, shouldn't we be able to call on them?" Kilgi suggested.

"I could ask my fate, he said he would help me learn to control my magic when we have quiet time," Mika responded.

"Your fate contacted you?" Clovis asked.

"This morning before all the chaos, his name is Ellis."

"I see, well then try to get in contact with Ellis. For now, let's all try to stay alive, we don't need another one of us semi-dead like Iathos, or dead," Clovis said, standing from his seat.

***

Sitting on the edge of Clovis's bedroom balcony railing, Kilgi tilted her head to the starry night sky, the breeze chilling her cheeks. Closing her eyes and focusing on her breathing, Kilgi let herself recall the conversation she had with the man from the pub, and Oliver's eager-to-please face smiling at the crowd. Gripping the cool railing, Kilgi let out a breath she didn't know she had been holding, a tear falling down her face. *When does my suffering end?*

The sound of the balcony door opening brought Kilgi's thoughts back to the present. Wiping her face, Kilgi turned to the prince. He wore deep green pajamas and his hair was mussed from being towel-dried. Closing the door behind him, Clovis walked over to Kilgi and leaned against the railing beside her. The smell of sage now filled the air. Leaning to the side, Kilgi sniffed Clovis, invoking a startled reaction out of him.

"What are you doing?"

"Smelled like sage, I was making sure it was you and not someone trying to cleanse a room." Kilgi laughed.

"You're odd sometimes," he mused.

"Says the guy who's making me share a room with him."

"It's safer if you're there to beat me up if I go crazy again."

"Probably, or more dangerous, one of these times you may kill me and no one would probably care." Kilgi laughed.

"I think more people care than you think."

"Come on, you're saying it to be nice. You don't have to coddle me, I was born hated and I'll die that way too."

"Why give everyone tough love all the time then? You've known everyone for about a month now and you are kind despite all the hate. I haven't seen anyone in this group treat you awfully for existing."

Kilgi did her best to keep at bay the tears threatening to spill in.

"I'm no more than a means to an end, that's all I am and ever will be."

"Perhaps at some point, I think I, myself am guilty of it. Perhaps we should start over?"

"Don't play with me like that," Kilgi whispered. *Oliver played with my feelings like that.*

"I'm not playing. There is something more serious going on than what race we all are, and if you feel this way, then it needs to be rectified." Continuing he said, "I'm not sure the kind of life you lived before all of this happened, but I'd like you to feel welcome within the company we have formed. Once all this comes to a head, then we can start paving a path for equality across the board."

"How can you say all this? You don't know anything about me," Kilgi said, tears starting to spill down her face.

"I know you are a half-princess from the Maholo family, you aren't an assassin, you just do whatever job is given to you. You used to live in Neron under the name Naomi and were engaged to a man named Oliver."

Choking, Kilgi felt a sense of fear raises the hairs on the back of her neck.

"I didn't hire anyone, I've been having dreams about everyone. It's like I can see the things everyone's keeping in the dark."

"Your fate?" Kilgi whispered.

"I think so. I don't know everything about you though, just the things you keep quiet."

"Clovis."

"Yeah."

"Oliver is working with the man I encountered," Kilgi said.

"I see, you want him dead?"

"Yes," Kilgi breathed.

"Okay."

"That's it?"

"I don't need to know what he did to you unless you want to tell me. If he is an enemy and you'd rather him dead then it's one less obstacle for us," Clovis reasoned. "You should go shower and get ready for bed," he continued.

"Yeah, you're right."

"Kilgi?"

"Yes?"

"Next time you're having a panic attack of any kind, let me know. Mika has been having them for years, we'll make sure you're taken care of."

Why are you being nice to me? I don't understand. You are supposed to be mean like the rumors.

***

Hearing a heavy knock on the door, Kilgi groaned but rolled out of bed. Answering the door, Kilgi suddenly felt more awake seeing Clovis's parents before her. Putting up a finger to indicate she needed a minute, she was interrupted by King Gorkem pushing the door wide open and walking past her. Stopping beside Kilgi, Lilith pushed a piece of paper into her hand before continuing to stand beside her husband. Pocketing the paper, Kilgi shut the door, walked across the cold floor, and stopped a few feet behind the royal family.

Shock filled her as the King grabbed Clovis by the collar and dragged him from his bed, throwing him to the floor. On instinct, Kilgi ran up and pulled the king backward, as he stumbled, she put herself between Clovis and what she now deemed a threat. Staring down the wide-eyed king, Kilgi put one of her hands behind her back, to help Clovis to his feet. Feeling the warmth of his hand take hers, she prepared for a fight.

"Tell your mutt to stand down son," Damien's thick voice demanded.

"I think it is you who should stand down, Your Majesty," Kilgi sneered.

"Speak again and I will have you killed."

"Say what you came to say, father." Clovis sighed.

"I was informed you plan on leaving for the mountains before the week is out, I will not allow this. Any thoughts in your head you should forget now."

"No can do, father, we will meet you back in Aeberuthey after I fix this curse."

"Why are you trying to stop me?" Clovis asked.

"Because you are chasing nothing, son. You are delusional. First, you say you got a curse after starting a fight with General Casxes, then you take on an attack on the city like it is your fight, and now you have it in your head that there is something big going on. Things like this happen often, you have disturbed regular citizens' lives for this delusion of yours. I am ending it now."

"I am not—" Clovis argued.

"I made Clovis promise he'd go to the mountains so he could receive treatment. He has been having mental breaks and could use professional help, and we have a contact there who can fix his delusions," Kilgi interjected, slightly squeezing Clovis's hand, "These regular citizens were all saved by your son during the attack, and they have pledged themselves to his service, myself included, but only your son and I will be going on this trip," Kilgi said, standing tall.

Narrowing his eyes, the king replied, "You know that he's delusional?"

"Yes, I had a feeling. After an episode he had yesterday, he finally agreed to receive help."

"I am right here," Clovis argued.

"How do I know you won't harm my son?"

"He offered me the only thing I have ever wanted, for the price of being his right hand. He will be safe so long as I draw breath. That means even from you, sir."

Pinching the bridge of his nose, the king took a moment to collect his thoughts. A feeling of cold ran up Kilgi's spine, and for a moment, she thought the king's shadow moved. Clovis stood just as still as her, watching the man before them.

"Only you two will make this trip, a month from now. Some things need to be settled before you can travel."

"Yes Father," Clovis responded coolly.

As the king and queen took their leave from the room, the pair deflated with relief.

"Why do I feel like it's going to be a long day?" Kilgi asked.

"Because it is. Father changed his mind very suddenly, which means he has found a way to control our situation. You spoke out of turn so we should be expecting danger to come your way."

"Great, I'll wear something I can fight in I suppose," Kilgi sardonically. "What's the plan for today?" she continued.

"Well, Mika and I are supposed to work on her magic this morning, and Ehiliana is going to see what she can find out about the underground city. Zeppo is researching to find a way to fight off the curse if you're not around and Iathos is still comatose.

"So this morning you can either be stuck with me or you can be stuck with Zeppo. You are not going anywhere alone until we can ensure your safety within these walls." Clovis shrugged.

"I'll go with Zeppo. I need some space from you, no offense."

"None taken."

Falling into a comfortable silence, Kilgi stepped into the bathroom, leaving Clovis to change in the room. Grimacing at the feeling of the cold stone floor against her feet, Kilgi stepped onto the white fluffy rug in front of the vanity, setting her clothes on the counter. Stripping from her borrowed pajamas, Kilgi picked up the dark blue slacks and made quick work of putting them on. Surprised at how well they fit, she took her time putting on the linen white wrap shirt, making sure it covered all the appropriate places. After sliding the familiar brown leather belt around her waist, Kilgi began brushing her teeth and planning what to do with her hair. Hearing a gentle knock on the door, Kilgi walked over and turned the knob revealing Clovis's face.

Motioning for him to come in, he passed her his toothbrush and silently joined her in what felt like an awkward domestic moment. After spitting out her toothpaste and giving her mouth a quick rinse, Kilgi grabbed her comb and brushed her hair from the bottom up. She raised her eyebrow at his blatant staring.

"Can I help you?" she questioned.

Spitting out his toothpaste he said, "I didn't know you had so many tattoos."

"Well, it is decided that if I'm going to be an outsider my whole life, I might as well appear the way I want to, do they bother you?"

"No, I've never met anyone who has tattoos, they are typically frowned upon."

"You can take a closer look, but no touching."

"I can see from here, do they have meanings?"

"Oh, uh, yeah, they do," Kilgi said, a blush creeping onto her tanned face.

"Well, do indulge me. I can help you braid your hair while you tell me, I help Mika all the time."

"You are an odd prince, I'll braid my hair though, thanks. Vivian's not around so you don't have to completely coddle me."

Leaning against the stony wall, Clovis motioned for Kilgi to continue.

"Below my breast is a wasp with wildflowers, it represents the control I want over my life and the flowers are to honor those of my race who have been lost. The sun and moon on my feet are a representation of balance, and the queen piece on my shoulder is well—"

"Yeah, I get that one. What about the symbols on your back? I've never seen them before."

"Oh, they are the star signs of my brothers."

"Star signs?"

"Yes, they are symbols made by my ancestors to represent star placements in the sky. They correspond with our months and years, depending on where, when, and how you were born to play into the star sign you are assigned at birth." Taking a breath, Kilgi continued, "It can help you tell who a person is, in general, not necessarily in-depth, but it's supposed to act as a guide. Mentally and physically since you can use the stars as a map to navigate the land."

"Interesting, so, then what's your sign?"

"I feel like I'm being mocked. I'm a Thuro."

"I'm not mocking you, knowledge isn't meant to be teased. We don't learn about Matuen culture for obvious reasons, but when is Thuro?"

Finishing her braid, Kilgi walked back toward the bedroom. "Thuro is between Edex twentieth and Tuloq twentieth."

"What does it say about you then to be a Thuro?"

"It means, outwardly I am stubborn, tenacious, loyal, occasionally sensual," she said with a shrug.

Following, Clovis laughed. "You are not sensual."

"I said *sometimes.*"

"All right, whatever you say, also though, if you're a Thuro shouldn't your birthday be soon?"

"Oh, uh, yeah, I think it's past, I haven't been keeping track of the days. It was on the eleventh."

"So, it was last week."

"I guess so, but it's not important, bigger things are going on right now."

"I suppose," Clovis said as he laced his boots."

"You lace very slowly." Kilgi laughed.

"Do you have a better way?"

"Of course."

Taking both laces in between separate fingers of the same hand, she lined the strings up with the hooks of her boots. Crossing the same hand across the front of the boot, Clovis watched as she, in a matter of seconds, had her boots laced up and was tying them off.

"Okay, you do have a better way."

"Hurry up, Mika is probably waiting for you."

"Go on without me, don't forget your coat, Mika would have me hanged if I let you forget it."

"Did she make this?" Kilgi said, picking up the coat matching her pants.

"Yeah, she refused to let the handmaids make you subpar clothing, so she's taken to making you a few outfits herself."

"How did she know my size?"

"I have no idea. There are things about my sister I'm not willing to question."

"Fair enough, I'm going to go see if I can catch Zeppo."

"See you later, be careful."

Closing the door behind her, Kilgi glanced down both ends of the hallway before pulling out the paper Lilith Gorkem had given her.

I have a gift for you in the marquina room.

What the hell is marquina? Kilgi thought to herself.

With a little instruction from one of the passing maids, Kilgi managed to find her way to Zeppo's room. Knocking, she heard some shuffling before he opened the door, poking his head out.

Confused, he asked, "You okay?"

"Yeah, I'm all right, there is some stuff I need to do today, but Clovis wants me with you, think you could cover?"

"I could just go."

"You sure?"

"Yeah, where are we going?"

"Apparently, something called a marquina room."

Shocked he gently pushed Kilgi into the room and shut the door.

"I'm not sure that's a good idea."

"No?"

"I ended up there and had an awful encounter with some shadowy thing."

"Hmm, what was the encounter like?"

"He said to join him or die. I told him no, and instead of killing me, he gave me a vision of Mika getting critically injured."

"The future isn't set in stone, and as bad as it sounds, we need information. Another encounter may help us gain ground."

"You're sure?"

"Mostly." She chuckled.

"This is all so messed up, I feel like the ground is falling from under my feet," Zeppo said, sitting down on the bed.

Tossing his shirt to him, Kilgi said, "We all do. Even if you aren't marked, that thing wanted to scare you. That means, you have something that scares him and that's something we could use. I will have your back, and if we die then it's not our problem anymore."

"You may be a little insane. But yeah, I guess if we die it's not our problem anymore," he said, with an unamused laugh.

"You don't have to go in, but I do need help finding the room."

"You may be a scary lady, but even if I'm scared, no good being deserves to face scary things alone."

Smiling and opening the door, she said, "Zeppo you may just be the coolest guy I have ever met."

"Thanks," he said, clamping a hand on the back of her neck.

***

The marquina room was quiet, the only sound was the water running from Umbri's still hands. Stepping in and closing the door behind them, Zeppo and Kilgi stared at one another with looks of reassurance. Sitting by the pool was a clear vial with red dust, a label on the bottle read: *Kilgi*. Picking up the vial, Kilgi passed it to Zeppo.

"That's either sitid or sypher, can you tell the difference?"

"Yeah, the colors are different. This is sitid, sypher is orange."

"Why would she give me this, I thought only the Greoll could use it."

"Common misconception. It is a drug only they know how to make. Sypher is a poor imitation, hence why it's illegal. Taking Sypher could mess you up. This should be fine though, I'm more impressed the Greoll were willing to give her some. Also, who is she?"

"Clovis's mother."

"Oh."

"She seemed secretive about it, so I doubt the king knows."

"Well, I brought my medical bag in case something happened. I can treat you if something goes wrong with these drugs," he said, sounding relieved.

"That's good to know. I'm a little nervous."

"Let's hope it goes smoothly."

"I somehow doubt it," Kilgi said while opening the vial.

"Throw it on your face, don't swallow it," Zeppo said, taking a few steps back.

Letting out a breath, Kilgi threw the powder toward her face and inhaled. Feeling a tingle across her skin, she turned to Zeppo who was no longer there.

"Zeppo?" Kilgi asked, suddenly, scared.

Standing up, the world around her surged, and suddenly, she felt sick. The black marquina floor was suddenly soft under her feet, and rays of sunlight were spotting her eyes. Squinting, Kilgi tried to focus, letting her new surroundings settle around her. The grass before her was stained a deep red, and the creek by her feet ran with black water. Off in the distance, stood a city surrounded by large trees and floating rocks. Stumbling a little, Kilgi walked toward the city. Taking in the crisp woodsy smell mingling with the damp wet moss along the creek rocks, to ground herself as she continued.

Once she neared the city, she felt her breath catch at its beauty. Everything seemed to be made from white stone. The gates stood taller than any other she had ever seen with plants carved into its structure. The city beyond seemed to climb into the sky with elegant bridges and moving machines. Going to take another step toward the city, Kilgi was stopped by a Greoll appearing before her. They had deep yellow skin and sandy-colored eyes, their blond hair was cut short and wild.

"Hello, Kilgi, my name is Ora. It's a pleasure to meet you."

"Hello?"

"I am the fate of prophecy, though we can't talk long. I was asked to give you a specific vision, though you seem to have wandered."

"Oh, well, what is this place?"

"This is the in-between, where spirits go to rest before living again."

"It's breathtaking."

"Yes, but entering the city will kill your physical body, so we need to get you to your actual vision."

"Wait! Is it true you and the other fates erected a prison for something or someone?"

Sighing, Ora responded, "Yes, but some of us weren't fates at the time."

"How do we stop it from being released?"

"I am afraid it is too late for that, we need to find a way to destroy that monster. We, unfortunately, don't know how yet either. Anyway,

I'm sending you off to your actual vision. I am going to resume work," Ora said, with a wave.

Stumbling as her vision blurred, the overpowering smell of lavender and smoke filled her lungs. Taking a few clumsy steps backward, Kilgi fell right through a woman, she saw a younger version of a pregnant Lilith Gorkem browsing the little shop. She wore an elegant red gown with golden leaves sewn along the dress's hem. The smell of jasmine wafted past as she moved.

Kilgi saw hundreds of colored vials lining the shop's shelves, and alchemic equipment sitting neatly on tables in the middle of the room. Settling her gaze back on the queen, she stood up and followed. Lilith ran her delicate fingers along the tables, walking toward the back of the shop. Soft clanking sounds came from behind the old wooden door. Lilith opened the door. Stepping in behind the queen, Kilgi spotted a man with long golden locks hunched over a table.

"Hello, love, did you miss me?" Lilith spoke.

Turning his head a smile graced his handsome face. "Always, dear."

Watching the two embrace, a diminutive feeling of terror filled Kilgi at how much this man resembled Clovis. As if reading her mind, the man's big worn hands settled on Lilith's stomach.

"How is Clovis? Have the Vulocri figured out the little one's gender yet?" he asked.

"Aurelius, you're always so eager, Clovis is just fine. Damien is teaching him magic, he's quite amazing at it, though I suspect he gets his talent from you. As for the little one, the healers said that it's a girl."

"I don't like not being a part of their lives." Aurelius frowned.

"I know, my love, but I can't leave. Damien is very dangerous, he'd have us all dead before the next sunrise if he had an inkling the kids weren't his."

"The world is much bigger than the lands that sit within Eckris's bounds. We could take the children and run, surely Isla can be saved this way too."

Placing a hand on Aurelius's face, Lilith said, " I wish things were that simple, truly I do, but they are not. This is the last time I will visit, Damien cannot become suspicious, and I will not have you killed for loving me."

Lowering her hand, Aurelius turned his back, tears threatening to spill from his red eyes.

"Aurelius, please do not be cold to me during this goodbye."

"I am leaving, if this is truly a last goodbye, I cannot stay where I will be forced to watch my children from afar."

"Aurelius." Lilith's soft voice choked.

"My last request for you is to name our daughter Mika, after my mother. I expect you to protect our children more fiercely than you ever could for Isla."

"You don't have to leave."

Turning now, he said, "I do, I cannot live here while another man raises my children, because you are too weak-willed to leave him. Should you ever gather the courage to tell them the truth, I will leave a way for them to find me.

"I-I am sorry, love," Lilith stuttered.

Lifting her chin to meet his sad eyes, he said, "I do not believe you, I never should've fallen for you, yet I did. How can you be sorry when you deprive me of your undivided love, of my children, and continue to do so selfishly."

"If I could give you what you want I would!"

"Please, Lilly, leave."

"No, not until you stay, I will command it as your queen."

"Will you hang me should I not listen?"

"Yes," she whispered.

"Then call your guards, my queen."

"Why must you break my heart, Aurelius?"

Silence filled the room, as Lilith stared at the man bowing before her, seeming so stubborn it could rival Clovis's. Kilgi watched as Lilith turned her back and angrily flung her arms forward, sending a wave of magic through the shop. The potions sitting neatly along the shelves, shattered upon hitting the ground, and the alchemical equipment clanged loudly. She didn't stop her tantrum until every vial within sight had been destroyed. Kilgi felt her stomach drop as the queen lit the tables aflame and blew out the glass of the latticed windows.

"Now leaving will be easier for you, I will give you until sunrise to disappear. Should I still find you here I will have you killed. From this day forward I shall recognize you as a stranger and forbid you from ever speaking to the kids should you happen upon them," Lilith's cold voice spoke.

As the door slammed behind her and the flames spread at a fast rate, Kilgi had the sudden urge to force the man from the building. Watching, as he stood in shock, Kilgi suddenly reached forward and tried to grab his arm.

"Damn, how do I get him out, he isn't moving?" She panicked.

She watched as Aurelius moved to one of the windows and climbed out, turning to watch the building burn. Citizens gathered to watch, all whispering about how he must have insulted the queen. The vision seemed to change again. Now becoming used to the magic, she could see bits of sand swirling around creating the images around her.

Before she was a humble cottage made of wood and cobblestone. Vines neatly covered the archway leading to the doorstep, and smoke came steadily from the chimney. The smell of a hearty stew filled the air, and Kilgi found herself wandering to the door. Knocking, she felt a little silly as her hand went right through the sturdy wood. Entering the home, she was greeted with herbs hanging by the windows and a dog sleeping on the couch. To the left of the door was a dining table, seemingly made by non-professional hands.

Smiling, she had the feeling she was in Aurelius's new home and walked into the kitchen. The older man sat close to the pot and occasionally stirred it. After a few minutes, he turned his head and looked right at Kilgi. His brilliant eyes crinkled with amusement, his crow's feet showing his age.

"Hello, young one."

"You can see me?"

"Yes, I saw you years ago in the shop too."

"Why, how?"

"I can tell the difference between those who are here, and those who are seeing what was, is, and will be. I didn't say anything because I knew you weren't really there."

"But now?"

"It would seem you are more than likely in the present."

"I do not understand, I wasn't born with magic."

"Come sit, and I will explain to you how it works then, and we can move from there."

"What if we run out of time?"

"I think Ora is deciding how much time you have." He gave a coy smile.

Opting to lean against the doorframe, Kilgi gestured for him to continue.

"There was a time when magic was there for all to use, it vibrated through all that which lives. The trees, rocks, water, you name it. The world was very vibrant then, and petty things like politics didn't exist.

That was, until around six hundred years ago, when a man by the name Charles Gorkem, rose to sudden power. He had the idea in his head, that if magic could be used by all, then it could be willed to be controlled by only one. There is still no answer as to how he managed to achieve such a feat, but he plunged the world into darkness."

"That sounds terrible."

"It was. The darkness lasted nearly a century. Many had tried to start a rebellion against Charles, many lost their lives. The bloodshed only seemed to empower him, though it seemed that there were a few who had learned how he stole such power. The first fates, if you will."

"The first fates?"

"Yes, Hunnopo and Echo, they were two general brothers, killed in a raid against the Gorkem's empire. While bleeding out, they could see wisps of magic and reached for that which was in front of them. Echo made contact with the magic first and became what he is now, his brother seemed to follow along. That day they gained power over death and darkness.

"They had to die, to grab the raw power?" Kilgi asked.

"That is how it seems to be."

"So, the other fates?"

"Yes, to gain their power, the brothers' closest confidants all faced near death to grab power, to defeat Charles. With Echo learning to watch over death, it was much easier for the others to obtain this goal."

"How is he still alive?"

"Well, his main power was hate manifested from those around him. You could consider him the fate of the dark or devouring."

"What of Hunnopo then?"

"Ah, yes, well, you could consider his power which is blind to those feelings, if you are used to living in the dark, how could you possibly see it for what it is? Hunnopo is the only fate that Charles cannot see. He knows that he exists, but he is blind to what Hunnopo is."

"He's a prison for Charles."

"Clever girl."

"His defeat came when Umbri, who used to be the love of his life, betrayed him so that he could be sealed away by the fates. That day he declared a new name, Merikh. He promised upon his return he'd hang the fates up to watch the world they tried so hard to protect crumble away beneath them.

"But what he left behind was Umbri and their son, Drevon. She only became the fate of life through her death at the hands of her son, who was unable to see his father for the monster he was."

"That is an awfully sad story."

"It is. She is considered the oldest of the fates because Merikh forced her to partake in life-prolonging rituals. Now she is ageless from the magic that she now protects."

"Aurelius?"

"Yes, young one?"

"If the fates are holding extreme powers, how are others able to use magic?"

"A good question, it is simply because magic just is, the world couldn't live otherwise. Though it seems as if only those who come from a fates' bloodline have access to powerful magic, the rest is practical magic."

"So it's blood magic."

"In a way, yes, the fates can love too, they were once mortal."

"You speak as if you were there."

Smiling, he said, "Are there any other questions you have?"

"Is Lilith of a fates' lineage? She seemed powerful."

"No, but her children are, her magic was vastly more powerful due to her pregnancies."

"Oh, but that means you are."

"Something like that."

"Clovis and Mika should know the truth."

"Perhaps"

"I think Lilith only meant for me to see the potions shop memory, Ora seemed to imply it anyway."

"Hmm, perhaps she is still too afraid to tell the truth on her own."

"I don't understand."

"Lilith lives in fear, and it tends to lead her to do things in troubling ways, more than likely, you are here because there is something she is hiding."

"Please, Aurelius, do not be coy, there is enough afoot already."

"Hmm, very well. I have a connection to the fates of my own, I can see you are Nell's replacement, and if you are here then there is something Lilith has tactfully kept from you." Taking a breath he continued, "Your powers are trying to lead you to the truth through Ora's powers."

"What could she be hiding though?"

"I couldn't say, but my guess would be it is what has kept her around that madman Damien for so long."

"I should probably wake up, is there a way I can find you?"

"Do not bother with that, there are more important things for you to take care of. Please, hug my kids for me."

With the wave of a hand, Kilgi felt the world swim around her, and the cool floor chilled her skin. Opening her eyes, she was met with

Zeppo's concerned ones. Grabbing one of her arms, and putting a hand behind her back, she shifted into a sitting position. As she took in some deep breaths to gather herself, she felt Zeppo's warm hand touch her forehead, and check her pulse.

"How long was I out?"

"About an hour."

"That wasn't as long as I thought." She sighed.

"What happened?"

"She showed me a memory, a modified one, it would seem, but I have some information that should only be spoken somewhere private . . . Magically private."

"Oh, Oh!" He seemed to realize what she was hinting at.

"I'd hate to interrupt everyone's day, so maybe we should call for a meeting once nightfall has come and the castle has all but gone to bed."

Chapter Fifteen

<u>Clovis</u>

Grabbing the dark coat from where it hung, Clovis swung the door closed behind him as he set off in search of his sister. Shoving his hands in his trouser pockets, he let out a huff as his thoughts planned on how to deal with the new day. Nearing the kitchens, the floors were worn with age, and the aromatic scent of fresh rosemary bread filled the halls. The lower arches led into a very spacious and well-lit room. Dozens of kitchen workers dashed back and forth preparing all the food for breakfast. Others seemed to do more menial tasks, such as milling wheat and hanging fresh-picked herbs for drying. Walking up to one of the younger Irkafen girls with black hair, Clovis touched her shoulder to get her attention.

Jumping, she turned and said, "Mrs. Crims, I'm sorry—" Stammering she blurted out, "Oh my! I am so sorry, Your Highness, I thought you were Mrs. Crims."

"I see, well, inform Mrs. Crims I will be having breakfast in the kitchen this morning, I will be sitting right over there," he said, pointing to an empty table by one of the windows.

"Oh, okay." She blushed.

Turning to walk over to his now chosen spot, he heard the girl loudly whisper, "Oh, my fate, Clovis Gorkem touched me!"

Grimacing, he took his seat and pulled out a yellow leather-bound sketchbook and a graphite pencil. Flipping to an empty page, he began to draw out and build his newest spell. Letting his mind wander as his hand-etched away at the page, he found himself thinking back to the Auramic ruins.

It doesn't make sense that a simple protection spell could inflict such a bad curse for a few drops of blood. The worst that should have happened was perhaps a few weeks of becoming physically weaker, he reasoned internally.

Granted, there isn't much of an equivalent exchange with magic, but it's not that imbalanced. It's pretty standard that those born into magical bloodlines can dive deeper into wells of magic, those who aren't can sometimes do bits of practical magic. So would it be reasonable that those with deeper ties would be more affected by curses than those without? Yeah, but it's been proven otherwise.

Gillian Clemish had little magic abilities for a maid and paid quite a high price for her misuse of the gift. The inability to feel happy emotions, and why she would ever cast a love spell of any kind, especially with blood, will forever leave my mind curious.

However, the spell's backfire was within range of what the original spell's purpose was intended for, and it seems to be that way, in most cases. However, it's been known that using blood always brings higher consequences. Still, though, it doesn't make sense for the protection spell.

Opening a portal and being cursed by something in the darkness is definitely out of bounds for a rebound. Could I have perhaps messed up somehow? No, I followed fathers instructions step by step.

His thoughts stalled, as an epiphany crossed his mind.

I followed my father's instructions, if they were messed up it could perhaps give me some answers. I should perhaps redraw it first so I have a physical copy to make marks on. Father would never give me the first copy back anyway . . . stingy bastard. Good thing he can't take away my impeccable memory, he thought, smirking.

All right, perhaps cool the ego a little, Gorkem, Mika would tug your ear if she could hear that. She'd pull your ear if she heard most of your thoughts.

"Here is your breakfast," a timid voice said, stirring him from his thoughts.

"Ah, yes, thank you," he said, dismissively.

"You're welcome. Your drawing is beautiful, by the way, though I thought your book was supposed to be purple," the maid said, studying the drawing of a sphere wrapped in vines.

"Yes, my spell book is purple, this one is not, thank you for the compliment. Have a nice day."

"Oh, sorry to be a bother, I have always been curious about the cool, mysterious prince from Aeberuthey," she said, with a nervous chuckle.

"There is nothing you need to know, you should run along before someone comes searching for you, take the drawing though," he said, ripping it from the book binding.

"You are secretly nice." She smiled.

"Don't tell anyone, kid, otherwise I'll tell Mrs. Crims to put you on dishes for the foreseeable future.

Leaning back in his chair, he picked up his fork and gave it a twirl, sighing, as he dug into the food before him. Glancing at the now-torn page in the book, Clovis couldn't help but eat with one hand and draw out the spell from the ruins with the other. Feeling as if something important was nudging at the back of his mind, a tingle of dread raised the hairs on the back of his neck, and without a second thought, he slammed the little book closed. As he did, a shadow seemed to pass over the table before vanishing.

"Clovis?" Mika said, concerned.

 Startled, he said, "Hey."

"Father is upset you skipped breakfast in the dining hall."

"Let him be." Clovis waved.

"You two have been fighting a lot recently," she said, taking the seat across from him.

"Mika, something isn't right."

"He is our father Clovis, you should at least try to have a conversation without it turning into some kind of argument."

"He doesn't know how to listen, he only knows how to hear himself talk. He isn't concerned in the slightest about anything going on, least of all, that I am cursed."

"Maybe I should try talking to him?" she asked, with downcast eyes.

"No, this is between us, not you or mother," he said, sighing.

"Yes, it is!" she snapped. "Ever since you have been cursed, it's like you are a different person, you have been moody and unwilling to listen to anyone. Father cares about you, he just thinks you are being rash and rushing into things, mother is uncomfortable with all of the arguments you two have been having. Not to mention the bouts of violence," she said, rushed.

"Mika, I haven't changed, I have been stressed. I only consider attacking Zeppo out of character, the only person I'd attack unprovoked is if Iathos did anything."

"You are an ass sometimes." Sighing, she continued, "No, Clovis, Father is doing what he thinks best, he has always taken care of us. Why can't you just be a little willing to bend? Would marrying Vivian be that bad?"

"Not you too." He seethed.

"Clovis."

"Forget your magic lessons this morning, if you want to learn so badly, go find your father. I am busy anyway," he said, standing from the table and making his leave toward the door."

"Clovis! Why are you so selfish!" her voice squeaked out over the now quiet kitchen.

Glancing back, his golden eyes met hers and he said, "Why does nobody but a stranger care that I'm dying," he said calmly, before moving forward.

I'm tired, he thought. *You're tired because it's true. When has anyone ever actually cared outside of basic needs? Father never played with you as a kid, you were always punished for anything he didn't deem acceptable behavior. How many times did you take a lashing for breaking his rules, or covering for Mika's mistakes?*

He never really cared, he did the bare minimum and Mother let it happen. When has she ever come to comfort us? Or protect us from his aggressive behavior?

Should a king even have such nasty tendencies? What is he doing to the kingdom if he is willing to treat his kids like a common thief? Why does nobody question his authority? He says he wants me to run the kingdom one day, but I seriously doubt that narcissist could ever give the spot up. I'm not even sure I want it anymore, I'm sure he will leave me nothing but a mess to clean up.

Now Mika is listening to him too, or has she always listened to him? Who can I trust? It feels like I'm bashing my head off a wall over and over again. What am I supposed to do?

Focus, that's what you need to do! His voice seemed to burst through the onslaught of rushed thoughts.

Focus on the spell and see if there are clues to the curse. After that, we can meet up with Kilgi and Zeppo, and from there we will discuss any discoveries. I'll send Zeppo to keep an eye on Mika and head into the city to find some necessities.

What about Ehiliana?

Ah, right, she's been stir-crazy since her leg broke. Perhaps I'll send her into town to listen and follow leads on that Noa boy.

Iathos can stay the way he is, that man is a loose cannon. His fear of magic is too dangerous, I doubt he will last any longer than he has around this chaos.

Feels like the only one I can trust is Kilgi and I just met her. Ha, how pathetic, all of these new presences and all of them but one seems more trustworthy than everyone I have known for years. Perhaps it's sad that I trust Kilgi more than Mika. I know she only wants the best, but her rose-colored glasses always sway her from the reality right in front of her.

You should have told Mika that your father called you delusional and threatened to kill Kilgi.

No, she'd make things worse and say something to Father. For now, it stays quiet, Father can't know anything that's happening currently.

Stirring from his thoughts as he opened the study door, he caught sight of Vivian sitting snuggly in one of the chairs by the fireplace. With a frown, he stepped inside and closed the door with a slam. Walking across the room, he took a seat in the plush desk chair and pulled out a few writing utensils.

"Are you going to pretend I don't exist?" Vivian smiled. "How long are you going to pretend you have any control over this situation?" she pressed.

"Your father has already called off the farce of an engagement you made with the freak, waving it off as you did it as a form of torment for the poor thing."

"Our engagement is to be announced over her death tomorrow during a death duel."

"What?" His head snapped up now, meeting her darkened eyes.

"Yes, winning gets the right to your hand in marriage, old Colkirk law."

Kilgi can handle Vivian's best fighter, we will cheat if needed, he thought. "Okay."

"That's it, no pleading to save her life, no threats to mine?" she asked.

"No."

"Hmm, I like this version of you," Vivian said, coming around the desk.

"You can take your leave now, I am busy."

"With what? I am to be your wife, might as well get used to me being nosy."

Curling his darkened hands into a fist, he resisted the urge to strangle the woman before him.

"Oh, come on, Gorkem." She laughed, grabbing a fistful of his hair and yanking. Now staring into his cold eyes, Vivian smiled and said, "Oh, you look good like this."

Can I never be left alone to work? "*She is like a peckish bird,*" a darker voice snickered at the back of his mind. "*Kill her,*" the voice suggested.

Her lips crashed against his, their teeth clanking together. Gripping tighter she yanked his head back, forcing the chair to recline a little. Taking her chance she plopped down on top of him and wrapped her other thin hand around his neck and squeezed. Clovis laughed as blood leaked from his lip.

"I don't think you could choke me with both hands," he said, suddenly serious.

"You are a freak." Vivian all but laughed.

"I don't even need mine to choke you." He smiled, his eyes darkening as they met hers.

Going to speak, Vivian opened her mouth but nothing came out, except a strangled gasp of air. Untangling her hand from Clovis's hair she reached for her throat. Peering into Vivian's eyes, Clovis flashed a vicious smile and grabbed her hips to keep her glued in his lap before she could run.

Attempting to pry his hands from her, her hands weakened and her eyes bulged from their sockets. Only then did he let up the spell, watching as she gulped the air before her greedily. Tears gathered in the corner of her eyes, and Clovis frowned, pushing her to the floor.

"What? Can't take what you give?" he asked innocently.

"You're crazy," she rasped.

"And here you wanted me as a husband."

"I-I can handle it, you can do it again."

Surprised, Clovis leaned forward. "You are the crazy one, now leave."

"I can do anything she does better. Besides, now I know you like it rough," she rasped.

"Did it feel like I liked it?"

A blush now crept up her face at the realization Clovis showed no physical sign of liking her bold display. "You just have good mental control over your body."

"You are delusional."

"I am better than her, and I will prove it right here," she whispered.

Thinking of that morning, his mind wandered to Kilgi's tattoos and toned stomach. He thought of the way her hair curled when it was down, and how she smiled while brushing her teeth. His heart beat just a little faster. "I seriously doubt that," he whispered back.

Fuck I find Kilgi beautiful. He sighed inwardly.

Suddenly feeling cool metal touch his throat, Kilgi's voice rang out, "Am I interrupting something?"

"No, just Vivian continuing her delusional quest."

Vivian stood and backed away from the prince, making her way to the door with Kilgi behind her. He met Zeppo's embarrassed gaze, as the man took a seat. The door shut behind the two, and Kilgi didn't return for a few minutes. Opting for the silence, he picked at his nails, trying to avoid thinking. Hearing the door's soft click, his gaze snapped to Kilgi as she whispered something into Zeppo's ear, and then the Vulocri fled the room.

"What did you do to him?" Clovis asked, clearing his throat.

"I sent him to grab lunch, neither of us has eaten yet."

"He seemed freaked out."

"We just walked in on you two engaged in some kind of mating ritual." Kilgi shrugged.

"That is exaggerated. Honestly, I was trying to scare her off so I could work," he said, with a slight blush.

Laughing, she said, "Sure, next time give me a warning. I do not want to see her naked."

"Neither do I, she is like a sick bird."

"Mm-hmm."

"Stop it."

"I'm not the one letting a sick bird in my room," Kilgi said, a smirk tugging on the corners of her lips.

"You're annoying." Clovis huffed.

"Says the guy who likes it rough," she said pointing at his split lip.

"Honestly, you get on my nerves."

"Well, perhaps, you should keep your private affairs more private."

"Well, if you would shut your mouth, then I could tell you, she came to let me know the father is dissolving our engagement through a death duel. You are to fight Vivian's champion tomorrow morning, the winner gets the right to marry me."

"Fantastic, I'll sharpen my blades tonight," Kilgi said, plopping down in the chair on the other side of the desk.

"You're not worried?"

"No. If I die then I die."

"You are something else."

"Says the guy getting freaky with a woman he hates."

"I wasn't."

"Your hair says otherwise."

"Can we please move on from this, I think I might have figured something out."

"I'll let it go for now, what did you find?"

"I redrew the spell I did from the Auromic ruins, and some of these symbols are like the ones from the rune Ehiliana and Zeppo decoded."

"Oh, that is interesting," Kilgi said, standing to walk around the desk.

"It's been bugging me all morning, but once I drew it out—"

"You knew that you could find the answer in Ehiliana's notes."

"Yes."

"Well, uh, I may have some hard to hear news."

"Go on," he said.

"Your mother gave me sitid, gifted to her from Ora."

"She what," he choked out."

"Just listen."

"I saw parts of her past, and well, it's not good news." Clasping her hands she continued, "You and Mika have a different father, your mom had an affair with a man who made potions."

"You took a drug to find this out?" he asked, running a hand through his wild hair.

"Yeah, Ora was there though, at first to guide me to the vision. After that, I ended up somewhere near Misty Cove, at your real father's cottage. His name is Auerilus and he could see me."

"This is too much." He breathed.

"I know, but it explains why you and Mika have such strong magic. You come from a family descended from the fates. Aurelius wouldn't say which one you are descended from, but he gave me a better understanding of what's happened."

Now, with both hands clasped in his hair, his elbows hit the desk with a light thud.

"I am sorry, Clovis, but It seems your mom is, for some reason, too scared of your father to have ever said anything until now. The weirdest part was that she seemed to have given up on Isla Gorkem, she spoke about her as if she were already dead." She paused. "I didn't even know you had an older sister," she said.

The door clicked softly as Clovis locked the door using magic. Kilgi reached her hand out to the prince but stopped when she noticed the symbols laid out on the desk. Just like the symbols from the rune, the symbols from the spell Clovis had sitting out and deciphered read Isla's name. The other names included in the decoding were Merkth, Clovis, and Drevon.

Clovis's hand crumbled the page, before moving his hands to his hair. Gently Kilgi pulled his hands away and hugged him. Running her fingers through his silky hair, he hugged her like his life depended on it.

"I'm here, I am sorry for your sister," she whispered.

"It's a suicide spell, it's a spell meant to give your life force to another." He seethed.

"Isla held that spell before me, she couldn't have known. I didn't. That spell was supposed to kill me."

Hugging him tighter, Kilgi said nothing, as the cold truth sunk in. *He's not our father, but he was Islas.*

Letting go of Kilgi he stared into her gray eyes and said, "This means, the spell didn't work because I'm not his kid, and because of Iathos helping fuck it up. It also means that he doesn't know Mika and I aren't his."

"What do we do now?" she asked.

"We figure out why he did it, and we figure out if he is working with the guy from your vision."

"That man's name is Merkth, used to be Charles Gorkem. Drevon is his son, and Umbri is Merkth's wife and mother to Drevon. She became the fate of life when she betrayed Merkth to help end his reign, Drevon killed her for revenge."

"How is she a fate if she died?"

"Those who are strong enough, can latch on and take control of certain kinds of magic. The fates did this to keep Merkth from continuing his reign of terror, they won't let magic flow as freely as it used to, until Merkth is dead."

"This is all so messed up." He sighed.

"But it's happening now, and we are a part of it. The fates think we are strong enough to do what they can't, let's have some faith in them."

"Tomorrow, during the fight, I'm not going to help you. While everyone is distracted, I am going to talk to my fa—Damien. I'm going to give him a skewed version of the rune we found and see if he will decipher it for me. I'll use some of the ones from this spell and see if he lies to me. Then I'll know, if he does, I'd like to find someone who can spy on him for us."

"Use the maids."

"What?"

"Use the maids, many of them have complained about how they are treated by the nobles here, they have some of the best gossip."

"Oh, I am sure they do." He rolled his eyes.

"So, you didn't have an argument with Mika in the kitchens this morning."

"Okay, well, the maid's gossip spreads fast it seems. Fine, I may know a maid that can help. If anything happens though, we get her out. She's just a kid, maybe fifteen at most."

"Perhaps someone older?"

"No, my father—Damien wouldn't think to be super careful around a kid."

"Then we should find a way to speak with her discreetly."

"I think I could use some time alone, and a drink first," he said, with a sigh.

"You are exhausted, I'll try to keep everyone who's here busy. Ehiliana will hopefully be back tonight with information on Noa."

"Thanks," he said, as he stood to leave.

"Please don't tell Mika, not yet," he requested.

"As you wish."

Chapter Sixteen

<u>Iathos</u>

As he stirred, darkness loomed at the edges of his vision. The landscape appeared as a muted, inky expanse before him. Gradually sitting up, a sense of foreboding settled in his stomach as he took in the familiar sight. In front of him stood a quaint cottage, its exterior adorned with winding vines and weathered paint flaking in worn patterns. The scent of damp earth drifted through the air, subtle yet unmistakable. He observed a younger incarnation of himself, accompanied by an older face, rushing toward the building.

"Luella," he breathed.

Standing he raced inside the cottage after the memory, where there before him stood the young woman touching the herbs hanging in the window. Her black-and-white features turned to color as she smiled at him. Luella's long curly brown hair, big brown eyes, and cheeks full of freckles caught in the sunlight making her appear almost ethereal.

"Do you remember this place?" her velvety voice asked.

"Of course, how could I forget." He breathed.

"You are older, taller too," she said, brushing a hand against his chest.

"You are beautiful."

"We were determined to make this place our home, huh? But I wasn't enough for you," she said.

"You were more than enough."

"Then why did you kill me?"

"Luella I-I—I would have never," he choked.

The room crumbled away, the world rebuilding itself around them. The cottage turned into a grassy field filled with wildflowers covered in blood. He watched it transform into a battlefield. The smell of fire, copper, and rotting flesh filled the air, and Iathos tried not to gag at the smell.

"Look at it," Luella demanded.

"I can't, please don't make me."

"LOOK AT IT!" she screamed.

Standing before him, Luella was now covered in blood, pieces of her flesh hung from her body, and patches of her hair were missing. Gesturing to the field, there were now dozens of corpses rotting along the horizon. Falling to his knees, he felt her icy hands grip his chin and force him to see her now alive face.

"You did it," she whispered.

"Luella, please."

"You liked it though, didn't you?"

"No, never. I would never like killing you."

"Liar, if you truly regretted it then why did you never give us a proper funeral? Why did you burn us off the map and let the royals hide our story? You killed us, under order from your king. You let someone *spell* you, and you enjoyed watching us die," she said sweetly.

"NO!" he bellowed.

The scene changed, to Clovis in the ruins. His golden hair moved in the wind as he conducted a spell. Luella stood beside him, stroking his face, smiling. Anger filled Iathos as he watched her. Moving toward the pair he was halted in front of Clovis. The memory now seemed different; tears slid down the prince's face.

"He's just found out the terrible news," Luella said, her face shifting into that of the late Isla Gorkem.

Stumbling back he said, "What dark magic is this?"

"You hate him because of his magic, but if he didn't have it, you'd probably have been great friends."

"No, he's an arrogant prick who only cares about himself."

"Still lying to yourself I see." Isla giggled.

The scene changed and he was standing in the ballroom the night Colkirk was attacked. His sword faced Kilgi, hers pointed in return. The feeling of betrayal churned in his gut at his fearless cousin. She dropped her weapon and walked forward onto his, blood spilling down her front as she walked the length of the sword, grabbing his shoulder.

"Don't worry, cousin, I will do what you can't, you'd prefer me this way than for me to have magic, right?" Kilgi said, blood dripping from her mouth.

"No, none of this would happen if magic wasn't accessible," he whispered.

"Well, I am a Matuen, my death is better than you being caught being friends with me. Then no one will ever know about you letting me into the palace to see my brothers. They will never know about the death of an entire village, that you killed Luella, or that I am leaving you behind for your *enemy*."

"Stop," he said through gritted teeth but only pushed the sword further through Kilgi.

"See, isn't that better?"

"Stop talking." He seethed.

As Kilgi's body froze, becoming lifeless, a wave of apathy washed over him, and the scene changed again. Alton's little body was sitting in the throne chair like a limp doll, his skin colored with decay.

"I just wanted you to be proud of me," his voice squeaked.

"Then don't ever do magic," he said, walking away from the boy.

As he barged through the throne hall's double doors, he was standing on the stairs, Facing Ehiliana and her broken leg. Trading apathy for anger, Iathos's chest began heaving with rage.

I wish I would have left you to die, he thought.

Drawing his sword, he walked over to her and peered into her four magenta eyes. Lifting the weapon, he stabbed her repeatedly, listening to her screams quietly as she bled out. Eventually, he dropped the sword and walked up the stairs into the empty library. Echo came before him, a frown on his face.

"Free me from this nightmare," Iathos demanded.

"I shall free you from my binding, as well. Merkth can have his way with you," Echo responded.

"Because I don't like magic."

"Because you have failed judgment."

"You're not a judge, you are death."

"How little you understand because of your prejudice. Though I will not explain to someone who is an enemy. You are a monster, Iathos."

"Magic forced me to do those things."

"No, you were never under a spell. You and your king needed someone to blame, and you chose the Gorkems."

"Stop!"

"You lied your way through those memories, and you've lied to everyone you know."

"I said stop."

"What are you going to kill me?" Echo now smirked.

"You filthy bastard, You are the monster."

"I'm not the one who wished I killed someone who is supposed to be my friend. In all honesty, I only saved you because we were worried about Clovis. You were never meant to be chosen, we all knew you were crazy."

"Of course! Because he is so precious." Iathos rolled his eyes.

"No, because he can get a job done, and hold himself and others accountable. You hate him because he is what you wish you could be."

"We are done talking," Iathos stated.

"As you wish, just know we'll meet again, once you die."

With a wave of his hand, a burning sensation began claiming every inch of his skin. Falling to his knees, the feeling of hatred made his heart pound hard against his chest. Letting out screams of agony, the pain resided as a pair of long slender fingers gripped his hair. Pulling his head up, a sharp smile fitted Merkth's pale face.

"Hello, want to make a deal?"

"What do you want?" Iathos rasped.

"The same as you, a world with no magic."

"At what cost?"

"None, there will probably be some fighting, but I plan to eat all magic and rid the world of it."

"You'd use magic to get rid of magic."

"Hypocritical, I know, but sometimes we have to do hard things to get what we want. Like letting the Irkafen girl live, you knew you'd die without her, so you let her live."

"You promise that your intentions are pure?"

"Yes, I will even help you take revenge on Prince Clovis, we will save the others and make sure they can never do magic again."

"What do you need from me?"

"I need you to get a book for me, the *Bralins Tome,* in the archives."

"Fine, but I want that prince bastard for myself."

"As you wish, my knight, now go and show me what you are capable of."

Letting the world go blank, a warm feeling washed over him, as he cracked his eye open, blinking rapidly at the sun's rays coming through the windows. Lifting his arm, he was met with a blood-red knight instead of a black one, inked into his tanned skin. Letting it fall with a thud, he sighed.

If I'm lucky I'll be dead after I save everyone.

Chapter Seventeen

<u>Mika</u>

What a complete asshole, he never thinks about anyone but himself. He isn't an all-knowing fate, yet he always acts like it!

Why does he have to be the most frustrating brother to ever exist? He won't even tell me what's going on, Mika thought, watching Clovis walk from the kitchens.

As she surveyed the servants, all meticulously feigning indifference to Mika's outburst, she smoothed her dress before making her way out of the bustling kitchens. Moving deliberately, she trailed her fingers along the banister, finding solace in its polished surface. Gradually, she ascended to the upper levels of the castle.

In the west wing lofts, suspended ropes held aging flags, their slightly musty scent mingling with that of weathered wood. The floorboards beneath her feet groaned as she approached a weathered door at the far end. Its tarnished wood was offset by a pristine silver knob.

Upon pushing it open, she entered a chamber where mirrors lined the walls, and the floor was fashioned from an enigmatic, jet-black stone. She knelt to touch its icy surface, captivated by the eerie bluish luminescence that bathed the space. Her head snapped up at the abrupt slam of the door behind her.

Rushing back to it, her hand met empty air where the doorknob once was. Whirling around in panic, she found Ellis standing on the opposite side of the room, a disarming smile gracing his lips.

"Hello, Mika," he said with a bow.

"Don't scare me like that!" she yelled.

"Should've seen the look on your face."

"We have met once, you jerk."

"Ah, yes, well, your brother ditched your practice, so I figured you could use a substitute."

"You saw us fight."

"Sure did, now we have some big things to cover today. There isn't much time before we are faced with danger again, so we will be learning deflection spells," Ellis said, with a clap of his hands.

"I am not dressed well for this." Mika sighed.

"Good, you won't always be prepared for danger, you should learn to adapt."

"I'll try; then I'll rub it in my brother's face."

"That's the spirit, think of deflection like these mirrors before you. You want to send back whatever is thrown at you or at least away from you."

"Is there a casting word for it?"

"Sure, but you don't need it, you don't have your brother's memory, you don't need a dictionary of spells. Make them, Mika, see it, and pull it into existence."

"You make it sound easy."

"It will be, you have the best teacher out of everyone!"

"Everyone always says that there is no point worshiping you because the ethereal is out of reach and meaningless."

"Oh, dear, I will shatter some of the illusion now assuming you can keep it secret from everyone."

"Yes, everyone else has theirs, I want something of my own," Mika said with a half-smile.

"Good. The fates only hold a fraction of magic. No one knows the truth about how magic works because it would be hard to keep people from doing what's happening now."

"Summoning monsters?"

"Well, certain ones, to be exact. Everyone can access magic, dear, and become quite good at it. The fates lie to create a placebo effect to keep most people complacent so they can do the work they need to without many other outside factors."

"So, anyone can use magic?"

"Yes."

"How does it make you important?"

"I am magic." He smiled. "I am all that you cannot see, everything in between. The world is just beyond all physical ones. People thinking I am not important cuts off their ties to raw magic, because they simply do not believe in me."

"Oh my; then are the fates, fates? How come they don't age the same as everyone else?"

"They are in a sense, I keep them younger but not immortal. They are my pillars, distractions if you will. Some of them know this, but not many. Now, we can talk again later, for now, you need to learn to defend yourself. I am going to start sending stinging spells your way, I suggest you start deflecting or you're in for some discomfort," Ellis said, raising a hand.

Without another warning Mika felt the hair on her neck stand up as Ellis lazily flicked his hand in her direction, a stinging sensation flaring up her leg."

"Ow!" she yelped.

Another came her way, and without thinking she dove to the side, the sensation brushing past her. Only to feel another sting hit her side.

"Ow, that hurts."

"Deflect, not run away, Mika."

"Right, yeah, okay."

Feeling the magic stir in the air, Mika tried to imagine a mirror in front of her, both hands outstretched. The sting never came, and she felt a rush of excitement at the accomplishment. Moments later the stinging sensation hit her shoulder."

"Hey!"

"If this were real, you'd be dead. Now that you deflected it, imagine it like a bubble surrounding all sides of you. It won't be easy. I will be hitting you from multiple sides."

Rubbing her shoulder, she straightened and imagined a shelter of mirrors surrounding her, for a second it almost seemed like she could see them. Her hair prickled all over as multiple stinging spells shot toward her, some deflecting while others hit her. Falling to her knees, the air left her lungs at the sheer impact of the spells.

"Not bad, three of fourteen hit you, however you need to block them all. If a sting spell can pierce your mirrors, then pretty much anything else could shatter them. Strengthen it, make something impenetrable," Ellis called calmly.

"Okay, okay, I'm trying."

I am strong, my mirrors are like the bubbles that held those monsters from the festival, she thought, pulling the magic around her.

Nothing in and nothing out, it could be those monsters.

Seeing a shine of blue light, Mika could see a bubble form around her, as the spells bounced off. Pushing further she pictured it with a more metallic feeling. She watched as Ellis kept sending spells. Pouring her focus into it, she felt the magic shift and it became more sturdy.

"Good, I'm sending a lethal strike. I will heal you if it hits you."

Not responding Mika held the shield as strongly as possible as the spell hit. The first one dissipated against the bubble, the second pushed her back a few inches. The shield managed to hold off eight before it shattered and she threw up another out of fear of getting hurt. Feeling nothing, wide-eyed at the fate before her, smiling like a madman, his fluffy hair falling into his face.

"I did it?"

"You did it."

"Yes! I did it!" She celebrated, falling to her knees.

"We will keep working on it, but you will need to rest first."

"Okay." She smiled.

"Also, I told you, there was no need for any verbal spells. You have more control this way."

Realizing that her magic didn't once go out of control, a grin spread across her face.

"This is the most progress I have ever made, who knew it took magic itself to teach me," Mika said, laughing.

"Well, I knew." Ellis smiled.

"Nice to know you have a sense of humor, but I should be going. I am quite sure I have a lecture awaiting me."

"That you do."

"If you are magic, then how come you don't stop people from using it?" Mika asked, abruptly.

"Ah, well, that is where it is complicated, I just am, I do not control other's abilities to use me, I can just sway things in my favor through those like you, who want to see a better world. You could consider what I am as a sword, I am what the wielder makes me. In your case, my dear, you need me to teach you, so I have manifested as a physical form to help you move forward."

"Why not do that more often?"

"You ask many questions, but it is because very few deserve the best of me. Take it for what it is, but you are quite worthy of the sentient attention of my being."

"Oh. Thank you." Mika smiled, flustered.

"I should go, thank you! I will have many questions the next time we meet."

Waving at the door, she closed it behind her and did a victory dance at her newfound sense of control. *I did it, I feel like I could do anything!*

Deciding to take a detour back to her room to change out of her now ruined dress, she ran her hand along the cool stone walls.

I should apologize to Clovis for my outburst earlier, I know he is stressed, but all this nonsense he is doing with Kilgi is making things harder than they need to be. Why would he go out of his way to hurt Mother and Father like that? Vivian can be quite annoying with her advances, but it's also endearing that she cares that much! Most women just gawk and are easily intimidated by him, so her courage is a breath of fresh air.

Taking her hand from the wall and curling it in her dress, the stream of thoughts continued on. *Kilgi seems nice, but we have only known her for a few weeks and she seems weirdly quiet. I guess she's been pretty kind though, and I liked making clothes for her. Perhaps I should kill my pride and ask Clovis what's going on and if he is okay.*

I would also like to know more about Noa, he is quite powerful for being younger. At least he is younger, even with little control, his abilities shouldn't have affected me that fast; maybe if he is good like he claims, he'd let me count his freckles."

Mika! You don't know anything about him, don't think like that. Yeah he's cute but totally made a fool of you!

Shaking her head, she entered her bedroom and closed the door, sinking to the floor, Mika leaned her head against the door and gave a heavy sigh.

"I am in so much trouble," she whined aloud.

Walking to the wardrobe she pulled out a green short-sleeved dress. Making quick work of the change, a shiver ran down her spine at the gentle breeze that passed over her shoulders as she laced the back of her dress.

I don't recall opening the balcony doors.

Turning around there stood Noa in a plain blue tunic and brown trousers, running his hands through his hair. Smiling, he waved and then immediately ran a hand through his fluffy locks.

I know I can't summon people, but what weird timing.

"I—how, how the hell did you get up to this floor from there!" Mika said, shocked.

"Took the stairs." He shrugged.

"Why do people keep surprising me? Give me one reason not to scream for the guards in the next five seconds."

"I come bearing important information about an attack that will be taking place soon."

That matches up with what Ellis alluded to earlier, Mika thought.

Staying guarded, she asked, "What's this information?"

Closing the balcony doors, Noa motioned for her to lock the door behind her while coming closer. Making her way to the door, she turned the lock and glanced back at the dark-haired man.

"Okay, make it quick though, someone is bound to show up any minute now, I've been away for too long already."

"Someone has hired Jasper's group to attempt an attack on the palace sometime soon. All I know for certain is Jasper has his eyes on you and Zeppo."

"You don't have a day?"

"I do, but I am one of few with this information, revealing it would give my position away."

"Oh, well, is there anything else?"

"We were also ordered to take any tomes being carried by anyone in your group."

"Our group?"

"Yes, the Irkafen woman, the general, the Matuen woman, you, your brother, and Zeppo."

"This is troublesome if you know all of this, why are you helping?"

"Zeppo is my friend."

"There's more isn't there?" Mika said, stepping closer.

"I owe him my life, and since he chose you over them then that's where I will follow."

"Why not give him this information instead of me?"

"He seemed busy," Noa responded, clearing his throat.

"I see, well, if you find any other information please come to me, anyone else may kill you on the spot."

"You will trust me that easily."

"No, which is why I am ordering you to stay here until I return."

"What makes you think I'll stay?"

"You'll stay if you want to gain my trust," Mika said, now standing close to Noa.

"If that's what you wish then, milady," Noa said, bowing

"Good."

Grabbing the door handle, the sound of Noa clearing his throat and laughing made her glance over her shoulder.

"What are you laughing at?"

"I didn't realize royalty walked around with their dresses half-laced."

"Oh! Gosh, how could I forget something so simple," Mika said, letting go of the handle.

Honestly? The cute boy you were thinking about showed up, gave you information, is going to be sitting in your room for a few hours, and you forgot to finish lacing your dress. Will you ever stop embarrassing yourself, Mika?

"Would you like some help?

"Y-You'll only lace my dress?" Mika questioned, a blush across her face.

"If that's what you want."

"Yes, it would make it faster if you could then, please."

"Does this go toward gaining your trust?"

"No."

"How harsh you are, milady."

Hold your ground, Mika, we don't stumble over cute boys, let alone commoners. If you can turn down every suitor that's come for your hand since you were ten, then you can turn down this boy. Or at least make sure he doesn't get too comfortable with you, even if his hands are warm, and he smells citrusy.

"Many maids have helped me with my dresses, my brother on occasion also, therefore it is not a special task."

"Do they tell you that you are beautiful too?"

"Yes."

"Good, because you are," Noa whispered.

Turning to face him, Mika pushed him away. "You're a flirt."

"Only for you, milady, how could I resist when you tell me I'm pretty."

Ah, no, I did say that!

"I do have to go, stay here, we can talk more when I return. However, I am asking Zeppo if you flirt with others or not, if I find out you lied about it only being me, you are losing trust points!" Mika said, her cheeks a rosy red.

Before Noa could get another word out, Mika left the room, shutting the door just a little too hard. Gripping the sides of her dress, she took off at a quick pace, trying her best to put space between her and Noa.

***

Standing on one of the many balconies overlooking the palace garden, Mika played with some of the ivy leaves wrapped around the railing. The salty ocean breeze calmed her anxious mind as she waited for her father to speak. He stood beside her, his hands behind his back, his suit sharp and dark as the expression on his face.

"Did you speak with Clovis as I instructed?" he asked.

"Yes, Father I did, he didn't take it well."

"Of course he didn't, he has a miraculous way of making things harder than they need to be."

"Father, why is it so important that he marry Vivian?"

"Vivian is the only noblewoman to handle someone like your brother, and if he is to take my role one day, he will need an heir or two."

"What will you do if you push him too hard and he steps down from being the crowned prince?"

"He will do what he has to. I can't live forever, he will have to come to his senses sooner or later. That Matuen girl is the problem."

"Are you going to have her killed in a death duel tomorrow?"

"Yes."

I hope she wins, Clovis seems to trust her, and she's saved our lives.

"I have these rules to keep you and your brother safe." Damien sighed.

"I know, Father."

"Then make him see sense before my hands become tied and I'm forced to stop this madness."

Why is he so dead set on this marriage? He didn't seem to care all the times Clovis broke the rules before.

"Father, you used to always let Clovis off easy, and myself, when we messed up. Why not just let him marry who he wants? I know that Matuen is frowned upon, but I doubt he would have ever asked her hand in marriage if he wasn't being pressured to marry a girl he's always disliked."

"You question my authority on this matter?"

"Yes."

"Then perhaps I've been too lenient on you," he said, hands now gripping the balcony railing."

What does he mean? He's going to punish me for not agreeing with him.

"Father, I just think if Clovis is going to rule one day, then he should have some room to rule the way he sees fit. It's not like he is going to change everything you have ever done, he just doesn't want the pressure of marriage."

"It seems I have failed you, for you are more blind than a corpse, and your magic is just as useless."

"F-Father, I don't—Why?" Mika stuttered, tears threatening to spill down her face.

Grabbing Mika's face, he said, "Your brother has done nothing but disobey me from the day your older sister died. He lied to protect you and I let him. He said he would teach you to be less ignorant and harness your magic, and he has failed. You think I was lenient, but I assure you, your brother is just a good liar. Perhaps now I will teach you why you do not disobey me. You have both done such a miraculous job, at giving me a mess to clean. Perhaps this will teach your brother to listen."

Grabbing Mika by the arm, he led her toward her room. Feeling like ice was creeping up her spine, she couldn't shake the feeling something awful was about to happen.

Noa is in my room, I have to warn him somehow before we get there or father will kill him. Ellis said, don't think just imagine and do. I will just try to speak to him without being in the room.

Letting her body relax, she closed her eyes and focused on Noa's appearance. Imagine she was in her room standing by the door, Noa sitting on the plush leather couch reading a book. His hair was tousled and his feet were resting on top of the coffee table, she could hear him turn the page.

"Noa, It's me, Mika. You need to listen now."

Startled, Noa sat up and asked, "Mika?"

"Listen, there isn't much time! My father is dragging me to my room. You need to make a run for it or hide NOW."

Opening her eyes, she let out a breath and peeked at her father only to meet his hard stare. Not saying anything he seemed to clear his head of thoughts and flung open her bedroom door. Shoving her inside, he closed the door behind him, turning the lock. Panicking as her eyes darted around the room, aside from the now closed book on the table, there was no indication of anyone having been in her room. Letting out a sigh of relief, it was replaced by fear as her father's large hand tangled in her hair and shoved her to her knees.

"I do apologize to you, my dear child, but this will not be pleasant for you. Perhaps, from now on, you will learn to not question my authority."

Chapter Eighteen

<u>Zeppo</u>

Standing in the kitchens watching the staff rush to and fro, to complete their tasks, Zeppo leaned against the cool wall. The smell of fresh herbs and fruit tinged the air with its sweet and earthy scents, calming his nerves.

That's the second time the prince has choked someone in such a short period, he thought, rubbing his throat.

Something feels wrong. This evil guy knows who we are and we barely have a grasp on who he is! How could he possibly know who the fates are going to pick? Unless there is a traitor among the fates.

That feels wrong as well. He was shadowy when we met, and from what Clovis and Kilgi have said he was laced in darkness when they also met him. Perhaps he can spy through the shadows? It still doesn't explain how he knew Umbri wanted me, but it's a start. I should bring this up to Clovis. Hopefully, he won't go crazy and try to kill me again.

"Sir, here's the food you requested," an older Irkafen woman said, passing him a tray.

"Thank you," he said, taking the tray.

He saw an assortment of tea sandwiches, a fruit bowl, and a white teapot, its citrusy smell sweetening the air. Nodding at the woman, he turned to leave the kitchens. his footsteps echoed loudly in the hall as he headed back toward the study.

Feeling a creeping anxiety quicken his heart, he sped up his pace. *"Mika is in danger, can you save her Zeppo?"* Umbri's voice said.

Stopping in his tracks, Zeppo felt an unnatural warmth seep into his skin. The hallway suddenly seemed brighter than before, and his anxiety spiked.

"What?" he asked.

"Go to her before her father kills her."

Feeling the warmth leave the hall, Zeppo, now almost running, hurried to her room. Seeing a maid come around out of one of the rooms, Zeppo stopped her.

"I hate to ask, but I need this delivered to the prince's study by the throne room. I had an emergency arise," he said, pushing the tray into her tanned hands.

"Oh, uh—"

"Thank you, sorry," he said, waving as he ran away.

As he approached the princess's room, his fear tightened his throat, upon hearing her muffled screams. Without a second thought, Zeppo tried to open the door, only to find it locked.

"STOP!" her scared voice screamed.

Umbri, if you want me, you better help me get this door open, he thought, steeling his nerves.

Taking a few steps back, he stormed forward and slammed his foot against the door. Seeing it give, he felt a rush of hope and slammed his foot against the door. Watching it splinter, he held it together as he listened to Mika's screams. Seeing the door now ajar from his kicks, he grabbed the handle and flung the door open.

Before him, Mika was kneeling on the ground before her father, blood seeping down her back, staining her green dress and the ends of her blond hair. A few feet in front of her stood Noa, banging against an iridescent bubble of magic, his voice muffled. Locking eyes with Noa, he turned following his gaze, the king watched him with clouded eyes, a sneer on his face.

His daughter, how cruel, Zeppo thought, anger replacing his fear.

"I came to treat the princess, I'm her healer," Zeppo half-lied.

"I never hired a healer," he said, stepping forward.

"Her Majesty did."

"I never knew my wife to be the kind of woman to make decisions without me."

"She tasked me with taking care of the prince and princess's medical needs after the attack last month."

"No one called for a healer," the king said, stepping closer.

"Mika called for me."

"Did she now?"

Meeting her tear-streaked eyes, she nodded at her father.

"Then it seems you are not all that incompetent,"

"This stays between us. Should anyone else know, it will be both of your lives that I take as punishment," he stated, nodding to Noa.

"Sir?" Zeppo asked, bowing slightly.

"Speak."

"Will you have a message delivered to the prince, that I will not be returning for some reason or another? He is no idiot, he or his bodyguard will come sniffing eventually unless I am given a proper excuse."

"It would seem my wife picked a smart healer. Treat her here," the king demanded.

Shutting the broken door behind him, Zeppo jumped at the sound of wood snapping back into place. Assuming the king fixed the door to keep this moment quiet, Zeppo locked the door and sprang into action.

Reaching her at the same time as Noa, Mika collapsed into their arms. Moving her messy hair off her back, Zeppo gasped at the cuts littered all over her. Sighing, he laid her on her stomach and peeled her dress forward.

"Don't talk yet, Mika, save your strength. Let's get you taken care of first."

Whimpering, she nodded.

"Will she be okay?" Noa whispered.

"I've dealt with worse. First thing, though, we need to stop the bleeding."

Noa got up and grabbed towels from the bathroom, Throwing a few over her back upon his return.

"I am sorry, Mika, but it's going to hurt to heal you. You got to bear through," Zeppo said, reassuringly.

Nodding at Noa, they both pressed strongly against her back. She let out a cry and sucked her bottom lip between her teeth, her fingers curling into her palms.

"You're doing a good job, Mika, try to take some deep, slow breaths for me."

Waiting until he heard her third deep breath, he and Noa peeled the first sets of stained towels and put the new ones on. This time Mika gasped, but let her hands relax. A little while later, the bleeding let up.

"What now, boss?" Noa asked, seeming a little calmer.

"We move her to the bathroom, so I can clean the wounds before I heal them. I'm not risking infection."

"Mika, do you have the strength to move with us, or will you be okay if we drag you?" Noa asked, pushing some of her bangs to the side.

"I-I can walk," she said, quietly.

"You don't have to force yourself, we are here to help," Zeppo added, grabbing her arm.

With joint effort, they managed to move Mika to the bathroom. Grabbing the stool from her vanity, Noa sat it down giving Mika a seat. As Zeppo filled the sink with hot water, he watched the way Noa whispered to the princess and smiled. Grabbing a washcloth, Zeppo soaked it and returned to the princess.

"I will heal the cuts as I clean them. We are lucky it's nothing worse, I'm sorry I wasn't here sooner," Zeppo said, standing behind the princess.

"How did you know?" she whispered.

"Umbri told me."

"You mean to say a fate told you we were in danger?" Noa scoffed.

"Yes."

"There is no way." Noa laughed.

"You don't know much for being a spy," Mika hissed through the pain of being healed.

"You got that right." Zeppo laughed.

"Hey! It's not about me or my ability to spy, besides, why would I be a good one if I am trying to help you, Zep?"

"Fair enough."

"Do you guys trust each other?" Mika asked.

"Yes," they replied in unison.

"Then, Noa, I will trust you, but you can't be a spy anymore. I want you here as my bodyguard."

"What?" he asked.

"I need a bodyguard with everything going on. I feel better having you two by my side. I would be dead if you didn't step in," she said with another whimper.

"Almost done," Zeppo cut in.

"Hardly, you shielded me from him, instead of protecting yourself."

"I had to, It's my job to protect the common folk. I am supposed to bear that responsibility everywhere I go. If I can't do that then with or without magic, I fail everyone."

"I knew what I was risking, princess."

"SO DID I!" she yelled, startling both men.

"My father is a lunatic, my mother is a coward, and my brother is in danger. Everyone pushed me aside for one reason or another, but I didn't stop caring. They are all incapable of seeing reason, so I have to be reasonable, or more bad things are bound to happen. I'm trying to be strong, but I am asking that you both help me do that," she said.

Meeting her bright eyes, Zeppo stepped before her, kneeling, crossing a hand over his heart. "I pledge my life to you, princess, I will become a healer worthy of you."

Kneeling Noa said, "I swear my allegiance to you, milady. I will protect you with my life but I cannot stop being a spy. We need information from the other side and I can get it."

"Give me your hands," she demanded.

Her eyes glowed an unnatural blue, the air stirring, lifting her hair in its breeze. Zeppo placed his big hand in hers, he watched as Noa bowed his head but didn't give her his hand.

"From this moment forward, Zeppo, you are under a magical oath. You shall answer only to me, should you betray your oaths, it will be punishable with a swift death."

Feeling her magic make its way up his arm, it felt like the buzzing in the air before lightning struck. The blue of her magic wrapped around his body, settling deep within his skin. He saw his hand had a tattoo of electric blue and white ivy vines reaching to his chest, ending right above his heart. Locking eyes with Noa, he gave a nod of his head and stood.

Reaching forward Noa placed his hand in the princess's.

"Do as you must, I will not place you under oath, but should you betray me then may magic itself punish you."

"Yes, milady."

Oh, he has it bad for her. Zeppo chuckled inwardly.

Swaying, Noa didn't miss a beat in catching Mika and steadying her on the stool. Smiling at the two, Mika reached forward and grabbed Zeppo. Pulling both boys into a hug, they found themselves all relaxing into the touch. Zeppo hugged a little tighter when he felt Mika's tears wet his shirt.

"Can you cut my hair for me?" She sniffled, pulling from the hug.

"You want us to cut your hair?" Noa laughed.

"Yeah, just up to my shoulders."

"I'm no stylist, I'm sure the blood will wash out," Zeppo said.

"I will have someone come to fix it tomorrow, I want it shorter."

"All of a sudden."

"No, my father grabbed my hair and yanked me around with it, I want him to know even if I'm scared, I'll cut out what doesn't suit me. I won't be a coward like my mother, and I won't sit idle while my brother needs me. This is a subtle way of saying that."

"You think he'll get it?" Noa asked,

"This is why I'm the princess and you're the bodyguard." Mika smiled.

"All right, we'll attempt to cut it." Zeppo laughed.

"Wish I could just pick myself up the way you do." Noa smiled.

Me too. Zeppo thought.

"I'll cut and you run her a bath," Zeppo said to Noa.

"What if I wanted to cut her hair?"

"My hands are steadier, you get to choose how good she smells afterward."

"Fine."

"Honestly. I'll take my bath quickly. If I don't come out shortly, come make sure I'm fine."

After putting Mika's hair up and cutting it as straight across as possible. She shooed both men from the bathroom, leaving them to wait. Walking over to the balcony, Zeppo opened the doors to air out the room.

"Should we get someone to clean the blood off the floor?" Noa asked.

"I'll send for cleaning supplies and a fresh towel. Though we are on our own as far as cleaning goes. The staff is bound to gossip if they see blood on the floor."

"Fair enough."

"I'm sure Mika will fill you in, but it's a mess, Noa. Every day that goes by, things seem to somehow get worse."

"You mean because of the guy attacking the kingdom?"

"Not only that, but the dark magic he possesses, his unnatural knowledge, and now King Gorkem's antics on top of it."

"I thought he was going to kill her. If you hadn't kicked the door in, I'm sure we'd both be dead right now."

"What kind of king tortures his daughter?"

"The cruel kind."

"What are the chances the prince has had the same experience?"

"Well, rumor is Prince Clovis is remarkably strong in magic, I'm sure his father hasn't done anything since he was little," Noa said, crossing his arms and leaning against the wall.

Leaning on the balcony facing Noa, Zeppo responded, "Clovis is pretty damn strong, but after today, I think everyone has underestimated Mika. She didn't mutter a spell for that oath. I've never felt such power in my life."

"She didn't use any incantation for whatever she used to protect me either."

"Everyone, including her, thinks she can't cast, though it seems that's changing and I'm glad. She'd make a good ruler with a little more time. More so than Clovis, in my opinion."

"Well, what's the plan then?"

"For now, make sure Mika is fine. Once she fills you in, then we can figure something out."

"Okay."

"You've got it bad for her, you know." Zeppo smiled.

"And you don't? She is gorgeous and courageous."

"Not really into girls, but I can agree she is beautiful and courageous. Clever too."

"Think I have a shot?" Noa grinned.

"Hell no. Not unless King Gorkem walks himself off a cliff."

"But you think I have a chance." Noa grinned wider.

"Shut up," Zeppo said, pushing Noa as he walked back inside.

"Hey!"

Walking inside, he saw Mika in her undergarments ruffling through her wardrobe. Turning around, he grabbed Noa and spun him.

"Princess?" Zeppo asked.

"Oh! I thought you two would stay out a little longer. You can turn around, I'm covered enough."

Turning around, the princess now wore deep red pants and was lacing a black corset. Smiling at them, she stopped to wave them in closer.

"How are you feeling?"

"A little woozy, and hungry."

"Makes sense, you lost quite a lot of blood, my magic only replaces so much."

"Well, then, we can get some lunch, and go to the library." Mika smiled, a fire raging in her bright eyes.

"You should rest."

"I will be fine, my father won't anticipate me being up and moving already. It will give us some time to cause trouble."

"What kind of trouble?" Noa asked, picking up and handing the bolero that matched Mika's pants to her."

"My fate said there is a hidden room in the library that has a book that can teach me magics that can hinder my father, and Clovis, if need be," Mika said.

"I doubt you need it," Noa said.

"It's a different magic, more strategic. Something that could put us at an advantage with a proper approach. Though let it be known now, anything we discuss in private is to stay private between us three."

"You sure you're up for this?" Zeppo asked.

"With you guys, yes."

"Then let's go get that book. Maybe, we can get ahead of that evil bastard for once."

"Is anyone gonna fill me in?" Noa asked.

"Yeah, I'll tell you a little telepathically as we walk, I'm not magicked out yet."

She is admirable, I'd be crushed if I was in her spot. I will protect her, I will not fail like back then, Zeppo thought, as they walked out of the room.

Chapter Nineteen

<u>Ehiliana</u>

Standing off to the side of the crowded docks, Ehiliana watched as the citizens of Colkirk went about their business in the sweltering sun. Since the attack a month ago, what was left of the market had moved to the docks, while the main streets were being repaired. Colorful shade blankets hung lazily over the sections of the street to provide some refuge from the sun's intensity. The smell of fish, fresh food, and baked goods wafted through the streets blending harshly against Ellie's nose. Listening to idle talk and gossip among the crowd, Ellie peeled herself from the shaded wall and slipped through the masses, listening for anything noteworthy.

Most of the gossip she heard pertained to the citizens thinking the Gorkem family planned the attack as a way to seize power from King Hawkore. Standing on the southeast side of the dock, it opened into a lively plaza where she could hear upbeat fiddle music drifting in between the chatter. Pushing to the front of the crowd, she saw a woman with unnaturally black hair that seemed to soak up the light itself. She wore a sheer cream dress that split along her tanned thighs, with golden stars embroidered all over, while solid cream fabric covered her breasts and buttocks. Her eyes were closed as she played and danced along the edge of the fountain, singing with a voice that sounded almost ethereal, and fingers that moved so fast along the fiddle they could catch fire.

"Underneath the moonlit sky, my fiddle starts to play, A nomad's heart, I wander far, across the starry way, In the twilight's mystic glow, my fiddle takes the lead

Through cosmic paths where wonders intercede. I'm a vagabond of starry nights, a wanderer of space, filling the void with tunes of a celestial embrace.

"Oh, I'm a fiddlin' traveler, a drifter without reins

Guided by the constellations, where magic remains.

I dance along the starlit path, where dreams are not confined

A troubadour of the universe, in melodies entwined.

Beneath the arch of a fateful dome, a symphony unfolds

Celestial strings harmonize, as tales of stars are told.

Through nebulae and cosmic dust, my fiddle leads the way

A nomad of the cosmos, forever here to stay.

Oh, I'm a fiddlin' traveler, a drifter without reins

In every twinkle of the sky, a story yet untold

Whispered secrets of the stars, in melodies unheard. With nimble fingers on my strings, I weave a cosmic thread

A nomad's journey through the stars, where mysteries lie spread.

Oh, I'm a fiddlin' traveler, a drifter without reins

Guided by the constellations, where magic remains. I dance along the starlit path, where dreams are not confined

A troubadour of the universe, in melodies entwined.

So, let the fiddle's sweet refrain echo through the night

A melody for those who roam, beneath the starry light."

Entranced, Ehiliana couldn't help but nod along with the beat, the crowd around her dancing to the musician's fiery tune. Only did she snap back to reality as the song came to an end, and the woman's eyes snapped over to Ehiliana briefly, before beginning her next song. Feeling an electrical buzz between her and the woman, she felt compelled to stay and speak with her.

What the hell was that? I've never felt a surge like this before, is she a magic user or something like us? Or am I going crazy? Ehiliana panicked inwardly at the charged eye contact the woman made.

I need to speak with her, maybe she knows something. I'm sure musicians hear stuff all the time, perhaps she could be helpful.

Walking to the other side of the fountain, Ehiliana took a seat and played with the water as she waited for the concert to end. Letting her thoughts roam as she did, the music only seemed to pull her further into her thoughts from the last few weeks, as if clearing a fog.

The green light from the cavern in the historical building spread out like roots on a tree. A large pillar had many bridges networked through its inky depths, elegant balconies lined the walls where halls led to some untold mystery. The doorways had runes etched in the stone above them, they were like the ones from the slab she and Iathos found.

Iathos's face flashed before her, with disdain in the darkened halfway as he sighed to pick her up because she broke her leg.

"Hi, I'd say I didn't mean to interrupt your thoughts, but I did," the musician said, tapping her shoulder.

"Oh, sorry I must have zoned out." Ellie laughed.

"No need to worry, I get that way too. I had a feeling you wanted to talk to me," she said, plopping down next to Ehiliana.

"Yes, actually I did. When you made eye contact with me the air felt charged, it's never happened to me before."

"Hmm, maybe the cosmos wanted me to share something with you?"

"You don't have magic?"

"I do, in my own right." The woman smiled.

That feels like a coy answer, Ellie thought.

"Musicians tend to hear all kinds of gossip. I was wondering if you could tell me where I could find someone named Noa, or at least any dangers that could be passing through."

"What do I get in return?"

"I don't have much to offer. Perhaps a favor, within reason."

"Hmm, since you are information gathering, you could find my friend. I traced him here to Colkirk, but since I've been here it's like he is gone. His name is Silas, I'd like to know if he is in the castle dungeons."

"I could probably swing that."

"Go to Grogan's Bookery, tell the desk clerk you're searching for a meddler's tale."

"We'll meet here tomorrow night, right after sunset," Ehiliana said, standing.

"Sounds good to me."

"I never got your name by the way."

"I never got yours. Let's earn each other's trust first, yeah?"

"Fair enough." Ehiliana waved a two-finger salute as she walked away.

How have I lived here my entire life and never heard of Grogan's? I know this place like the back of my hand. Also, how the hell am I supposed to find this place?

By turning around and asking her before she disappears.

Fine, but don't be awkward.

Turning around to ask the mysterious woman about the location, she was nowhere to be found. Though the air itself seemed to hum with a similar electrical buzz as before. Huffing, Ehiliana tilted her head toward the sky and took a deep breath. Focusing on the buzz, Ehiliana felt the wind shift ever so slightly.

Just follow your instincts, there isn't a road map for suddenly having magic, and Makani hasn't been that helpful. I can manage on my own.

Letting her newfound magic narrow in on the electrical buzz, she watched as a beautiful shifting hue of blues and greens manifested above her head. Facing forward, she noticed how everyone else seemed oblivious to the line of magic trailing over them. Walking forward she followed the line to the far side of the market, entering the crowd.

The air carried the sweet aroma of exotic spices, mingling with the fragrance of blooming jasmine and the musky scent of old leather, as she was pulled further into the bottom ring of the city. Ellie's eyes traced the elegant archways that framed the bustling market stalls, each one brimming with treasures from afar. Lively chatter filled the air as locals bargained passionately, their voices rising and falling like a melodic tune. The vibrant array of merchants beckoned her with their wares, displaying silken fabrics, shimmering jewelry, and delicate porcelain pottery.

Dancing above her the luminescent magic took her through a labyrinth of narrow alleys adorned with vibrant tapestries and intricate mosaic tiles recounting old tales of Colkirk's history. As she navigated through the bustling crowd, the character's gaze fell upon a hidden alcove nestled between two ornate buildings. It seemed as though time had stood still in this enchanted oasis. Vines entwined around the stone walls, creating a lush canopy that shielded the entrance from prying eyes. A sense of curiosity surged through Ellie, drawing her closer to the mysterious sanctuary.

This is it! I knew I could do it!" she thought, proudly.

As Ehiliana stepped inside the magic bookery, a hushed reverence filled the air. Sunlight filtered through stained glass windows, casting an ethereal glow upon the shelves that held ancient tomes and mystical scrolls. The scent of aged parchment hung delicately in the air, mingling with the aroma of incense, hinting at the profound knowledge concealed within those pages.

In the flickering candlelight, Ellie's eyes danced across shelves adorned with books bound in shimmering gold leaf and embellished with intricate leatherwork. Ancient manuscripts whispered tales of forgotten lands and arcane spells, while leather-bound grimoires promised the secrets of enchantment. Every corner of the bookery seemed to hold a fragment of magic waiting to be discovered. Mesmerized by the aura of wisdom and enchantment, Ehiliana cautiously ran her fingers over the spines of the books, feeling the weight of centuries' worth of knowledge. Her heart quickened with anticipation as she realized that within these sacred pages lay the power to unlock secrets, weave spells, and shape destinies.

"Can I help you?" a feminine voice asked.

Spinning around to face the woman, she was stunned by her almost electric green eyes that popped against her wavy black and white locks. Taking her in, Ehiliana noticed how the navy blue robes complemented her paler skin; the robes ended near her ankles. The robes' edges were embroidered in delicate gold ink pots, books, and quills. Her outfit was a simple white blouse and black slacks, with matching boots. Her waist held a wide leather belt that had multiple books attached. She studied Ehiliana with a raised eyebrow, through round golden spectacles.

Clearing her throat, Ehiliana answered, "Oh, yes. I was told to ask you about a meddler's tale."

"Is that so? Who told you to ask me about that?"

"A fiddle player," Ellie said, feeling a blush creep up her face.

"How descriptive. Come follow me," the woman beckoned.

Following silently, the shopkeeper led Ehiliana to the back of the book-filled room and down a set of dimly lit stairs. Paintings of otherworldly creatures filled the hall, and the familiar scent of oranges lingered in the air.

"Is someone making food somewhere?" Ehiliana asked.

"It's a simmer pot, helps with wards, and makes this old place smell less old."

"Oh, that's interesting, I am still learning about magic, so I didn't know that."

"It would seem you have much to learn then."

"Yeah."

"Well, anyway, kitchen's through here."

Pushing the door open, Ehiliana was surprised to see a brightly lit room. Big arched windows filtered in sunlight, which gave the room a spacious feeling. Marble countertops lined the walls, with beautiful floral carved cabinets. Above the counters to the left were overhead pantry cabinets, and to the right were open shelves where numerous herbs were stored in glass jars. In the middle of the room was a matching island, with three chairs on one side. On this island was a bubbling cauldron, the scent of orange lightening the grounded aura of the room.

"How is the cauldron bubbling without a fire?" Ehiliana asked, nearing the pot.

"With ingenuity and rune magic. My son came up with the idea."

"That's amazing! Are runes really that powerful?"

"I'd hardly call this a feat, compared to the shop and house. It's called a stove, it heats things for cooking on top and baking inside. I'll put a kettle on and make us some tea. Do you have a preference in flavor?"

"Jasmine green tea, please."

"Hmm a sweet but delicate flavor, I'm partial to say you're very logical, loyal, and contemplative."

"You got all that from a tea flavor?"

"You carry yourself much the same too. Though, I will say the lavender day dress suits you well, and gives you an air of intelligence."

Leaning against the counter, Ehiliana responded, "Thank you, can I ask what tea you prefer?"

"Pirate's tea."

Smiling, Ehiliana said, "What is in this pirate's tea?"

"It's spiced black tea, cinnamon, nutmeg, and clove."

"It sounds pretty good."

"Oh, it is."

"So does it mean you're a pirate?"

Handing Ehiliana her cup of tea, the woman laughed. "In some ways, maybe."

"Well, madam pirate, I am Ehiliana Pinkali, former bookkeeper for the Colkirk Historical Building."

"A pleasure to meet you, Miss Pinkali, I am Octavia Blackthorn."

Picking up her cup, Octavia motioned for Ehiliana to follow her. Together, the pair walked out of a glass backdoor, onto a terrace that matched the kitchen's woodwork. The siding of the house was an elegant dark green, and the railings of the terrace matched the floral kitchen cabinets. A multitude of herbs, flora, and vines grew around the pillars to the second floor. To the left of the door was a couch and two chairs all a silvery color. A low sitting oak table in between them. Above her, golden orbs hung dormant, waiting for night to come. Walking to the banister of the terrace, Ellie took in the hillside forest.

The trees towered in a way she had never seen before. They seemed as if they could reach the clouds and they arched making the forest feel otherworldly. Sunlight filtered through the canopy, illuminating patches of wildflowers, ferns, and other diverse plant life. A gentle breeze rustled the leaves on the forest floor and filled the air with damp earth and tea. Listening carefully, Ehiliana could hear running water, indicating a body of water was nearby.

Taking a deep breath, Ehiliana turned away from the tranquil forest and sat on the couch with Octavia.

"You like it?"

"Love it, I'd work here in a heartbeat."

"Hmm, well, if we can come to trust each other, perhaps one day I could give you a position here."

"You're being serious?"

"Absolutely, but first things first, what are you here for?" Octavia asked, taking a sip of her tea.

"Information."

"Do you have something of value in exchange?"

"Only myself."

"You would sell yourself for information?"

"No, just a service for a service."

"What if I want something cruel?"

"Well, if my circumstances were different, I'd refuse, but I want to give someone I love a chance at a future that isn't bad."

"I knew you were loyal. Well, Ehiliana, you are honorable, I have a simple request."

"Okay."

"I'd like you to deliver a letter for me."

"Where to?"

"Lady Cromsel. No one must know you deliver this letter."

"I can manage that."

"Good, now what is it you need to know?"

"I need information on a Jesatyl named Noa and anything on any dangers passing through."

"I haven't heard of anyone named Noa, but I have heard rumors of an army gathering on the East Coast led by someone named Oliver Thornbrook."

"Any idea of why?"

"No, but we can go find out if you are up for an adventure. Though it will require a change of clothes on your part."

"I don't have anything to—"

"Good thing we can alter some of my clothes with magic. We'll have some lunch then go somewhere exciting."

***

Standing in front of the bathroom vanity, Octavia stood behind her, pulling her fiery curls into a neat bun at the base of her neck, as Ehiliana examined her new outfit. She now wore tight-fitted black plants with silver vines creeping up the legs. Her matching shirt cropped tightly against the underside of her breast exposing some of her pale skin, and the sleeves were snug against her wrist. Despite the snug fit, she was surprised by how well she could still move in the garments.

"You befitting of a higher-class delinquent."

"Am I supposed to be one for this adventure?"

"Only if need be; I'll do most of the talking. You'll be my guard if anyone asks."

Hmm, she must know this place well, if I'm pretending to be something for her.

"I see, you have an established identity where we are going?"

"You do catch on quickly." Octavia smiled.

Walking away, as Ehiliana strapped a black leather belt to her waist and clipped a sword to it, Octavia crossed the room and grabbed something. Walking back, she placed a mask in her hands. It was a solid piece of black metal with silver-filled runes etched along the edge pieces. There were no eyeholes, or straps to hold the mask to her face.

How the hell am I supposed to wear this?

"I'm sure you're thinking, how am I supposed to see or keep this thing on my face," Octavia said.

"So, you're also a mind reader?"

"No, I just asked my son the same thing years ago."

"Is your son some kind of genius?"

"Something like that. You just place it on your face, the magic will keep it there until you alone take it off, and it won't even seem like you are wearing a mask."

"So, will I have a full vision?"

"Yes. Where we are going there are very few Irkafens, so if you stick out, the mask will help with that. Plus, it will make you more intimidating and protect your face from some attacks."

"Octavia, no offense, but I feel like I am being recruited for something more than being a potential bookkeeper one day."

"That is up to you and what kind of relationship we have. I will not push you to do anything you don't want. This, however, is to keep any enemies from recognizing you anywhere else. Which means you will also need a name of some kind."

"Hmm."

"What about Shadow Dancer?"

Snorting, Ehiliana shook her head, "I am no dancer."

"I thought it was good."

"You can do better than Shadow Dancer for a name."

"Hey! What about Crimson Tempest?"

"Did you name your son, Raven Feather?"

"Ha-ha, you name yourself then."

"What about Obsidian Rose? Black clothes, matching mask, the only color to this getup is my red hair."

"Well, I'll be damned, maybe you are a little better at naming things."

"Obsidian Rose it is, then."

"Well, then, we should be going."

Turning, Ehiliana followed Octavia through the winding halls of her home. Buzzing with magic, Ellie felt like her skin was vibrating with its power. Before long, the pair stood in front of a door made completely of rifilium. It was an off-color of copper, and runes made of crystals were fastened to the door. Placing a hand on its knob, Octavia whispered something intelligible and opened the door.

Before them was an underground network of shops. On each side of the dim tunnel system were hanging shop signs in almost every language there was. They were bustling with life, just not as much as Colkirk's main market. Everyone looked shady in one form or another and eyed each other with suspicion. Octavia nodded her head and the pair made their way into the crowd.

Unlike most topside markets, everyone seemed quieter, and the air held a stiffness that warned those around to be weary. Keeping only a step behind Octavia, Ehiliana held her head high walking with purpose. Many seemed to part for Octavia as if she held some power in this realm of space.

I seriously need to find out what she does, Ehiliana thought, holding a soft creaky door for the woman.

Before she could step through, a man with almost translucent skin exited through the door Ehiliana held. His gaze roamed over her with white cloudy eyes and he nodded his head in thanks before disappearing into the crowd. Glancing at Octavia, she shrugged and walked through the entrance, Ehiliana slipping in behind her.

The building had shorter ceilings and was almost bursting with how many items it held. There were shelves of books, scrolls, jars, cauldrons, crowns, clothing, and dolls. Keeping a neutral expression, Ehiliana tried her best to not wrinkle her nose at the building's aged smell. Near the back of the shop was a greasy blond man, leaning forward on the counter watching the pair with his beady dark eyes and a smirk."

"Must be troubling times if the great archivist is traveling with a bodyguard," his whiny voice snickered.

"Troubling times indeed, Thaddeus."

"What are you here for this time?"

"Rose, can you please go lock the door for us?" Octavia said, without turning around.

Without a word, Ehiliana turned to lock the door, returning after a few seconds.

"Now that we're alone. I need information on a Jesatyl named Noa and about the gathering armies on the East Coast."

"The Noa boy can be discussed, the other is a very big ask. What do you have to offer me?"

"For Noa, I will offer you a vial of equinox."

"You are offering me a rare potion? Hmm, for him, I can accept that."

"For the army, I am offering one vial of bone wither, and one vial of epithelix."

What are these potions? Ehiliana thought.

"I will accept, under one condition." Thaddeus smiled a yellow grin.

"That is?" Octavia said, raising an eyebrow.

"I want to see Rose's face."

"No."

"No deal then."

"You're kidding, there is nothing else you'd be willing to negotiate for?" Octavia asked.

"You can touch my butt, but you can't see my face," Ehiliana cut in.

"A girl of my own heart."

"Not particularly, we just need the info. You can touch my butt first, vials come after the info. If you get any more handsy than one grab, I will take your hands off myself. Understand?" Ehiliana said, with one hand planted on the desk, leaning over the weasel.

"Yes." He gulped, leaning back just a little.

Walking around the desk Ehiliana turned so he could take a grab, all while staring at Octavia whose face matched hers.

This is why I like women, she thought, as the man felt her up.

Stepping out of his grasp, and returning to stand behind Octavia, she put a hand on her hip and waited for the grease ball to spill the information they wanted.

"Noa is a spy working for the army on the East Coast. They have yet to acquire a name. Noa, from my understanding, is spying on the royal families and finding weak points for an attack sometime within the next week or two. He is considered a higher-up in the army."

Setting the first vial on the desk, the man continued.

"Oliver Thornbrook is the army's general, he hails from Nearon, a local rich kid. Rumor is, that he gained power by tricking a Matuen into trusting him, only to turn her in to gain status. Since then, he has been working with a sponsor to start his campaign. He's been giving speeches about uniting the kingdoms under one banner. Rumor is, Oliver is coming here soon to give the same speech and make a declaration of war."

"That's all?" Octavia asked.

"So far, yes, they seem to be good at keeping things close to their chest. Reminds me of you a little, dear. I'm still wondering if you are taken or not."

Setting the last two vials down, she said, "Careful how you use those, we'll be back eventually."

"Do you have a last name, Rose?" He smiled, as the pair turned to leave.

"It's Obsidian Rose."

Opening the door to leave, Octavia, for a second, let her neutral expression falter into a scowl, before fixing it. Shutting the door behind them, they walked back toward the area they arrived at and made quick work of opening the magic door. Once inside Octavia's home, both sighed.

Taking off the mask, Ehiliana said, "I hate that guy."

"Yeah, the feeling is mutual, but he's the best in the market."

"Thank you for the help. I will deliver the letter to Lady Cromsel for you."

"Much appreciated. I hope we come to have a good relationship, I can always use more intelligent and trustworthy friends,"

"The feeling is mutual. If things are going the way I'm thinking, we may all be in trouble before too long. I'll be on my way, I hope you and your fiddle friend stay safe."

Chapter Twenty

<u>Kilgi</u>

Sprawled out on the moss garden floor, Kilgi took in the bright blue of the sky. Clouds floated through every so often, and the sea breeze cooled her warm skin only a little. The chatter of noble women gossiping acted as white noise for her thoughts.

How the hell did I end up in such a mess? I can barely keep the prince from going feral over a curse and now I have to fight to the death with someone over a marriage! She scoffed inwardly.

Why would you even agree to something so stupid? Well, I know why, it's because I'm not dumb enough to say no to a guy who could kill me with the snap of his fingers. Plus there is a part of me that wanted to piss that Vivian girl off . . . though probably a dumb move, in hindsight.

In hindsight! You broke one of your big rules. No royals! *I am fucked if we don't find a way to get things on a better track. Clovis seems determined to lose his seat as heir to the throne, and his father may be a madman. Honestly, I'm starting to think most of these upperclassmen are just lunatics who think they can do as they please."*

Come on, stay focused, I need to survive a duel, cure a prince, and protect the rest of the group. I need a plan because I doubt Clovis's father will let us go to the mountains, considering there has been talk about them going back to Aeberuthey amongst the wandering gossip. If we can keep things on plan though, maybe we can switch flights and make our way there with the group, that way everyone is together.

If things do go south and Clovis can't keep you or anyone safe? Yeah, there is a possibility. Then I take Ehiliana and Zeppo and run, I have some safe places in Lunoath. I will talk with Ehiliana when she returns. She's smart as a whip and would be a good ally.

What about Mika, would she be fine if things went south? I'm sure Clovis would protect her more fiercely than any of us.

"Hi, am I interrupting something?" Iatho's voice said, interrupting her thoughts.

Jumping to her feet, Kilgi smiled. "Iathos! You're okay. Thank goodness."

"As fine as being stabbed by a fate as one could be."

"Ellie told us what happened, do you know why he would do something so insane?"

"No, it's hazy, if I'm honest," he said, shifting slightly.

Is he nervous?

"Oh, well, that's okay. Has anyone caught you up on what's happening?"

"Yes, my king did, though I'm sure with you being involved there is more to tell."

"Well, a little. We found out some important stuff, but it's better left for another time."

"Makes sense. There are quite a few ears here. I heard you are in a death duel for a hand at marrying Clovis."

"He-he, yeah," Kilgi said, rubbing the back of her head.

"Are you stupid?"

"I was already scolding myself for being an idiot, I don't need you to scold me too. It was this or put myself at risk for something worse."

"Is there worse than a death duel?"

"You and I both know there is worse for someone like me. Besides, if I can beat you, I can beat anyone here."

"Kilgi this is too much, I never wanted any of this for you."

"My life doesn't get to be easy, cousin. For now, let's take it a day at a time and make sense of this mess."

"Would you like a sparring partner then?"

"Always." She smiled.

After an intense sparring session with Iathos, Kilgi sagged with exhaustion as she entered her shared quarters. Lifting herself off the door, she Spotted Clovis across the room sleeping on top of the bed covers, as if he just plopped down and passed out on the spot. His face seemed more relaxed in the evening sun, and his neat hair was splayed out on the pillow. Smiling at the gentleness of the sleeping prince, Kilgi walked toward her wardrobe.

It is a shame, I can't trust him as much as I'd like to. If he wasn't being messed about by a curse, I am sure he would be far less impulsive. She thought making her way to the shower, with her clean clothes in hand.

Turning on the water, Kilgi stripped down and inspected herself in the mirror. Her hands softly traced over the scars from the past, many lining parts of her upper shoulders, hips, and thighs. Now faded with time, they were thin white lines wrapped around her legs, but still, she frowned at the memory of a terrible life as she stepped into the hot spray.

"No one should be forced to live like this just because they are different."

"Do you think I'd love someone like you?" Oliver's face sneered in the back of her mind.

"I had hoped."

"The prince is no different, he'll probably do worse to you than I ever did."

"He won't, I don't even love him."

"You trust him, even though he is going insane. I bet he'll take immense pleasure in torturing you once he finally loses his mind. Maybe he'll give you to Vivian."

"Stop."

"Maybe he'll find your last two kin and kill them in front of you as a peace offering to his father for disobeying him."

"He isn't that petty."

"But you don't deny he could do these things. I'm sure even if he wasn't cursed, he'd find a way to rid himself of you once you're not useful anymore."

"He won't, he promised."

"You thought I wouldn't and where did that get you? The scars suit you, they remind you where you belong."

"Stop." She thought, sliding to the shower floor.

"You can't hide from the truth, He will betray you and everyone will stand by, so it's only your head that rolls when this is all over."

"I said, stop," she whimpered, curling in on herself, as the hot water pelted her skin.

The feeling of dread pulled on her navel, and she felt like ocean waves were pulling her further into despair. Feeling too tired to fight the feeling, Kilgi hugged her knees tighter and sobbed until the water began to cool.

A gentle knock on the door pulled Kilgi from her monstrous thoughts. After a few seconds, she heard the knob turn and feet pad toward the shower.

"You may turn into a prune if you stay in there any longer," Clovis's voice said.

"Maybe I want to be a prune."

"I doubt it, now get out, my love, we have something to discuss."

That's not Clovis.

Standing up, Kilgi reached for the bottle of shampoo by her. Stepping forward, she flung the shower door open and slammed the bottle into the stranger's head. Stumbling back blood flung to the floor as she pulled the bottle back. The assassin's blond hair clung where blood flowed out, and his dark eyes glared at her. Feeling off, Kilgi knew she was dealing with a Jesatyl. Still feeling her strength and focus, she guessed he was more than likely blocking her stamina.

I have to make this quick, she thought, as she heard a loud crash outside the bathroom.

The assassin lunged forward, forcing Kilgi to dodge almost falling out of the shower. As he attacked again, Kilgi stepped to the side of him and slammed the bottle into his head. Letting out a grunt he stumbled again. Taking her chance, Kilgi threw the bottle at him and lunged for his sword. Grabbing his wrist, she pulled his arm up and slammed it down on her knee, the crunch of his bone echoed across the room, then his scream. Letting go of his hand she grabbed the sword, turned, and drove it through his neck. Eyes wide with fear, Kilgi pulled the blade from his throat and tried not to grimace at the blood that splattered against her naked body.

Guess I need another shower.

Throwing on her underwear and shirt, Kilgi went into the bedroom. Before her, Clovis was kneeling on the ground a sword at his throat and another keeping him pinned to the floor through his hand. Shadows were leaking off him like wet ink, and his icy gaze met hers. Two dead Jesatyl were sprawled over his furniture and the other three were now fixed on her.

"Stand down, scum," the one holding a sword to Clovis said.

"I'm not the one to fear here,"

An ugly smile distorted his features; the shadows growing rapidly up his arms, inking across his jawline.

"Stand down," he said again.

"That isn't Clovis," she said, a chill running up her spine.

Dashing the door, the sounds of muffled cries screamed out as Clovis's shadows drenched the room in darkness. Still trying to beeline for the door, cold hands reached for the back of her head and slammed it forward against the door. As the light came back into the room, the world was fuzzy as Clovis stood over Kilgi's slumped body.

Turning her over to face him, Merkth's voice spoke instead. "I missed you, little one," he cooed, stroking her face. "You see, I am under the impression there is something you know that I don't and I need you to tell me. See, my curse should've eaten Clovis by now, yet all I can do is this. He'll regain control eventually, he is quite strong, but not before I kill at least you and maybe one or two people in the rooms nearby."

"Fuck off," she spat, blood hitting Clovis's face.

"Now, now, dear, that is no way to speak to your future leader." He smiled, squeezing her face with enough force to make her head spin.

"I said, fuck off," she said, grabbing his face.

Focusing all her energy, she called forth all the light she possibly could and poured it into Clovis. Demonic screeches came from his mouth along with Clovis's screams. Not caring, Kilgi dug her fingers into his face and kept pouring all her energy into the man until his grip loosened on her. Feeling her heart pound in her chest, and the smell of blood filling the air, Kilgi finally let go, completely drained. Watching as his body slumped to the floor, she scooted forward and pulled his head into her lap. Checking for a pulse, Kilgi let out a breath of relief and moved some of the hair plastered on his forward out of the way.

"How did they get past his wards? How was Merkth able to possess him?

"What do I do, Nell? How do I rid him of this curse, we can't keep on like this, we will all be dead soon if Clovis is compromised like this."

"Chase the darkness from the depths of his mind, body, and soul, you will need Umbri unless Zeppo accepts her power."

"This is too much, Nell, I can't survive this half-assed, I don't care if it's early but if you want me to do something that crazy, I am going to need your full power."

"Always so quick to figure things out. I will pass my title to you tomorrow evening after you and the boy have seen a healer, and you win your duel."

"Thank you, Nell."

"Thank you, my dear, you will make a much better fate than me."

As the room quieted, Kilgi sighed, pulling herself to her feet. After a minute, she pulled the prince up and dragged him through the door. Setting him in the hall, she collapsed beside him, the world spinning. Trying her best to stay awake, she tried to call out but was hit by a wave of nausea and the world went black.

Chapter Twenty-One

<u>Mika</u>

Mika stepped into the castle library, her heart racing with excitement. The grand entrance opened up to a vast chamber filled with towering shelves, lined with ancient tomes and glittering manuscripts, reaching up to the ceiling far above. The scent of old parchment and leather enveloped her, creating an atmosphere of knowledge and wisdom.

Her eyes were immediately drawn to the far side of the room, where the large windows bathed the library in natural light, illuminating the countless books in a golden glow. The windows offered breathtaking views of the castle grounds, with gardens, rolling hills, and distant forests stretching out to the horizon.

Near the entrance, a welcoming hearth crackled and danced, casting a warm glow across the room. Cozy sofas encircled the fireplace, where a few guests sat to relax and enjoy the company of a good book. The flickering flames created an ambiance of comfort and serenity.

As she strolled deeper into the library, Zeppo and Noa at her side, she noticed a few people scattered around the room. Some were engrossed in their readings, their fingers lightly tracing over the intricate lettering of ancient texts. Others were engaged in hushed conversations, exchanging knowledge and ideas. The library seemed to be more lively than most other days.

Mika could hear the gentle rustling of pages turning and the soft murmur of voices, creating a symphony of knowledge and curiosity. The library was alive with the stories of countless generations, and Princess Mika felt a sense of reverence and awe for the wealth of knowledge contained within its walls. Buzzing just under her skin, was the sensation of her magic pulling her further into the library.

Lost in the enchantment of the place, She was pulled near one of the back walls on the west side of the chamber. Zeppo and Noa had spread out to search in other places within the book-filled room. Running her fingers against the book's spines, their worn leather soft but sturdy gave her a sense of ease. She followed the buzz, its sensation growing stronger as she neared the west corner. Feeling a rush she focused on the sensation, letting the room spill its secrets to her, the magic humming wrapped around the sconce on the back wall. Reaching for the warm metal, she pulled it forward and heard a soft click from her left. Glancing over, one of the bookcases dislodged itself from the wall just enough for Mika to see light peeking out from behind it. Jamming her fingers into the crack, she pulled the heavy door and slipped through, closing it behind her.

As Princess Mika's fingers brushed along the dusty tomes on one of the towering bookshelves, she noticed a faint, almost imperceptible seam in the woodwork. Her curiosity piqued, she pressed her hand against the suspicious section of the wall, and to her astonishment, it gave way, revealing a concealed door that blended seamlessly with the rest of the library's architecture.

The hidden chamber was like a realm from a forgotten tale, an enchanting haven known only to a select few. It was a magical enclave, bathed in a soft, ethereal glow, emitted by intricate, glowing crystals embedded in the walls and ceiling.

The hidden room was more quaint than the main library, but no less impressive. The shelves here were filled with ancient tomes, written in languages long lost to time. The air carried a faint scent of aged parchment and the promise of secrets waiting to be unveiled. Antique maps and scrolls adorned the walls. A plush, velvet carpet covered the floor, leading the way to a central space where a delicate, round table stood, surrounded by cushioned chairs. On the table lay a large, leather-bound book, seemingly calling out to be explored. Runes and symbols were etched onto the table's surface, adding an air of mystique to the room.

A crystal chandelier, suspended from the ceiling, shimmered with soft, multicolored lights, illuminating the space with a gentle ambiance. The reflections of the crystals danced upon the walls, casting intricate patterns. Against one wall, a curious collection of peculiar artifacts was displayed on a wooden shelf.

The hidden room felt like a haven of knowledge and enchantment, a sanctuary where secrets were safeguarded and where one could delve into the most profound mysteries of the world. It was a place where time seemed to stand still, and the boundaries between reality and imagination blurred, allowing one to explore the depths of knowledge and wisdom.

This place is amazing, I could lose myself here. There is so much to explore and I think Clovis would like it too. Maybe I will show him once we are getting along again," she thought.

Walking over to the book on the table, she ran a hand over its red cover. When she opened the front page, it was blank. Deciding to turn a few pages, she furrowed her brow at the vastly blank pages.

What is this, I can feel the magic in it.

Picking it up, she turned it over in her hands, searching for any indication of how to reveal its contents. Finding nothing, she tucked it into her satchel and went to inspect the shelves' contents. The books varied in color, unlike the books within the library's main room, the dust settled on the shelves. Some of the books were in a language she couldn't understand while others had runic symbols on them. Letting her magic roam around the room, she tried to sense any books that felt more magical than the journal. The buzzing led her to a bright blue book in Auramic, the title read *A Beginners Guide to Teleportation.*

Interesting, she thought, tucking the book away.

Mika also found a book on conjuration and a ritual knife. Both of which she placed into her satchel. Deciding she probably spent too much time in there, she slipped out of the room, shutting the door behind her. Making her way back toward the entrance, Mika saw both boys leaning against the wall beside the doors talking quietly.

Zeppo's white locks were pulled back in a ponytail, and he had one leg crossed over the other matching his crossed arms. He wore a plain white button-down and dark trousers that gave him a clean but casual appearance. Leaning forward he seemed very focused on what Noa was saying to him.

He does listen quite well, Mika thought fondly, watching the pair.

Noa stood away from the wall beside Zeppo but facing him. His curly black hair moved as he talked. His freckles matched his shirt, and his pants fit nicely, making Mika blush a little.

Get it together, he is cute but we don't trust him, she thought, shaking her head.

Fixing her posture, Mika walked toward the boys, clasping her hands in front of her and rocking on her heels for a second as both of them turned to face her. Feeling insecure, Mika took a step back to not crane her neck as much and smiled.

"Hello, boys."

"Princess," Zeppo said, with a bow.

"Milady." Noa bowed.

"I am not sure if I found what Ellis wanted me to find, but I did find a cool little place. For now, though, we should find somewhere more private to talk."

"Shall we go then?" Zeppo asked.

"Lets."

Opening the door for Mika, Noa gestured to let the other two lead the way. Mika stepped out of the library, finding herself in a magnificent hall that overlooked an open room on the floor below. The hall itself was a masterpiece of architecture and design, adorned with grandeur and elegance. Tall, arched windows lined one side of the hall, allowing natural light to pour in and illuminate the space.

The windows offered breathtaking views of the castle grounds, with lush moss gardens, sparkling fountains, and winding pathways stretching out before her. The sight was both awe-inspiring and tranquil, making the hall feel like a bridge between the enchanted world of the library and the beauty of the world outside. Intricate pillars rose majestically on the other side of the hall, adding a touch of regal splendor. The polished marble floor beneath her feet felt cool and smooth, reflecting the soft glow from the crystal chandeliers that hung gracefully from the high, vaulted ceiling. The chandeliers sparkled like stars, casting a warm and inviting glow throughout the hall.

As she approached the railing that overlooked the open room below, Mika smiled at the room beneath the hall. It was a vibrant and inviting space, a cultural and social hub for the castle's inhabitants. Comfortable seating arrangements surrounded a large, ornate stage where performers and musicians would entertain the castle's residents and guests.

The open room was adorned with intricate tapestries and elegant drapery that lent a touch of opulence to the setting. Delicate candelabras hung from the ceiling, casting soft, flickering light over the grand space.

Shutting the doors behind them, Mika jumped a little at the sound but proceeded to lead the group toward Clovis's study chamber only to see a few guards rushing through the halls. Feeling nervousness rush through her, she peered over her shoulder at Zeppo.

Halting one of the guards, she asked, "Is something wrong?"

"Let me escort you somewhere safe, princess. An issue of security has come up," he stated.

"What is the issue?" she demanded.

"Uh, Prince Clovis and his bodyguard were attacked by Jesatyl assassins."

Peeking over her shoulder at Noa, she saw he had a schooled expression.

Did he know?

"Is my brother all right?" Please escort us to him."

"He is alive. I think the healing halls will be safer."

"Thank you."

The Halls of Healing were adorned with intricate carvings of healing symbols and gentle, pastel-hued tapestries that depicted scenes of rejuvenation and recovery.

The brightness of the place was not glaring or harsh but rather warm and inviting. Luminous crystal chandeliers hung from the ceilings, diffusing a soft, golden light that bathed the space in a comforting glow. Ethereal, glowing orbs floated in the air at regular intervals, adding an almost magical touch to the ambiance.

A sense of tranquility and peace pervaded the halls, emanating from the soft hum of healing energy that seemed to infuse the very air itself. The walls were lined with shelves holding precious vials of herbal remedies and potions, along with ancient scrolls of medicinal knowledge. Books written by skilled healers from generations past stood tall on sturdy wooden bookshelves, their words waiting to be unlocked and shared.

In the center of the Halls of Healing stood a grand fountain with cascading water, its gentle sound providing a soothing backdrop to the hushed conversations of healers and patients. Delicate, fragrant flowers adorned the edges of the fountain, adding a touch of nature's healing essence to the room.

One healer stood out in particular. His black fluffy mop of hair stood out against the white hall. His large slender hands cradled a book, and his glasses reflected bits of light, as he stood over a wooden bowl of herbs, his face a little perplexed. Forgetting the two boys behind her, Mika rushed across the hall to Ethan and flung her arms around him.

"I'm so sorry I haven't been by to say hello. Things have been so crazy, and I'm worried about Clovis. Please tell me you are overseeing him. I missed you," she spat out as she hugged the life out of the Vulocri.

"He is fine, we think, and he is in my care. It is okay, things have been hectic here anyway, I miss you too," he said, pulling from the hug and smiling down at her. "You cut your hair, I like it."

"Thank you."

Coming up behind the pair, Zeppo waved at Ethan, and Noa gave him a sizing glare.

"Hey, Zep." Ethan waved.

"Hey."

"Who's this?" he asked.

"This is Noa, he works for me." She smiled.

"Nice to meet you, Noa."

"Yeah," he responded, cooly.

"Anyway, could you take us to my brother?"

"Yeah, follow me."

Approaching Clovis's bed, he seemed a little more pale than normal and his skin was cool to the touch. Mika laid a hand over his and gave it a gentle squeeze. Glancing back at the group of boys staring at her, she gave a smile.

"Zeppo, Noa, could you both check on Kilgi, please?" she asked.

Nodding, Zeppo grabbed Noa by the elbow and led him away from Mika, leaving Ethan at her side.

"I am really worried, Ethan." Mika sighed.

Putting his arm out for her to take, Ethan led Mika toward his office near the end of the hall. Closing the door behind them, he moved to sit on the sofa sitting off to the side of the room. Sitting beside him, she slumped, feeling more comfortable.

"What's on your mind?"

"The attacks. This one, and the one a month ago when Ehiliana got attacked. They keep coming and this won't be the last."

"What do you think is coming?"

"An attack on the castle, a war, I'm not sure, but bad things are stirring."

"Well, when you figure it out, let me know how I can help."

"You're not worried?"

"Of course, I am, but I know between you and Clovis, whoever it is will have a hell of a time accomplishing anything without a fight."

"You have too much faith in me. Clovis is the real leader here."

"You would be surprised, I think you are the reason he goes so hard against the political grain."

Shoving into his shoulder, Mika laughed. "I think he just likes ruffling everyone's feathers."

"He will be fine, Mika," Ethan said, turning to the princess.

"I know, but I am still concerned."

"Do you remember when we were ten and Clovis got hurt fighting against Lord Preston because he tried to kidnap you while we were playing in the gardens?"

"Yeah," Mika responded. You kicked him hard and grabbed my hand to run. You took us straight to Clovis. He dragged Preston's body back himself and delivered him to Father's throne before passing out. I stayed by his bed for hours and demanded you keep checking on him."

"You said I have to always take care of you and Clovis because no other healer would care for you guys the same. It was a lot of pressure for a kid, but I was happy to be important to you guys."

"Sorry I put so much pressure on you, and you always will be, we have been through a lot together as kids. I'm just sad you had to leave."

"Don't apologize for asking me to be in your life, Mika, I got lucky to have people to care about, regardless of their position. I don't have the same treatment here, while they leave me be, if I mess up it's almost world-ending to them."

"When Clovis is king I'll make sure he brings you back home where you belong," Mika said, pouting.

Laughing, Ethan leaned back, "I can't wait. I probably shouldn't keep you any longer though, we both have things to do and your friend seemed like he was ready to clock me earlier."

"Zeppo would never."

"Not Zeppo, he and I know each other from the mountain temples. Talking about the moody Jesatyl, Noa."

"Oh, well, I will tell him to leave you be. He is still new to the group, anyway, and his flirting is very blunt and surprising."

"He is flirting with you?"

"Enough that I noticed, yeah. Luckily, Clovis taught me how to pick out smooth talkers, though I don't think he was trying very hard to hide it."

"I'd be careful then, I trust you to take care of yourself though."

"I will be' Zeppo seems to trust him. Hopefully, he can help us out," she said, with a blush.

Standing up Ethan offered his hand to Mika. "You know where to find me if you ever need anything, and I mean anything, Mika. I'm no Clovis, but I do want you safe and happy. Please, don't be a stranger."

Taking his hand, Mika stood and pulled him into a hug. "I know, I will come visit. I want you to be happy and safe too. Thank you for always supporting me."

"Always, Meeks," he said, pulling from the hug and opening the door.

Walking out of the office, they stared at the pair of boys talking by Kilgi's bed. Waving bye to Ethan, Mika could have sworn she saw Ethan frown in their direction. Turning to study the boys she could see Noa frowning at Ethan.

I really should say something, so he doesn't start any trouble. I trust Ethan as much as my brother, Mika thought

Chapter Twenty-Two

<u>Clovis</u>

Awaking with a start, Clovis sat up his eyes darting around the room. Seeing the healing hall, he let out a huff and fell back on the bed.

What the hell happened? he thought.

As if on cue, Ethan plopped down in the chair next to his bed, his fluffy black hair bouncing a little as he did. Without speaking, he wrapped his warm hands around Clovis's wrist and pulled his arm up, inspecting the runes on his arms.

"Well my runes did nothing, so I have no idea what happened to you. Would you like to tell me? Rumor is, there are quite a few dead mercenaries in your room."

"I was sleeping, when I woke to them barging through my bedroom door and balcony window. I was struggling against them, and then Kilgi burst through the bathroom. After that, everything went black."

"That's more than we got from Kilgi," he said, gesturing down the hall to the girl glaring at the pair."

Clovis said, "That sounds about right. Ethan, what time is it?"

"It's been a day, sir. Kilgi is expected to be in the field for her death duel in less than an hour. None of the healers would take her. I had to fight to get her into my section of the hall. You had a few visitors, and Zeppo stopped by with some concerning news but perhaps that's for another time."

I forgot how well of a secret this kid could keep Clovis thought.

"Well, I should also prepare for the day."

"I figured you'd say that. Mika brought you and your friend some clothes." Ethan blushed.

"I'll have to thank her. Have you talked to Mika since we've been back? I know you guys were close when we were kids."

"We talked a little, but with everything going on I haven't had time. When the hall is quiet, we are down in the city caring for the folks with the limited supplies."

"You should take some time to talk, Mika could probably use a good friend right now. Things have been rough for all of us, don't deny yourself some leisure time."

"I'll think about it, Clove," Ethan said, patting his arm.

Standing up, Clovis staggered a little, but grabbed the pile of clothes and made his way toward Kilgi. She was standing up as he got to the side of her bed. He lifted his arm for her to take. He watched as she gave him an odd look but reached for his arm, hesitant.

What happened?

"Ethan let me know the room was cleaned up overnight," Kilgi said.

"Was anyone we trust keeping watch over the cleaning?"

"I have no idea."

"We will have to check the room later, someone messed with the wards I had up."

"Clovis, we also need to talk about this curse."

"I know, but first we need to deal with this duel."

"Yeah, I've been thinking, though. This engagement was meant as a statement to your dad and it has only made him . . . well, crazy. I think once this is over, either way, we call off the engagement and explain the reason why to the audience. It would piss your dad off but garner a different attention he couldn't deny."

"You want me to deal with multiple suitors?"

"You've been pushing them off for years, and if you call out your father on old practices, all the families who want a chance for a better position will take your side for their chance to marry off their daughters. They would consider an equal opportunity over an arranged marriage. I also don't think those assassins would've come for you if I wasn't there," Kilgi said, rubbing the back of her neck.

"Kilgi, things are getting dangerous. While I think you have the right idea on this, my curse is also getting harder to control. What would happen if you weren't there to stop me?"

"Well, I barely managed to this time, Clove. You had me dead to rights, I got lucky."

"No, you know how to survive and you would've killed me if it came down to it, that is what I need beside me."

"Well, that's just it, Clovis. What happens if you can't keep your promise or I can't cure you before having to kill you? I need a backup plan. I can't keep doing this without a contingency plan in place."

Smiling, Clovis finished lacing his boots. "I won't stop you from having a backup plan, but all you've done is prove I can trust you more than any person I've known, up to this point."

"You are frustratingly optimistic and it's making you sound like your sister."

"Well, there's a first time for everything, because I think you figured something out and that's why you want a contingency. You're not afraid of the duel, but something about me is scaring you."

"Right, your new fear-seeing power," she quipped.

"Yeah, so what's on your mind?"

"Nell said there is a way to cure you but we will need Umbri or Zeppo's help."

"That is good news. We don't need to go to the mountains."

"Yeah, but what if it goes wrong? You can't tell me you don't feel the tension in the air. Something is going to happen soon."

Waving a hand and muttering a spell, Clovis locked and silenced the room, before turning back to Kilgi.

"You're not wrong. While I'm still feeling out this power, the air has been stirred. The longer this goes on, the more dangerous it is for you, Mika, Ehiliana, and Zeppo, so I have an idea but you need to listen closely."

"Okay."

"No matter if this goes south or my father makes the call to make us go home, you have to make a run with the others. He and the others will not hesitate to kill you guys if it means keeping trouble out of their way. Before this happens, though, I will make sure you have enough money to survive and get you knowledge on every kingdom's siege tunnels. Things don't change if we don't shake every one of these bastards up, so when you run, you have to build a way to fight back. I won't be able to join you guys until I make a public statement against my father, and I'd like to leave Mika out of it because I know he'd use her against me."

"You are going to rebel?"

"Yes, after everything that we have found out, I am certain he killed Isla. I know he isn't who he says he is, and he isn't even my father, but I still have a claim to the throne. Sometimes, we have to take that leap, and we won't be alone. I just know, for now, I have to pretend I think all of you are incapable of moving things behind the scenes without me. Like I said, though, I trust you. Don't take that lightly, I've never trusted anyone, really, not even Mika."

"You're fine with being in the dark on me wanting to make a backup plan?"

"Yes, because we are going to get through this, and between all of us, I think with time, we can become a smooth operating unit. Let's get this duel over with and I'll turn the other way while you make the moves I cannot."

"Clovis?"

"Yeah?"

"Thank you. I've been doubting all of this, and I have been consistently on edge. I'm not sure if it will ever go away but thank you for letting me have some room to breathe."

Watching as Kilgi adjusted her braid, he felt warmth rush to his cheeks and shook his head. Walking to the door he let up on the spell and the pair made their way to the death duel.

I've spent my whole life questioning what everyone says and yet she speaks, and all I do is listen. What the hell is wrong with me?"

***

As Clovis and Kilgi stepped through the ornate double doors of the dueling arena, the atmosphere immediately changed. The air became charged with anticipation and the echoes of past clashes seemed to resonate in the ancient stone walls. The arena was nestled within the heart of the imposing castle, a place where knights and warriors came to test their mettle and prove their valor. The circular dueling ground stood surrounded by elegant stands, accommodating a limited number of spectators. Each tier was adorned with plush, deep-red velvet cushions, providing comfort to those lucky enough to secure a seat to witness the bouts. Elaborate banners bearing the sigils of noble houses fluttered overhead, lending an air of grandeur to the scene.

The dueling ground itself was a combination of packed dirt and smooth flagstones. The border of the dueling ring was etched with ancient runes and intricate carvings, rumored to keep the specters safe in the event of a magical battle. Torches mounted at strategic intervals along the walls cast flickering light, providing an ethereal glow to the dueling arena during evening bouts. The smell of the earthy ground mingled with that of the noble's expensive perfumes wafting by as they filled the seats. Gripping Kilgi's shoulder, he gave a curt nod and turned to head for his seat.

Approaching his seat, he pulled out a piece of parchment and handed it to his father. Taking a seat, he watched as his father studied the fake content he created. While he studied it, Clovis glanced over at Mika who was pointedly not looking at him but clutching the fabric of her dress.

"This is what my people found after the attack. I figured since you are more knowledgeable than me, you may know what these symbols are." Clovis said leaning back in his seat.

"Seems they have been busy, no wonder you have been fighting me every step of the way," he said, handing the paper back.

"I have been reluctant to listen because of your disloyalty to Mother," he said.

Going stiff, Damien responded, "I see, perhaps we should talk about that another time."

"Later tonight works for me. You know what the runes are though. They are similar to the spell you had me do before I got cursed."

"Are you insinuating something, son?"

"Nothing sinister. I figured you could help me figure this out, and in return, I will quit making things more difficult for you."

"You'll end the engagement and get rid of the Matuen?"

"I'll end the engagement and I will keep her as a bodyguard though. You'll find she is very skilled."

"You'll marry Vivian then?"

"No, but I will start meeting with other options.""

Sighing, Damien said, "It's a start."

"What does the paper say?"

"It's a simple love spell, that binds the blood."

Bastard, Clovis seethed inwardly.

"Thank you, Father," the prince stated.

"I heard of the attack yesterday, you'd do better to keep stronger wards from now on. I also apologize for my actions toward Mika yesterday."

Watching as both his mother and Mika stiffened up past his father, Clovis quirked an eyebrow.

"What do you mean?"

"We disagreed. I know you are very protective of your sister, I lost my temper with her. As you can see, she is fine, I caught her with some boy in her room."

Mika clenched her skirts tighter, but refused to acknowledge the conversation, and instead, stood to move closer to the railing of their private balcony.

"You mean the healer?"

"No, another, a Jesatyl boy. Went as far as protecting him from me, I'd like to not deal with any more secrets from the lot of you."

Seeing Mika grip the railing, he could tell she was barely holding it together. Then he noticed she cut her hair. It now sat neatly along her shoulders, the strands swaying with the gentle breeze.

"We are getting older, Father, we are not obligated to tell you everything. Besides Mika is hardly the type to have some secret affair, if she was, there isn't much room for you to talk. You should have more faith in her, she has always been dutiful. She even risked an argument between us to get me to marry Vivian for you. Honestly, by now, you should see how loyal she is."

"She is loyal to you, not me. What else am I supposed to think of a boy in her room, especially with the attack on you by another Jesatyl?"

"Have you ever thought to just talk to her?"

"She didn't say a word."

"With your methods, I suppose not. Our agreement is still on for ending the engagement after the battle. However, if you touch Mika again, I will commit treason, Father. You can take your grievances with her out on me and I will deal with it accordingly, we have had this deal for many years now. Break it again and you will have as much trouble as I can make for you."

"I see," he said, turning his cold gaze to meet Clovis.

"You made me this monster, you'd do well to remember I do not die easily," he said, getting up from his seat.

Walking to Mika's side, he pressed his side into her and covered her hand with his.

"I am sorry," he whispered, as the announcer introduced the crowd to the fighters.

"I am too," she whispered.

"I like your hair, I think it suits you well."

"Thanks. Zeppo helped me cut it, the other boy was Noa. He tried to protect me from Father."

He came back then?"

"Yeah, I don't know what to make of him."

"We will figure it out. First, we just need to make sure Kilgi gets through this fight."

"I doubt she will need our help."

"She may, after yesterday."

"I heard, I'm glad you guys are fine."

"We need to up the wards on the rooms and put up contingency plans for the others." He nodded.

Kilgi would be laughing if she heard you openly echo her ideas, he thought.

"We will, let's focus though, the fights starting," Mika said.

***

In the heart of the arena, the crowd hushed in anticipation as the combatants prepared to face each other. On one side stood Kilgi, her striking purple hair flowing in the breeze. Clad in dark leather armor Clovis had provided, Kilgi exuded an aura of quiet confidence. Twin gleaming blades, one in each hand, were held at the ready, their edges catching the glint of sunlight that filtered through the arena's high arches.

Opposite Kilgi, stood Malcom Granis, the pride of Colkirk's finest swordsmen. A veteran of a few battles, Malcolm's presence commanded respect. He wore a polished suit of steel armor, each plate perfectly fitted to ensure maximum mobility. A long, elegant sword was strapped to his back, a testament to his renowned skill with a single blade.

As the horn sounded, signaling the start of the duel, Kilgi lunged forward, a whirlwind of motion and grace. The purple-haired duelist's agility was a sight to behold, gracefully weaving through Malcom's initial strikes with a dancer's finesse. Kilgi's dual blades moved with precision, parrying, and deflecting Malcom's powerful blows with a calculated ease that hinted at extraordinary training and skill.

Yet, for all Kilgi's prowess, Malcom was no ordinary swordsman. He adapted to Kilgi's unorthodox fighting style with experience and tenacity. The clash of metal reverberated through the arena as the two warriors engaged in a fierce dance of blades. Each step, each swing, and each parry was executed with calculated precision.

He sure as hell wasn't that good when they spared a few weeks ago, Clovis thought.

The crowd watched with bated breath, witnessing the spectacle of two extraordinary swordsmen locked in combat. Although Kilgi managed to land a few telling strikes, it was evident that Malcom's strength and experience were presenting formidable obstacles against Kilgi's ruthless blows.

As the duel raged on, beads of sweat glistened on Kilgi's forehead, a testament to the intense effort being exerted. The purple-haired duelist's breaths came quicker, determination crossed Kilgi's eyes. The spectators began to sense that Kilgi's victory would not come easily.

"Come on, Kils," Mika muttered, beside Clovis.

With a sudden burst of energy, Kilgi launched a daring attack, pushing Malcom back with a flurry of rapid strikes. The crowd gasped as Kilgi's relentless assault nearly overpowered the Colkirk swordsman. But Malcom, undeterred, dug his heels in the ground and rallied. In a swift counterattack, he forced Kilgi to retreat momentarily, regaining his footing and resolve.

The battle reached its climax as the sun dipped behind some passing clouds, casting long shadows across the arena. Kilgi and Malcom circled each other, the tension palpable. Lunging forward, Kilgi executed a daring maneuver, disarming Malcom's sword with a swift strike. The crowd quieted as it seemed Kilgi had secured her victory.

However, the duel was not yet over. Despite being disarmed, Malcom displayed the true spirit of a warrior. Drawing a concealed dagger from his belt, he lunged forward, catching Kilgi off guard. In a desperate move, Kilgi evaded the strike but not without a grazing wound to her arm.

Stumbling back, clutching her injured arm, the pain evident in her gritted teeth, Kilgi gripped her swords tighter.

"Come on, Kilgi, he's gonna kill you if you lower your sword," Clovis whispered.

Grabbing his sword, Malcom ran at Kilgi but was too slow. The crowd collectively gasped, as Kilgi dodged under his swing, and plunged her swords through the knight. After a few moments, she pulled them out and he staggered backward, sword falling from his hands. The crowd broke out in low murmurs as the winner was announced.

Checking for a pulse, he watched as Kilgi declared him dead, and then left the arena. Gripping Mika's hand before letting go, he saw her also relax.

"Quite skilled indeed," his father said from behind.

"Told you she made a good bodyguard."

Using a spell to make his voice louder, Clovis called attention to himself, quieting the crowd.

"Hello, everyone, I have an announcement to make. I am ending my engagement to Kilgi, though she will remain my bodyguard. The engagement was made for personal reasons, but rest assured, nothing has happened between either of us. I will not be taking proposals at this time. We have other issues going on that need my attention first. Once things settle down, I will announce to start meeting with the noble houses. Thank you all and have a good evening."

As the crowd exploded in noise, Clovis turned to his father, nodded his head, and left the arena.

Chapter Twenty-Three

<u>Ehiliana</u>

As the sun dipped below the horizon, casting a warm, golden glow over the castle's towering spires and walls, Ehiliana emerged from the shadows of the alleyway. The air was crisp with the ocean's breeze and distant flowers. Walking through the gateway, the fading sunlight caught the intricate patterns woven into her new outfit, hinting at the experiences she had encountered beyond the castle walls. Her steps echoed in the mossy courtyard, a rhythmic cadence of determination and a hint of exhaustion.

Ehiliana's hair cascaded in loose waves around her shoulders, kissed by the wind and Tousled by the day's exploits. Her cheeks carried a rosy hue, from walking in the heat. A satchel hung from her shoulder, and within it were a few books she had been allowed to take with her from Octavia.

Her eyes, a shade of deep magenta, held a spark of vitality despite the fatigue that weighed on her frame. They scanned the courtyard, taking in the familiar sights and sounds of the castle, a place that was both her sanctuary and her launching pad for exploration.

I need to find out who is in the dungeons without getting in trouble. I'll tell Clovis most of the truth, but I think it would be best to keep Octavia's place a secret, she thought, entering the castle. Hopefully, Regina had a good day. It will be nice to spend time with her. We have both been running around a lot recently.

Ehiliana approached the door and was halted by the guards posted there. She put her hands up, and they checked through her bag before letting her pass. She felt confused as she walked in and found herself turning.

"Is everything okay?" she asked.

'Everything is fine," the guard said, turning from her.

Shaking her head, she entered the castle. With it being later in the evening, the halls were quieter than the bustle of daytime activity. The sound of her footsteps echoed off the halls as she headed for the prince's room, anxiety making her heart beat a little faster. She heard chatter near the top of the stairs of the east wing and peeked her head around the corner. Gasping, she saw bodies being dragged out of Clovis's room by some of the castle guards.

Among them stood King Gorkem, he stood tall and menacingly, yet seemed to sense her presence. flicking his gaze in her direction, he raised a hand and beckoned her forward.

Stepping around the corner and bowing, she said, "Your Majesty."

"Why are you here?" he asked.

"I was sent on an errand by the prince, I just got back," she said.

"What was this errand?"

Feeling a cold shiver up her spine, she met the king's eyes. "He was searching for some books that aren't in the castle's library," she lied.

"What are these books?"

"Potion-making, conjuration, and curse-breaking," she stuttered.

"Now, no need to be scared, dear. Find what he was searching for?" he asked, placing a hand on her shoulder.

"Yes, I did. I even managed to find myself a book."

"Good. It is good to have well-studied people around you."

"Your Majesty?"

"Yes, dear?"

"Is the prince, okay?" she asked, glancing at the guards moving dead bodies.

"There was an assassination attempt. My son is fine and with the healers."

"Oh, that's good, I was worried."

"No need to. Why don't you go get some rest, my son's books can wait until he is better."

"Yes, Your Majesty." Ehiliana bowed before walking away.

Ehiliana headed toward the servant's quarters, glancing around before she turned and headed for the halls of healing. Without wasting a single second, she burst through the doors. Seeing Mika on the far side of the hall with Zeppo and a Jesatyl, she walked over to them.

"Ehiliana, are you okay?" Mika asked.

Please be competent, Ehiliana silently begged before speaking.

"I heard what happened and came to check for myself."

"Oh, well, Clovis and Kilgi are fine. Kilgi will probably wake soon, we don't know about my brother yet."

"Okay, who is your friend?"

"This is Noa."

Noa waved and smiled, and Mika blushed.

You're kidding me! I just spent the day finding a way to get information about this guy, and he's just tagging along now. Is she that naïve to trust a guy who managed to stop her from using magic she can't even control?

Shifting on her feet, Ehiliana said, "I see, well, I am going to check on them myself and head to bed. You get some rest too."

"Are you sure you're, okay?" Zeppo asked.

I have a princess who is unreliable and a cursed prince who would be reliable if he were not cursed. The ones I need right now are hurt, and the guy I am supposed to figure out is standing in this group like he did nothing wrong, and no one is questioning it. No, I am not okay.

"I am fine. Just trying to finish out the work Clovis wanted from me today."

"Maybe we can help," Mika suggested.

"Sorry, princess, but there isn't much you can do. I wanted to see if he was up or not, they are just books."

"Oh, well, I'm sure he will be glad to have them soon."

"Indeed, where is the healer who worked on him?" Ehiliana asked.

"He wandered back toward his office a while ago," Mika said, pointing.

"Great, I am going to go talk to him. Go rest," she said, not waiting for a response.

Knocking, Ehiliana opened the door and shut it before Ethan could respond. He was sitting at his desk, filling out some paperwork. Leaning back in his chair, he adjusted his round glasses and motioned for her to sit.

"Can I help you?" he asked.

"Nothing you haven't already done. I'm just stressed and needed somewhere not suffocating."

"You want to talk about it?"

"Not sure that would help me or get me in trouble."

"Well, if it helps, I am by an oath sworn to keep patients' information private."

"I am not a patient."

"From your perspective perhaps." He chuckled.

"You swear it stays secret."

"On my magic," he said calmly.

"Fuck, okay. The prince sent me on a mission for information, and I got it, but I must pay it back with information. This person is trying to find their friend—they were kidnapped. They want to know if they are in the castle dungeons or not, but without Clovis, I can't find out."

"What about the princess?"

"I can't trust her," Ehiliana said, flopping back.

"Why can't you?"

"She is too naïve and has trouble controlling her magic. Then, to top it off has brought the person I was supposed to get information on into the fold. How can I trust someone who doesn't know better than to just trust someone like that? I can't exactly go, 'Hey your brother seems to have issues trusting you even if he won't say it aloud, and now, I'm information gathering on the idiot you trusted for no reason.'"

"Was the information you found on him that bad?"

"Yes. He is meant to be spying on the royal families and finding weak points for attacks."

"With Clovis, wouldn't telling the king be the next step?"

"No that is the complicated bit. None of us have said it aloud, but we are pretty sure there are royals involved in all this, so we must be careful, which is why talking to you is dangerous for me."

Leaning forward, Ethan said, "What is it you need help with then? I will try my best."

"I can't ask you to do that."

"You can." Rubbing his eyes, he continued, "Clovis and Mika are the closest things I have to family. Without going into detail, you should know I would do anything for either of them. Mika has always been a little too trusting, I agree, but she is tougher than she seems." A blush crept up his face.

"You love her," Ehiliana said, plainly.

"Yeah, I do, I'm not expecting anything, but I can do this for them. They have always made sure I am safe and taken care of. The least I can do is support them back."

"You won't tell her any of this?"

"Promised on my magic, didn't I? I may love her, but it doesn't mean I have to spill my guts."

"Okay, I need to know the names of everyone in the dungeons. Can you get me that information?"

"I will have it by tomorrow morning."

"Thank you," she said, sighing in relief.

"I am Ethan, by the way," he laughed.

"Ehiliana."

"Nice to meet you, officially."

"Likewise. You seem the better choice than freckle face out there."

"I'm not sure she even knows how I really feel. Probably for the best, the king may try to kill me otherwise."

"You have no obligations from me. Mika seems nice, I don't mind that. I just wish she'd be a little more aware."

"You almost sound like Clovis."

"All right, I'm going now before I believe you." She stood. "Thank you again," she said and opened the door.

"Of course," he said.

***

The moon hung low in the velvet sky, its soft glow spilling through the tiny casement window of Ehiliana's modest servant quarters. The flickering candle on the worn wooden table cast dancing shadows across the room, creating an ambiance of warmth and intimacy.

Ehiliana's steps were muffled by the threadbare rug that covered the cold stone floor. Her boots, previously stained with the marks of her adventures, now rested by the chair. With a contented sigh, she closed the door behind her, shutting out the world beyond and embracing the haven of her own space.

Regina was nestled against a mound of pillows that adorned the narrow bed. Her eyes lit up like twin stars as Ehiliana entered, and a soft smile graced her lips, inviting and affectionate. The air was infused with a subtle blend of lavender and vanilla, the fragrance of Regina's gentle presence.

Ehiliana's heart swelled with a sense of comfort and longing as she approached the bed and slipped beneath the worn covers. Regina opened her arms, and Ehiliana nestled against her girlfriend's welcoming embrace.

Their bodies molded together as if they were two puzzle pieces perfectly designed for each other. Ehiliana's head found its place on Regina's chest, just above her heart, and she could feel the steady rhythm of its beat—a comforting cadence that seemed to sync with her own.

Regina's fingers wove through Ehiliana's tousled hair, each stroke a silent reassurance that she was home, safe, and cherished. Ehiliana's exhaustion melted away in the presence of Regina, replaced by a profound sense of tranquility that settled over her like a soft blanket.

They exchanged whispers in the quietude of the room, sharing snippets of their days and dreams. The world outside seemed to fade as they created their cocoon of tenderness, a sanctuary where worries were forgotten.

Time became a distant concept as they lay there, wrapped in each other's warmth. The candle's flame flickered, casting a gentle, almost ethereal, glow upon their entwined forms. Ehiliana's fingers traced delicate patterns on Regina's arm, a silent declaration of affection that needed no words. Eventually, Regina curled into Ehiliana, and the pair fell asleep.

***

As the first rays of dawn cast a gentle glow through the tall arched windows of the halls of healing, Ehiliana navigated the hushed corridors, with a clear purpose clear resolute step. The scent of herbal remedies lingered in the air, an earthy embrace that enveloped the space in an aura of tranquility.

Ethan stood by a polished oak table, meticulously cleaning his instruments. His long white coat billowed as he moved, the embodiment of unwavering dedication. Ehiliana approached, her presence a silent summons, and she hooked her fingers around his elbow. Then, she guided him away from the table and into a quieter corner, but not before locking eyes with Clovis.

He is going to ask questions, she thought.

Ethan's eyes held a mixture of curiosity and concern as he turned his attention to Ehiliana. His tousled black hair framed his features, a testament to the busy hours he had already spent tending to the castle's wounded and ailing.

"Ehiliana," he greeted with a warm smile, his voice a soothing balm in the early morning stillness. "What brings you here so early?"

Her expression was serious yet determined, Ehiliana leaned in slightly, her voice a hushed undertone amid the hallowed halls. "Ethan, did you manage to get the names of those imprisoned in the castle dungeons?"

Ethan nodded, his gaze shifting to the pocket-sized leather-bound journal in his hand. "Yes, I went down this morning to check on their well-being and got a list."

Ehiliana's heart quickened with a mixture of anticipation and trepidation. She was aware of the complexities that lay within the castle's secretive dungeons stories untold, lives obscured from the light of day. "Tell me, Ethan," she urged, her eyes locking onto his, "who are the prisoners?"

Ethan flipped open the journal, his index finger tracing down the list as he began to share the names.

"Seraphina, Alistair, and Gregory."

Sighing with relief, she said, "Thank you."

"Anytime, I want the kingdom safe too. Just ask and I will do what I can."

"I need a letter delivered to Lady Cromsel. I have somewhere to be, unfortunately."

"I can pass it off on my medication deliveries for some of the residents."

"Seems I owe you again."

"I'll keep it in mind, but don't worry about owing me, honestly."

"Thank you, Ethan."

With a nod, Ehiliana turned and left the hall. She had to make it back to the fountain to meet the fiddler. Ehiliana maneuvered through the vibrant streets of Colkirk, a coastal gem nestled upon the shores of a desert island. The salty tang of the sea breeze mingled with the warm scents of sand and sunbaked stone, creating an intoxicating symphony that enveloped the bustling city. Tall palm trees swayed in the wind, their fronds whispering secrets to the cerulean sky.

The cobblestone pathways beneath her boots were interspersed with grains of sand, a reminder of the island's unique blend of environments. The sunlight danced upon the intricate mosaic of streets as Ehiliana made her way toward the fountain at the heart of the square, and her surroundings shifted. The air grew more humid, carrying with it the distant call of seagulls and the rhythmic melody of waves crashing against the rocky shore. The scent of saltwater grew stronger, intermingling with the vibrant blooms that adorned the corners of buildings and balconies.

The fountain itself was a work of art, a masterful creation of stone and water that stood as a testament to the city's connection with the sea. It depicted mythical creatures and aquatic motifs, each detail etched with care and reverence for the island's maritime heritage.

And there, perched on a weathered bench near the fountain, was the fiddler woman. Her eyes held a certain depth, a reflection of the vast ocean that stretched beyond the horizon. The rhythm of her music seemed to mirror the ebb and flow of the tides, a soulful melody that resonated with the island's essence.

Ehiliana approached, her footfalls soft upon the sand-dusted stones. The fiddler woman's fingers danced across the strings, coaxing forth a tune that spoke of long-forgotten stories and whispered legends. Their eyes met, and without a word, the fiddler ended her song. Sitting on the far edge of the fountain, the woman caught the corner of her eye as she walked the edge and sat beside her.

"Do you have what I want?" she asked.

"Their names are Seraphina, Alistair, and Gregory."

"So, not there. Where the hell could he be?" she muttered.

"There is a place beneath the city. Maybe he is there," Ehiliana said without thinking.

"Can you get there?" she asked, now paying more attention.

"Not me, I am not skilled enough if trouble came my way. I'm a planner more than a fighter, but I know someone who could."

"I want to meet them; I want to know about this place."

"We need a more private place to meet."

"You know where we can meet," she said, huffing.

"If they agree to come, we can discuss trying to help you find your friend."

"What is your price?"

"I am not sure yet, can we meet tonight after dark?"

"Done," she said, smiling.

"Okay," Ehiliana said, standing to leave.

"See you tonight."

"Indeed," she said, running a hand through her fiery curls.

Chapter Twenty-Four

Kilgi

As Kilgi stood in the tunnel, being healed by Zeppo, her mind raced at the whirl of events. The attack the night before, the fight with the man, and Clovis's announcement. Her hands were shaking like a leaf, and before long, Zeppo's warm hands closed around her.

"Let's get you somewhere quiet," he said, placing a hand on her back and leading her away.

As they made their way out of the arena, Zeppo waved toward Clovis and Mika, who were talking to some nobles. Catching Clovis's gaze, Kilgi grimaced and let Zeppo continue to lead her from the area. Once inside, Ehiliana appeared from one of the alcoves and joined the pair.

"Congratulations on surviving," Ehiliana said, smiling.

"Yeah, something wasn't right though," she said with a tremble in her voice.

Kilgi met Ehiliana's solid stare, seemed to understand, let the conversation die, and fell into a quick but silent walk to Clovis's study.

Letting the door shut behind the trio, Zeppo sat Kilgi in one of the chairs by the fireplace, still walking her through breathing techniques. Ehiliana, sitting across from her, waited for a conversation to spark. Not waiting long, Kilgi tapped Zeppo's arm, letting him know she was fine.

"The attack yesterday," she said, breathlessly. "Clovis was the one who hurt me, but it wasn't actually him. Merkth possessed him; he thinks I know something he doesn't. Then, to top it off, the man I just fought, when I checked his pulse, I noticed he had a red pawn tattoo on his forearm."

"We can't keep dealing with Clovis as a liability," Ehiliana said, leaning on her knees.

"No, we would be the first in the line of fire, we need a contingency plan, the three of us."

"I hate to admit it, but I agree. I have been mulling things over, and it would be good for us to have an escape from here because things are going to get worse," Zeppo said solemnly.

"I may know someone. I was going to ask Iathos for his help, but since the historical building, he puts me off."

"Iathos means well, he just has a hard time with change," Kilgi said.

"I'd prefer your help if that is okay."

"Yeah, what's the problem?"

"I made some friends of sorts who could be of help with a contingency plan. They need some help, however, that can't be explained here. They want to meet us tonight."

"These people, I assume, helped you find the information Clovis wanted?"

"Yeah, I will reveal it when he shows."

"Fair enough. We will go tonight then."

"Before the prince and princess get here, I also need to let you know I have a condition. Whatever this plan is, we need to include Mika, I think if she stays any longer she will be in the same danger as us. I cannot say why, for it could very well be my life if I do, but she is just as unsafe as the rest of us."

"Zeppo," Kilgi said, reaching for his hand. "Please, she needs us. She is still learning how the world is. She is powerful, and kind. We need her. Believe me when I say it, we need her."

"She isn't reliable," Ehiliana stated.

"She isn't the kind of reliable you want, but she is reliable. She doesn't have any of our cynicism, but she does listen and try. If we don't take her, she may be one of the first casualties of whatever is coming."

"Okay," Kilgi said.

"Okay?" he asked.

"Okay, she seems nice, and we need someone in a high position on our side. I have seen how King Gorkem acts with Clovis, and I am sure he is similar to her. We will take her with us. I think it would also give Clovis strength to make hard moves with his sister out of the way."

"This, however, stays between us three until we have an actual plan in place."

"It's nice to know they agree we need a backup plan in the event something goes wrong. It is also nice they came to the same conclusion that something is seriously wrong here."

Without a second thought, Kilgi stood to remove the leather armor. Zeppo stepped up a second later to help her. Laughing, Kilgi smiled at her companions. "You guys were just going to let me sit around in this all day? It's not that comfortable."

"Was more worried about healing you up than undressing you." Zeppo laughed.

"You lot are ridiculous." Ehiliana smiled, standing to help.

As they were helping Kilgi, the door clicked as Clovis and Mika walked in. Clovis's bright gaze landed on the trio. The white shirt he wore under a vest that matched his eyes was tucked neatly into his dark trousers, his boots just as dark. Somewhere along the walk, he took off his overcoat and threw it over his chair before taking a seat.

Mika matched her brother. She wore a beautiful summer dress of the same elegant blue as his which stopped near her ankles, and a pair of silver heels to match. Her hair was shorter and sat neatly on her shoulders, and her smile radiated around the room. Shutting the door, she locked it and waved her hand over the handle.

"Guess it is time to get down to business," Clovis said as everyone found a seat.

"We are missing Iathos," Kilgi said.

"Well, no one told him there was a meeting today," Ehiliana said.

"I will catch him up," Kilgi offered.

"All right then," Clovis said. "Ehiliana, what did you find?"

"The Noa boy has instructions to get close to the royal families and report weaknesses for attacks of opportunity," she said.

"I know," Mika said, "He told me he doesn't have much of a choice, but he said he was willing to give them limited information and help us instead. He doesn't seem keen on hurting me or Zeppo. Plus, he owes me his life now," she said with a creeping blush.

Schooling his expression, Clovis raised a brow. "He is to know nothing of what we speak of, he will only be allowed to pass information to Zeppo. He will not see you alone. Keep him close and play him, do not let him play you."

Spluttering, she said, "Yes, brother."

"He is mad, and she is surprised he didn't say anything worse," Kilgi thought.

"Anything else," Kilgi said, meeting Ehiliana's pissed gaze.

"The enemy is making a move very soon, there is an army on the eastern coast. A man by the name of Oliver Thornbrook is leading."

Kilgi tensed, and her eyes met Clovis. "He is coming here?" she whispered.

"We think so, there is a good chance he is already here or on his way, but that is just a guess on my part. You talk as if you know him."

"Yeah, I do. He isn't a joke; he has a lot of sway behind him."

"Well, what do we do?" Zeppo asked.

"We make them think we are biding our time. While we collect what information we can."

"Kilgi and I can take a stroll through the docks tonight, and if we don't hear anything then I will return tomorrow morning."

"Good cover." Kilgi smiled, shaking off her anxiety. "I'll need a wig or hat," Kilgi said.

"I can handle outfits," Mika said. "Come to my room before you go tonight."

Nodding their heads, Clovis cut in, "Zeppo, I want you to go separately from them, check around the markets that are not on the waterfronts."

"Yes, sir."

"Mika, you and I are going to be moving everyone to the same floor as us and warding the rooms."

"I actually may have something to help with that, but I am not sure how the book works," Mika said, standing.

Taking out a red book, she placed it before Clovis, who inspected it while Mika retreated to her seat.

"Okay, we will inspect it some more here shortly."

"If that is all," Clovis said before being interrupted.

"It's not," Kilgi said hastily. "The man I killed today, he had a red pawn on his arm."

"Shit, you're certain."

"Yes."

"That is problematic."

"Not if he is dead," Ehiliana said.

"No, but it means there is a chance there could be more among us."

"He was Vivian's champion, should we put her on the list."

"Probably for the best if we did. The kings and the Noa boy as well. We still need our pawn."

"I think it may be me," Zeppo said.

"Do you have the mark?" Mika asked.

"No, but Umbri wants me to be her champion, and I have been nervous about accepting."

"Zeppo, you need to accept. Nell said I need Umbri as well as myself to cure Clovis."

Everyone exploded in chatter at that comment.

"Why would you wait to say that!"

"When, how?"

"What do you mean, you need both!"

"Shut up!" she yelled.

The room fell silent. "I wasn't for certain, and I am feeling overwhelmed today, but I heard Nell tell me before blacking out yesterday."

"I don't feel right pressuring you to accept something if you don't want it though," Kilgi said, smiling at Zeppo.

"No, I have been thinking about it for a while now. I want to accept her, but I think I need to prove to myself I am worthy first. We could maybe go to her shrine and call on her though."

"We haven't had the best experiences in that place yet," Mika said.

"Well, then, I am trusting my princess and prince to figure out how to ward the room to the point nothing can harm us for whatever this curse healing would call for."

"It is a chance we may have to take before anyone gets a jump on us."

"Tonight, we do what we have to, tomorrow night, we all meet in Umbri's room after sundown."

Collectively agreeing to the meet-up, Clovis said, "All right then, let's get on with our days."

Ehiliana and Zeppo made their way from the room, and Kilgi hung back with the royals. She flicked her gaze to the ceiling before closing her eyes, and she listened to the quiet chatter of Clovis and Mika talking over the mysterious book and smiled at the ease of their siblingship.

"They are good siblings. They probably don't even realize how lucky they are to have each other."

Before long, Kilgi drifted off to sleep in the chair. Amidst the dream's landscape, the grass stretched out in a vast expanse of vivid red. It's a sight that embodied both solitude and beauty, the breeze soft against her skin. The red grass rustled in the breeze, creating a soothing melody reverberating throughout the quiet surroundings.

The water that encircled the land was a deep and mysterious black. Its surface was like a mirror, reflecting the shadowy clouds above. Kilgi gazed upon the stillness of the water, feeling an inexplicable connection to its enigmatic depths. Squatting on her heels, she let her hand drift upon its cool surface.

Kilgi peered up from the inky depths, the air stilled as she studied the group she had come to know, with Clovis at the front. They stood with pale, sunken faces and eyes that matched the water's lightlessness. They reached out their hands, and banshee screams came from their mouths.

Kilgi turned to run and faced a field of corpses and monsters similar to the attack on Colkirk roamed the field. A hand flew to her mouth to keep any sound from coming out. An evil laugh drifted through the air, and she tried to quietly make her way through the corpses. Tears pricked at her eyes, but she kept moving, and before long, a door appeared in the field. Taking it as a chance to escape, she took off running for the door, and the monsters turned to face her as she ran. The ground rumbled as they stampeded toward her, barely making it through the door before they slammed into it, splintering the door as it vanished.

She stood in a white cathedral with black stained glass filtering in the moonlight. The room stood empty except for the circular pool of water raised slightly from the floor. Catching her breath, Kilgi put a hand to her chest and squeezed her eyes closed.

"This is a nightmare," she said, "I can wake up."

"Can you?" Merkth's voice soothed as he grabbed her hand with his icy one.

With a sharp yank, he pulled Kilgi toward the pool of water. Her feet slipped against the cathedral's smooth floor as she attempted to dig her heels into the ground. Tutting at her, Merkth only tightened his grip and dragged her faster. Struggling the whole way, she stumbled over the edge of the pool; the cool water soaked her to her knees.

"There, there, my star, everything is going to be all right," he said, dragging her to his chest.

"Let me go," she pleaded.

"Now, now, no need to fear me. Though I should be angry with you for burning me quite fiercely, I have decided to be forgiving." He smiled.

She peered at Merkth's endless eyes, which seemed to absorb light itself, and said, "I will do it again."

"Do you wish to see your friends end up how you saw them by the water?"

"You will make them that way," she said, pulling away.

Adjusting his grip on her wrist, he said, "Hmm, no, my star, you will, let me change that."

Cold seeped into her bones, and a drowsiness seemed to fog her mind. Merkth's dark fingers grazed her cheek as her eyes seemed to fall closed. As she became calmer, Merkth pressed a kiss to her cheek and plunged her under the water. His strong hands pressed her firmly against the stony bottom of the pool.

"Rest now and be reborn someone free." Quiet ambiance surrounded Kilgi, her hair floating around her as her thoughts faded. Merkth's words, muffled by the water, seemed to reach toward her in a slow, cold crawl, wrapping around her arms, legs, and mouth. Before long, her lungs seized with the need for air, and her awareness snapped back like a stretched band breaking.

"Where am I? What is happening? I can't breathe." Her mind raced.

Darkness surrounded her, fear shot through her, and she let out a scream, water filling her lungs. Flailing her arms and legs, she shot up out of the water. Shuffling backward from where Merkth had been, Kilgi coughed up black water.

"This is a nightmare," she thought frantically.

"Why can't I wake up," she cried.

Seeing no sign of him, she found the cathedral furnished with pews and full of citizens. Stumbling out of the pool, Her gaze fell to the alter where Clovis was standing with the same black eyes. Behind her, the door opened, and Vivian walked in wearing a beautiful wedding dress that shimmered in the moonlight. Ignoring Kilgi, she walked to the altar and stood beside Clovis, kissing him briefly. Turning toward her, a rush of pain hit her as Iathos kicked her knees from under her and pinned her with a sword.

"Come now, did you really think we cared about you." Clovis's laugh echoed across the hall.

"Did you think, I'd choose you over your father's cousin? You're disowned. I owe you no loyalty," Iathos said, digging the blade into her back.

A sob escaped Kilgi's lips at the pain.

"Come on, answer, scum, did you really think we would care about you?" Zeppo asked, standing from one of the pews.

"Or you would have a chance at freedom or saving your extinct people?" said Ehiliana, standing beside Zeppo.

Their inky eyes stared endlessly at her as she sobbed. Another sharp pain tugged at her skin as Iathos pushed the blade deeper.

"Give up, Kilgi," Oliver said, pulling her chin up to meet her eyes.

Unlike the others, they stood out vibrantly against the dark sea of eyes. Kilgi's chin quivered as fear strung her tight.

"Did you think anyone could love you?" they all asked in unison.

"I had hoped," she said, letting her body slump.

"Well, I love you," Mika's voice called out from the crowd.

Oliver spun on his heel, and Kilgi glanced up to see Mika striding across the room. Her blond hair swayed as she walked, and her blue dress moved with practiced ease. She had her hands out on either side of her as if shielding herself from the horrors before her.

"Who is there?" Oliver called, confused.

Walking past Oliver, Mika shoved him and knelt before Kilgi. Taking her face into her warm hands, Kilgi sucked in a breath at her glowing blue eyes. Touching her forehead to Kilgis, Mika let her magic pour into her, slowly spreading warmth through her cold core.

"Kilgi, listen to me. None of this is real, something is happening to you, and I am expending a lot of magic to reach you. I care about you, and I want you safe. You give me hope for a better future, I want to give you a good future. Please, do not give up because you are scared, it's okay we will get through it together. Reach as deep as you can for the light and blast this place to pieces. I will hold on to you until you find it, okay?"

"Mika, I can't. I am so tired," Kilgi sobbed.

"It's okay to be tired; it isn't okay to give up. You must keep fighting."

"Mika."

"Kilgi, listen to me. Nell chose you for a reason, and I think it is because you have faced more horrors in this world than any of us combined, and you kept getting back up. Be tired, and scream as much as you want, but you must get back up. If you give up then everyone who ever wronged you has won, and you wouldn't have given us all the chance to prove ourselves to you."

"Mika," Kilgi said, leaning into her. "I'm sorry."

"You have nothing to apologize for. Give that asshole something to be sorry for instead," she demanded.

She felt the warmth of Mika's magic flow through her and closed her eyes to chase the sensation. Grounding herself, she kept reaching into the furthest depths of her mind and the scenery manifesting before her.

A quaint cottage sat in a field of wildflowers, the sound of a creek nearby joining into the soft noise of the nightlife. Walking past the house, she jumped over the stream and followed the blue spark of magic. Off in the distance, a light glowed, and the sound of music filled the air.

"We are of the stars, my child, we can never truly be lost," a soft, motherly voice whispered in her ear.

Reaching the fire, she saw many Matuen dancing around it, their array of colorful hair bouncing as they went. The sound of flutes, mandolins, drums, and fiddles joined in a fast, happy harmony. Her kindred, every so often clapped their hands in time with the song, skirts billowing with their turns. Feeling the warmth on her skin, Kilgi raced forward, grabbed onto one of the woman's hands, and started dancing.

"Welcome, who are you?" She laughed.

"Kilgi, one of the last of us," she said, squeezing the woman's hand.

"Is that so? Well, then, what has brought you here?"

"I need help reaching my light."

"Oh, dear," she said, spinning Kilgi. "It would seem you have already found it."

"What do you mean?"

Stopping Kilgi to show her all the dancing folk around her, the woman said, "We are of the stars; if you can see us even in our deaths, then you have already found your light. Just because we are dead, doesn't mean our light is gone."

"I think I understand what you mean," Kilgi said.

"Then it is time to wake up." She smiled.

Sharply, the world before her exploded in light. Closing her eyes against its harshness, she could feel hands on her shoulders. Opening her eyes and letting them adjust, she peeked blearily at Clovis and Mika, who stood over her.

"Kilgi!" Mika said, hugging her. "I knew you could do it."

"Kilgi, are you okay?" Clovis asked as Mika moved away from her.

"I will be. I think Merkth trapped me in some nightmare when I fell asleep listening to you guys talk."

"I felt your fear spike; it plunged the whole room into a bad feeling, and then you screamed. Your eyes turned black, and your body went cold." "Clovis couldn't reach you for some reason, but I managed to get inside somehow," Mika said.

"Thank you. In all honesty, right now, I could use a drink," Kilgi said with a half-smile.

"I'll go get some and give you a minute." Mika smiled.

"Thank you, Mika," Kilgi said, grabbing her hand before letting go.

"Of course, you would have done the same for me."

Chapter Twenty-Five

<u>Zeppo</u>

Walking through Colkirk's market, Zeppo took in the hectic scenery. Shop signs creaked in the wind, and the crowd of voices created a lively ambiance. The market setup was like the roots of a plant. There was a center of wide space with a beautiful fountain that musicians took turns playing by and alleyways that branched off the open area. The alleys seemed narrow, with their numerous shop signs and tapestries shading the passages from the harsh desert sun.

The aroma of baked sweets and dinners overpowered the scent of the sea. Zeppo decided to take a quick detour for some street food; he leaned against one of the shop walls and watched the square's activities while he ate.

"Think this is the calmest everything has been in a few weeks. I'm sure the girls are finding more than me. Pretty sure I am just a watcher at this point," Zeppo thought.

"Hopefully, we can take care of Clovis's curse tomorrow. I am sure Umbri will help us out. I hope we find out what's going on with the red tattoo thing. Fits Kilgi's guess that we have opponents of some kind. Though, part of me wants to not take the mark, because it would seem I am on the board, and we could use some people who aren't."

"How is everyone taking this all in stride, myself included? I feel like I should be having some sort of mental breakdown, yet here I am, eating a burrito and searching for suspicious activity."

"I mean, seriously, I betrayed my kind to save a princess, healed multiple wounds, entered a magical oath to protect said princess, and got choked out by her cursed brother. I should have run for the hills, so why do I keep staying?"

Sighing into his burrito, he felt the air shift as Noa appeared before him. "Hey, I'm surprised to see you about and not cooped up in the castle."

"Needed some air and some good street food." Zeppo shrugged.

Coming to lean on the wall, Noa said, "Living the good life suffocating you?"

"Wouldn't call it the good life."

"Trouble in paradise then?"

"Noa, you saw what the royals can get away with. I may not be suffering yet, but if they are willing to do such things to their own, what do you think is going to happen the minute they want one of us gone?"

"No one would blink an eye if we were gone," Noa said, inspecting his nails.

"Noa, you should take this a little more seriously, you are playing a dangerous game."

"I couldn't care less about what happens to anyone in that castle except you and Mika. I will make sure you both are fine, but otherwise, I will keep my distance from the rest."

"Noa."

"Don't 'Noa' me, we are friends, not each other's parents. I will do things my way, and you do them yours and we will meet in the middle like we always have. Now, you should pay attention, you have a good spot for what's about to happen, and I am sure the dark prince wants to know about this," he said, disappearing into the crowd.

Before him, people stopped walking to stare at the man standing on the fountain's ledge, two fingers against his throat. He had quaffed brown hair, fair skin, and green eyes and stood tall in his uniform. His clothing was blood red with a black star on the shoulder. A sword was strapped to his hip, and he was escorted by two more officers.

"Hello," his voice echoed over the crowd, the use of magic evident.

"My name is Oliver Thornbrook, general over the Blackstar. Now, I am sure many of you are thinking, what is the Blackstar?" I am here to tell you."

Hushing the crowd as they exploded in a wave of murmurs, he continued, "The Blackstar is the future, one that will form these countries for the better, but we need your help. As of right now, the systems of government we have now only benefit those who have wealth and keep the rest of us at the bottom, not only that it limits our rights as mortals."

"What will you do differently?" someone yelled.

"Build a fair system, increase incomes, and bring better living conditions to the countries who accept our help. We will also do our best to protect you from attacks in the future should you all choose to help us."

"How could you protect us?" another voice called.

"After the speech, come to the docks, and I will show you one of the monsters we captured over in Nearon."

"Now, I would like to tell you about your kings. We will start with King Quade of the Kamouraska Kingdom, a man of many children but a sympathizer to the Matuen and their heathen ways. He has a half-daughter, who, instead of killing, he disowned and banished. She is a Matuen. Her name is Kilgi Mohlo, and from my understanding, Prince Clovis Gorkem has sympathized with her too. If a king can't even be loyal to his wife, how could he be loyal to his country?" Oh, but that isn't all, folks, he ordered some of his men to take a town off the map about ten years ago because he wanted the land for his greedy ways."

The crowd broke out in yells and were quieted, Zeppo had his hands clenched at his sides.

"Let's move on to the Gorkems, shall we? Everyone has suspected the Gorkems of dark magic for ages, but despite their practices, they may be the most all-right family. Their people seem to have good living conditions and withstood the attack on their country, despite the royal family being here. Though it's King Gorkem himself, we would like to negotiate with him because we believe his son is a problem. Inside information has let me know he has become cursed with a sickness that is driving him mad. The rumor is that he was cursed by making a deal with a demon of darkness."

"I know, I know he is handsome and loved by many for his fairness, despite his cold attitude. Can you tell me you trust a man who is cursed to run his country, especially with the rumors surrounding it?"

"He isn't cursed," a woman yelled.

"Well, should we ask him to show himself as proof? Perhaps, those who work in the castle could speak up, we all know Krystru who have been cursed have their physical features altered. From my understanding, he is sporting some golden eyes instead of his renowned icy blue."

"He does, I have seen it," a man's voice yelled further back.

"This is bad," Zeppo thought.

"Who is to say he isn't responsible for the attack on this place?"

"And King Hawkore has just locked away those he deemed important and has left you all to struggle with the cleanup."

"Enough," Zeppo called.

"Umbri, give my voice some meaning, I will take your place," he said, walking toward Oliver.

"As you wish, my dear," she whispered.

Feeling a shift in his body, it was like someone took a match and lit him a flame for a brief second. Inspecting his arm, an iridescent knight sat on his forearm.

"Iathos had a knight. Are there two of us? I thought I'd be a pawn."

Zeppo stepped onto the ledge and said, "Enough."

"Who are you?" Oliver asked.

"I am Prince and Princess Gorkem's healer, Zeppo."

"Oh, then you can tell us, is the prince cursed?"

Turning to the crowd, he said, "I cannot speak for the kings, but I can speak on behalf of the prince and princess of Aeberuthey. I have never met anyone who has treated me with the level of respect that they do. They prefer to see us as we are and what we bring to the table for the better. They are motivated and ruthless in cutting down those who wish to bring bad into this world. Yes, the prince was cursed, but not because he made some crazy deal. He was cursed because he was attacked while doing a spell; he and the other party both suffered the effects of the curse. As of this week, we believe we have a cure for the curse, and both parties will be taken care of."

"What is the curse?" Oliver asked with a smile.

"The curse was meant to steal his life force and feed it to something trying to wake itself. The thing that sent those monsters used the botched spell to latch onto a strong magic source. He experiences temporary loss of control but has only had one incident, which was taken care of by the Matuen, Kilgi, who can tame shadows with light. She has been acting as a Band-Aid for the curse, while we searched for a cure. Now we think we have one, and by the end of the week, he will be cured."

"How can you trust that scum?" someone shouted.

"Easily, she is braver than all of us here combined. She is the reason the city survived the attack. She has continually shown her bravery in the face of the court and those would oppose her because of how she was born, as if she could control that. Honestly, all of you are no better than the kings, if what this man says is true. So, let me say this: should you choose to turn your backs on your kingdoms, then turn it to racism as well because your kings are the ones who decided to hunt them down, to begin with."

The crowd quieted, and Oliver whispered, "I have to hand it to you, bud, you are good at speeches."

"Zeppo here is right, we should turn our backs on everything the kings have taught us is right. Maybe Kilgi shouldn't be judged for her race, but what about the crimes she committed up until this point," says Oliver.

"Then we should judge everyone here for theirs too, including us," Zeppo called out.

"If you want to follow someone, then please follow the prince and Princess Mika. I have seen how they are, and the world they want to create. After the prince is cured, I will implore them to give a speech on the things they wish to change for all of you to hear yourself," he continues.

"Are you capable of curing them, we don't even know who or what you are."

"I am with Kilgi's help. I am Zeppo Vidali of the Vulocri and blessed by Umbri," he said, summoning his wings.

"Please match the tattoo," he thought.

The crowd gasped as Zeppo flew up for the crowd to see. White feathers that shimmered iridescent trod the air with ease. Everyone broke out in loud conversation, and Oliver seemed surprised.

"Please think for yourselves, everyone. I would hate to see this world fall apart because we all lost our heads to pretty words and let someone, we don't know well steer the ship of the future. I want to heal others and heal this world. I can't do that if we are condemning others because of someone else's words. Can you protect these people and heal your prince should an attack happen? I will, I know that those of us employed by the prince and princess would agree. Besides they can hold their own, cursed or not," Zeppo says, ending his speech.

Landing next to Oliver, he stood and stared him down. Before long, he said goodbye and walked back toward the dock. Making sure they left, he rolled his eyes and decided a fly back to the castle would be a good idea before anyone else told the prince what had happened.

As he headed back, the cool sea breeze felt good against his face. The sun had set, and the city lights were like stars from his view.

"So much for a peaceful moment, huh?"

Chapter Twenty-Six

<u>Ehiliana</u>

"So, is there a reason we are leaving the docks?" Kilgi asked, following Ehiliana.

"Yes, we have a meeting, and the meeting isn't here."

They fell into a silent walk as the pair weaved through the crowd into one of the narrow market alleys. The smell of food was overwhelming, and the noise from the crowd was enough to give one a headache. Both women made haste in the direction of Octavia's bookery to escape the crowd.

Kilgi gasped at the shop's neat but filled-to-the-brim shelves, and Ehiliana smiled, knowing she was just as enamored with the place as she was. Before them, at the counter, stood the fiddler, her hair was neatly tied back and her outfit a lot less revealing. It was a simple blue short-sleeve dress, paired with some brown sandals. Her eyes twinkled with delight as she stepped around the counter and went to the door to lock it.

"Welcome," she greeted.

"Thank you," Ehiliana replied.

"Who is your friend?" the woman asked.

"I am Kilgi."

Walking up to Kilgi, the woman placed her hands on Kilgi's head and pulled her down to touch their foreheads together. Ehiliana watched as Kilgi stiffened before suddenly wrapping her hands around the woman and speaking to her in a language she had never heard before.

"Do you two know each other?" she asked.

Pulling from the hug, the fiddler said, "It's a Matuen greeting."

"You're a Matuen, then? Because you do not look like one."

"Ah, well, yes, I can shift since I am full-blooded, which means I can change my colors too. The eyes take a little more magic," she said with a wave.

A woman with tanned skin, teal eyes, and matching hair stood before the pair. She smiled, gave a twirl, and bowed.

"You can call me Wren."

"Call me Kilgi."

"I am Ehiliana."

"Well, now, that we are aquatinted, we can get on with the meeting. Octavia is in the kitchen."

Ehiliana led them through the building, following the same path as the last time she was there, and they found themselves in the spacious room. Octavia sat at the counter with a cup of tea in one hand while she flipped through a book with her other. She wore eye-catching red slacks paired with a crisp white blouse, and her dark locks were pulled into a bun, the white streak making her seem more sophisticated. Closing her book, she beckoned them over. Everyone pulled up seats facing each other while Octavia poured everyone a drink.

"Welcome back, Obsidian."

"Thank you," Ehiliana said.

"Obsidian?" Kilgi asked.

"A nickname for Ehiliana," Wren answered.

"I see."

"Who are you?" Octavia asked.

"Kilgi, the help."

"I see. Well, it is a pleasure, Kilgi."

"Who are we searching for exactly?" Ehiliana asked.

"My son, Silas. You mentioned the underground place and it could be possible they are hiding him there."

"The place was pretty big, so, yes."

"What do you want in exchange for going in there to find him?" she asked.

"Security," Kilgi cut in.

"I have no issues going on a rescue mission for your son without asking too many questions if you can offer some of us refuge when shit hits the fan."

"How many are some of us?"

"Six of us. I doubt Iathos would come."

"Who is it you are asking me to protect?"

"This place is very magical, so it can. We are asking that you protect us, alongside our healer friend and the prince and princess of Aeberuthey, in the event of a worst-case scenario," Ehiliana said.

"No," she said.

"Then have fun getting your son yourself," Kilgi said, setting her cup down.

"You would condemn my son like that, you don't even know what you are asking me to do," Octavia said, flustered.

Sitting back, Ehiliana smirked at Kilgi and thought, *She has this handled.*

"I know exactly what I am asking you."

"You do not know anything about that family," Octavia seethed.

"You do?"

"They're evil."

"Their father is evil, and their mother is complacent. The prince and princess want a better world, I have seen it with my own eyes."

"You are with her on this?" Octavia asked.

"Mostly. Clovis is dealing with a curse that we are going to try and cure tomorrow morning. Mika has issues controlling her magic and is a little naïve, but she means well. I just personally wouldn't tell her important secrets until she proves herself."

"They are children of a monster," Octavia said, running a hand through her bangs and shaking them loose.

"Actually. they are not," Kilgi said, red in the cheeks.

"What are you on about?"

"What?" Ellie thought.

"I know it's not my place to say, but you all can keep a secret, it seems. The prince and princess are not the king's children. They are someone else's, the only tie to the kingdom they have is through their mother."

"You know this for certain? It doesn't change that they were raised by him."

"I know for certain; the queen informed me of this, I think, with the implication she wants me to protect them. The king had no hand in raising them, otherwise Clovis would have killed me on the spot just for the insult of being born a Matuen. Instead, he asked me to enter an engagement with him just to piss his father off and use it to manipulate him into having some wiggle room politically."

"I believe her," Wren said.

"This does change things."

"We will help you, but you must help us. There is an evil coming and I know the kings won't help us. They are covering up everything the best they can."

"I've seen some of the things down in the cavern, you would be sending Kilgi to fight monsters to find your son," Ehiliana said.

"Were they liking the ones from the attack?" Wren asked.

"More sentient, it had intelligent eyes. It was also guarded by archivists and guardsmen from the palace."

"That means there is a big chance our leaders are in on this," Wren said.

"Or they are dumb enough to mess around with something they think they understand but don't."

"Gorkem would know what he is doing," Octavia said, sighing.

"Well, there is only one way to find out, and it's to shake them up," Kilgi said, leaning back.

"What's the plan and deal then?" Ehiliana asked.

"Simple, we cure Clovis tomorrow, then go find Silas. After that, we stage a kidnapping of Princess Mika, become enemies in every kingdom, and disappear while the kingdoms freak out and start a war over which country planned us kidnapping her. Lay low for a while and train while Clovis stays and gains popularity among the citizens and becomes a public enemy from every king and Merkth."

"You're joking," Ehiliana said.

"Not even a little. Merkth wants to start a war and he has been terrorizing Clovis and me through his curse and my dreams. If we beat him to the punch and cause the stir first, Clovis has grounds to gain sympathy with Mika missing. If he plays his cards right, he could probably undermine King Gorkem as well."

"That isn't a bad idea," Octavia said.

"You think he could do it?" Wren asked.

"Yes, he played me before I even knew I was being played. I didn't realize he never meant to keep our engagement until I told him it would be good leverage against his father to get something he wanted. He agreed with me, but I could see it in his eyes, he already planned too."

"You're fine with him playing you?"

"I trust him. He wants to help. I didn't want to, but the more time goes by, I have come to believe he is a good leader."

"Is she blushing?" Ellie thought.

"I'm not sure I am ready to be wanted in every country," Ehiliana said.

"You'll be fine, it's not that bad," Wren said with a wave of her hand.

Kilgi laughed and nodded her head in agreement.

"She is right, you get used to it," Octavia said.

"Are, are all of you wanted?" Ehiliana said, sitting up.

"Born wanted," Wren and Kilgi said in unison.

"I'm the last of my kin in Eckris as well, and the kings don't like what they can't control."

"You're not a Matuen, then?" Ehiliana asked.

"I am an Aurami," stated Octavia.

"They went extinct hundreds of years ago!"

"Yes, we went extinct." Octavia smiled.

"So, you are all wanted and—wait you said in Eckris. Everything beyond is a dead zone."

"That is for another time, there is much to teach you all, it seems. For now, it seems we have a deal and a plan."

"I don't think it would be wise for us all to go and become wanted. Clovis will need at least one friend. I worked with the city for years, and I have a more trustworthy reputation. Perhaps I can report the kidnapping and spy from within," Ehiliana suggested.

"That is a good idea. We can use eyes on the inside," Octavia said.

"So, there we have it, and you are fine with housing us?"

"I have known bad things were coming for a while and hoped to avoid it, but it is what it is. You save my son, and I will help you attempt to tear these kings down and rebuild a world worth living in. As for this Merkth, that is a problem we will discuss another time."

"Guess that's our cue to leave," Kilgi said, standing.

"It was nice to see you again," Ehiliana said.

Walking Wren and Octavia to the door, they all said silent goodbyes and parted ways. As the door closed behind them, they both turned to see the door had vanished.

"Seems things are getting interesting. You have made some intriguing friends, and well, thank you."

"What are you thanking me for, I'm asking you to do something dangerous."

"Because you care too, and well, I never thought I'd see one of my kin again."

"Don't get sappy, I don't do sappy," Ehiliana said, lightly shoving Kilgi.

"Fine, fine. I won't be even a little thankful then to have a good friend."

"Good, because I'm not sure when you and I became friends."

"Probably somewhere in between the crazy monster attack and getting the bulk work of the aftermath."

"Fair. At least I don't have prince sitting duty." Ehiliana laughed.

"Well, you did sign yourself up to take that spot once we put the plan in motion."

"Fair. Are we gonna tell her, do you think she can handle it?"

"She can. I know she is still young, but she wants to help everyone. It would be wise to tell her though, I don't want to end up accidentally dead."

***

Kilgi and Ehiliana maneuvered through the bustling crowd, their presence subtly commanding attention. Kilgi, tall and proud, exuded a quiet strength, while Ehiliana, calm but poised, moved with a graceful determination. As they navigated the lively market square, their steps synchronized, each one purposeful yet unhurried. Kilgi's hair billowed slightly with her movements, a striking contrast to Ehiliana's lighter attire, which seemed to dance around her like a delicate breeze. Their shared confidence was palpable, creating a subtle aura that set them apart from the crowd.

Approaching the market square, the distant echo of a speech grew clearer. The fountain's splashing water provided a soothing backdrop to the speaker's words. Kilgi and Ehiliana arrived just in time to catch the closing sentiments. On the ledge of the fountain stood a man dressed in a red uniform with brown locks and bright eyes. Beside him stood Zeppo, who appeared to be angry. Around them, the crowd stirred, some nodding in agreement, others engaged in fervent discussions sparked by the speaker's words.

"Oliver?" Kilgi's voice whispered.

"You know the guy up there?"

"We have to go," Kilgi said, grabbing Ellie's hand.

"Hey, what's going on?" Ehiliana asked, being dragged.

"H-He is working with the guy we are trying to stop," Kilgi said, voice quaking.

"Why was Zeppo up there then?"

"I don't know," Kilgi said, her hands shaking.

Ehiliana pulled Kilgi into a quiet alcove and pressed her against a wall. Taking in her friend, Kilgi seemed to be spaced out and anxious. Her fingers were digging into her palms, and she was restless with constant shifting.

"Kilgi, you don't have to tell me how you know him or whatever it is you saw. I'm not the kind of person to push like that, but you need to take a few minutes to calm down. We are going to draw attention if you can't pull yourself together, so tell me what to do, how do I help you right now?"

"I need to breathe, he-he is evil, Ellie, I can't face him, be around him, it-it sets me off. I can't stop it, and all this is happening, and it's like Merkth knew Oliver would set me off and keep me weak," Kilgi said, eyes brimming with tears.

"Okay, then we will deal with him, and you deal with Merkth," Ehiliana said, leaning against the wall blocking the public's view from Kilgi.

"She has been through some shit, must have been lonely. Yet she still wears her heart on her sleeve and doesn't even realize it," Ellie thought.

"You don't understand, Ellie, he won't be that easy to deal with. He isn't a prince, but he has influence, power, and now an evil backing his evil. Merkth chose him for a reason."

"We will deal with it. You handle what you can handle. None of us asked for this, but we are all here trying to make it work. If this guy is too much for you, then we will pick up there while you pick up the work elsewhere. That is what teams and potential friends do."

"Ellie, I don't want to see anyone hurt, especially by him."

"Life doesn't get to be fair, especially to us that are different. The difference is, we won't be alone this time when bad things come for us. I can handle Oliver, never been the biggest fan of most men in any race anyway."

"How many men have you met that are actually that terrible?" Kilgi asked, wiping a tear.

"Just a few, but they aren't my type. Makes it easier to see past a handsome face and make their lives hard. Now, if Oliver were an Oliva and named Regina, then maybe, just maybe, I'd struggle."

Bursting out into a laugh, Kilgi swiped her palms under her red eyes, "Thank you."

"I know we are still getting to know each other, but I know you mean well. I am sorry that your life hasn't been easy, Kilgi, but I have never been one to care about race, gender, etc. I like to judge on personalities, and you deserve the same care you give the world. I know I can trust you, and I hope with time, you trust me more."

Lopsidedly smiling, Kilgi said, "I'll get there. It would be easier maybe if my past wasn't being thrown in my face every few days. Though I thought you weren't sappy."

"I wasn't being sappy; I was just stating my thoughts on some observations," Ehiliana said, nudging her.

"We should probably go find out why Zeppo was at that speech, and how the hell his wings are not a normal Vulocri color," Kilgi said, nudging back.

"Probably."

"Well, while we walk back, I'd be interested in hearing how you and Regina met. It would be a good distraction from my thoughts."

"Ah, well, good thing it's a longer walk because it was a trip. You see, Regina is a fiery and determined woman and was the one to romance me."

Chapter Twenty-Seven

<u>Iathos</u>

Stepping across the threshold, Iathos was immediately enveloped in an atmosphere of calm. The room was spacious, its walls adorned with rich, dark wood paneling that exuded a timeless elegance. A large, intricately carved canopy bed commanded the center, draped in sumptuous fabrics of deep burgundy and gold. The headboard, a masterpiece of craftsmanship, bore the emblem of the Hawkore family.

A fireplace made of polished marble stood against one wall, offering both warmth and a touch of opulence. Above it, a portrait of the knight in full regalia served as a reminder of their distinguished service. The flames danced with a gentle flicker, casting a warm glow that played off the gleam of the polished paneled walls.

A desk sat near a wide window, offering a commanding view of the castle grounds and the light of the city in the distance. The desk was meticulously organized: parchment and quills were neatly arranged, and adjacent to it, a sturdy wooden chest housed maps, scrolls, and other strategic documents.

Iathos sat on the pristine couch that occupied the space in front of the fireplace and leaned over to start unlacing his boots. The quiet of the room was peaceful compared to the noise of council meetings and training knights. He sighed as he kicked off the boots and flopped back on the couch.

"What a day. King Gorkem is a piece of work. He has a way of making everything harder than it needs to be. Not to mention Clovis and the problem he is becoming. How am I going to make Kilgi see the monster he is?" he thought, running a hand down his face.

"I get he is charming, but most people in higher social status are. I can't stay and protect her either. King Mohlo and the princes leave tomorrow, and I leave the day

after, once I get the book. Kilgi will be on her own, and I can't bring her with me since she is disowned."

"I think if I could get her alone, then maybe I could explain that Merkth has a good plan. She has always been one to listen. He wants to help make Eckris better without the dangers of magic. Kilgi is sensible enough to see reason in that, and she would be safe from Clovis's influence. I mean, King Mohlo already agrees magic should be banned. Perhaps Merkth would provide her with the safety she desires. I could speak with him on the issue, he already promised her safety anyway."

Sighing he thinks, *"This feels wrong; I don't entirely agree with or trust Merkth, but he seems like the one who can accomplish getting rid of magic for good. He is already acting and hasn't hurt anyone but Clovis whom I know of. I will go along with him for now, and if he becomes a threat, I will deal with it, but this, this feels like it goes against who I am."*

"Is it against who you are if you are doing it for the ones, you love and have sworn to protect? That you will be right there to save them instead of killing them, unlike Luella." Merkth's voice echoes across his thoughts.

"No one else I love will end up like them, like her. I won't let them be plagued by the evil of magic, I can't. I will fight to the death for that. No one will stop me from finding a way to keep everyone safe from this evil."

Shaking his head, he leaned forward and took the stopper of the crystal pitcher that held Colkirk's finest whiskey. Flipping over one of the glass cups, he poured himself a glass, grabbed his book, and relaxed.

***

Iathos's attire for the day consisted of a deep forest green tunic intricately embroidered with golden thread in patterns of heraldic symbols. The fabric flowed generously, giving him an air of nobility, while a leather belt cinched his waist, holding a pouch and a short dagger with an ornate hilt.

Over the tunic, he wore a richly dyed brown leather jacket bearing the crest of his house on the chest and back. The collar was clasped with an elegant pin, a family heirloom passed down through generations, bearing the symbol of a falcon.

His lower half was adorned with dark, well-worn trousers tucked into sturdy leather boots that had seen their share of journeys. A pair of matching gauntlets encased his hands, offering both protection and a touch of splendor. At his hip, a sword, its hilt encrusted with semi-precious stones, in an intricately adorned scabbard.

He stood alone in his chamber, oblivious to the distant ritual that was unraveling the cruel curse that bound him to Clovis and Merkth. The room, usually a sanctuary, seemed to close in around him, the air growing thick with an unexplainable heaviness.

Without warning, a sharp pang surged through his chest, stealing his breath. It was as if an invisible force was trying to rip something vital from within him, causing his knees to buckle. He clutched at his heart, eyes wide with disbelief, unable to fathom the source of this sudden agony.

"What is happening?"

Every heartbeat sent reverberations of pain through his veins as if his very essence was being drawn away. The room seemed to sway with the pain behind his eyes. Unseen tendrils of energy pulsed through Iathos, tugging at the core of his being with a burning intensity. He staggered, feeling a profound disconnect between his body and soul. Sweat formed on his brow, mingling with the distress etched across his features.

"Help," he gasped quietly as his body hit the ground.

As the ritual progressed, the pain intensified. It was as though an ethereal hand reached into his very soul, extracting an intangible, binding force. In his solitude, he called out a voiceless plea from his inexplicable torment. His fingers clenched and unclenched, searching for purchase on reality, while his breaths came in ragged gasps.

Squeezing his eyes closed, Iathos lay in pain, but instead of darkness, he saw different colors unraveling from one another. Purple, green, and a blue littered with stars. The pain still coursing through him with a burning like no other. He watched behind closed eyes at the energies before him.

"Where's Isla? Bring me the girl Drevon," Clovis's and Merkth's voices screamed over the pain.

"The curse," he thought, sluggishly, as the split slowed.

As time slinked by, Iathos spent hours immobilized from the pain of being unraveled and put back together before finally subsiding. Laying, panting heavily, Iathos, finally feeling okay, fell into a dreamless sleep.

***

"Wake Iathos, you need to make a move for the book, they know," Merkths voice whispered. "Wake now my knight, or we will lose much progress in our fight against magic."

"Where am I? What happened?"

Feeling cool fingers grip Iathos's chin, Merkth said, "In your room, the royals, save for Gorkem's children, are gone. My plan is set in motion, I have let you rest, now you must go below the city and get the Bralins Tome. Kill the boy who protects it, if you must."

Opening his eyes, he peered into Merkth's endless dark ones. "I feel as if I have been ripped apart and sewn back together by a toddler."

"You basically were. Seems the dark prince has found a cure to the predicament of us all being entangled. Though you were left unsupervised, and had I not come, you could have perished. He has a tight grip on that group, the poor dears probably don't even realize just what he is dragging them into," he said, running his fingers through Iathos's dark locks.

Leaning into Merkth's touch, Iathos said, "I want to save them, but I do not understand what it is Clovis is after. What do they know?"

"He is after my power, dear, and that of magic itself. He is chasing complete power, even the fates have been fooled by him, enough to give their power to his pawns. The only way we can save them now is by destroying him. They know about the book, seems one of them is going after it very soon. I need you up and moving now, my knight."

Groaning at the tingles within his skull, Iathos managed to pull himself up, with the help of Merkth. Iathos let his head fall on the other man's shoulder, his thinner frame embracing Iathos's broad one.

"Good, I cannot hold this form much longer. I still lack the strength to stay within this realm, so I must go, but I know you will do me proud. I see your worth, Iathos. Luella couldn't see what I do, but you are what this world needs. Let me help you show you your worth," he said, pulling Iathos away and running a thumb over the scarred part of his cheek.

Feeling fuzzy around the edges from the warmth that radiated from his tattoo, Iathos said, "I will get you what you want, then I have to go back to the king, I cannot stay by your side."

"You can't, my dear. If only you knew the horrors of what your king has done. He preaches his hate for magic, yet he intends to use your dearest cousin Kilgi to gift youth to his wife. He used magic to make everyone, including you, forget the town he ordered you to slaughter, but he doesn't know that you remember, does he?"

"Why deny yourself the truth before you? If you stand at his side, you will always have a collar that will keep you from protecting who you love. Kilgi, her brothers, Ehiliana, and Zeppo. They need you to be strong and go against their brainwashing and free them. Get me that book, and I will give you what you need to start freeing them. I find you hard to resist, my dear knight. Every day we are connected, I feel the need to fulfill your dreams and bring you peace," Merkth whispered against his lips.

"I want to help them. I am scared to leave the boys alone with the king, it's why I never left. Kilgi, I never worried about her, not until Clovis. I will try to get that book; I can't lose them like Luella."

"Focus on me, dearest," Merkth said, cradling Iathos's face.

He took in Merkth's sharp jawline, which was perfectly framed by his unnaturally dark hair and gray skin that seemed to blend and shift into different hues. Turning black halfway down his forearms, the coolness of his form settled comfortably against Iathos's warm temperature. His touch seemed to pull all of Iathos's focus and brought tingles from his head to his toes.

Flicking his gaze to Iathos's mouth, Merkth said, "We will take care of these problems, but for now, let's get that book. I will not replace your beloved Luella, but I'd like to hold a similar regard for her. I find myself preening in your light and I am sure you taste delicious."

Feeling fuzzy and enamored, Iathos let Merkth lead him into a tender kiss. His lips were cool and soft, and they tasted sweet like strawberries on a hot summer day. Lifting his hand to drag Merkth further into the kiss, his hands met fine silky hair. A warmth burned into his core, only doused when Merkth pulled away.

"Go now, dearest. Time is wasting. I can't wait to taste you again." He smiled before vanishing.

Letting his fingers drift to his lips, Iathos felt a little less fuzzy. Clenching his jaw, he gripped the hilt of his sword and made his way out of his room. Still feeling off from being untangled and kissing the man who promised him the world, Iathos moved quickly. The sound of his heavy footsteps echoed on the stone paths as he hurried toward the historical building.

"I will not fail them. I will stop Clovis, and I will make sure they are all safe. Merkth will show me the way. He will give up magic when this is over, I can feel it. He hates it just as much as I do. We can make a world that's better for everyone. Kilgi won't have to fear her father. The boys can live happier lives. Alton will find something better, and I can give them something better."

Iatho's thoughts continued to race as he felt the wind pick up and carry his hair back from his face.

"I want to kiss him again. He makes me feel alive and worth something. I can be something for him; he sees me as an equal. Luella was like the sun itself: calm,

warm, and always out of reach. I never burned for her. Despite my contentment, I never burned the way I did just now with him."

"I need that book."

Chapter Twenty-Eight

<u>Clovis</u>

"There is no guarantee this will work, Clovis, but it will be painful. We are untangling your soul from two others. If it works, hopefully, it will free Iathos too," Kilgi said.

"We do what needs to be done. I will be fine," he said, lying down. "Besides, I have to prove Oliver wrong on behalf of Zeppo, and maybe we can start getting somewhere with this mess once I'm free."

"You're sure about this?" Zeppo asked, placing warm hands against Clovis's pale chest.

"Not even a little, but hey, the worst that happens is I die, then it's not my problem." He smiled at Kilgi.

"Don't talk like that!" Mika said, flicking his forehead and peering down at him from where she sat.

"We'd take good care of you, princess." Kilgi smiled.

"You guys are going to joke around like this before a ritual two fates made up and passed off to you without a single instruction besides his soul."

"Probably the best time. Honestly, I'm nervous and feel jittery," Zeppo said.

Laughing, Clovis let his head flop down into his sister's lap. "Just in case, it has only been a little over a month now, but you guys are pretty all right and reliable, so thanks for dealing with me."

"You're welcome, drama king." Kilgi smiled, placing her soft hands alongside Zeppo's.

"He is dramatic; he tried to kill me once," Zeppo said, shaking his head.

"Definitely should be drama king over dark prince." Ehiliana hummed.

Shoving a leather belt into her brother's mouth, Mika said, "Don't you dare die, I'm not ready to be an only child."

Reaching his hand up, he let his hand land on top of her blond waves and ruffled her hair. Letting it fall with a thump, he locked eyes with his sister's bright eyes and gave a nod before the world went black.

"I won't leave you alone, ever."

Clovis's vision blurred, his senses a storm of conflicting emotions and fractured memories. It was as if his very essence was being pulled in opposite directions, torn between two other forces. Each thread of his soul felt like it was entwined with another, a complex knot of existence that seemed impossible to unravel. They ranged from varying purples, greens, and blues, all as if scattered among stars.

The pain surged through him, a relentless wave of anguish that seemed to emanate from the very core of his being. It was a searing, white-hot fire that consumed him, burning away the boundaries that defined him. Every fiber of his being screamed in protest, resisting the violent separation that was taking place. He felt as if time had slowed and sped up all at once, leaving him with the same never-ending agony again and again.

His thoughts, once clear and distinct, now melded together in a chaotic whirlwind. Memories bled into one another, identities blending and overlapping. It was a disorienting dance of past and present, a jumbled tapestry of experiences that threatened to swallow him whole.

"Luella, please. Drevon, you fool, you leave me no choice," Iathos and Merkth's voices screamed, overlapping in his essence.

As the process continued, Clovis felt like he was teetering on the precipice of oblivion, suspended in a liminal space between existence and dissolution. His very existence hung in the balance, caught in the agonizing struggle to disentangle himself from the other two beings.

Each heartbeat was a thunderous drumbeat of pain, reverberating through his weakened form.

Yet, amidst the torment, there was a strange sense of liberation, a glimmer of hope that shone through the darkness. As the knots unraveled, Clovis could feel the weight of the other souls lifting, the oppressive presence of their entanglement receding. It was a painful process, a violent shedding of old skin. Finally, with a wrenching surge of agony, the last vestiges of the entanglement snapped free. Clovis gasped, his chest heaving as he was released from the suffocating grip of the other souls. He was left trembling, raw, and vulnerable but also free. The pain, though still lingering, was now a distant echo, fading into the recesses of his memory.

"Come back to us, Clovis," Mika whispered to him.

Clovis took a shuddering breath as he unclenched his jaw. He could feel the sweat that had soaked him through and Mika's smaller hands cradling his dampened locks. Taking the time to let his muscles relax, he let his eyes flutter open. Meeting his sister's worried gaze, he tried to smile at her and only managed a grimace.

"You were out for a while, I sent Zeppo and Kilgi to rest. Ehiliana is grabbing food, and Ethan is a few feet away from us, helping while Zeppo rests. Don't move too fast, let Ethan help you, okay," she said, pushing some hair from his face.

Clovis croaked and watched as his sister smiled at him. After a few seconds, Ethan's sunset eyes were scanning over Clovis, glowing. Feeling spent, Clovis barely registered his surroundings. His mind only found its way back to focus as Ethan spoke.

"I don't see any signs of a curse. Your eyes also seem back to normal; some rest and food should help you gain your energy back."

Feeling Ethan's surprisingly strong hands haul him into a sitting position, Clovis heard Mika groan behind them. Laughing, he heard her shuffle about and watched Ethan's eyes follow her for a few moments.

"Still harboring a crush on her, it seems," he thought, as his mind seemed to settle.

"My legs have been numb for ages," she whined, walking around with wobbly legs.

"No one said you had to be his pillow." Ethan laughed.

"We didn't think to bring one. We figured he'd maybe be out for an hour at most, not almost an entire day."

"You figured untangling someone's soul would take an hour to rest up for?"

"Hey, I'm no doctor don't laugh at me! We figured he'd be up after an hour, and we could move him somewhere more accommodating."

"Sorry, Meeks," he said, cheeks coloring.

Coming to stand in front of Clovis, Mika ruffled Ethan's hair and said, "You're lucky we are friends."

"Blind as always, dear sister." He smiled at the thought. *"You'll figure it out though."*

With sudden clarity, Clovis asked in a croaked voice, "Who is watching Zeppo and Kilgi while they rest?"

"Regina. Ehiliana's significant other," Mika answered.

"Is she capable of protecting them?"

"You are worrying too much, brother, everything is going to be fine."

"Meeks, I need to make sure they are all right," he said, staggering to stand.

"Easy, Clovis, we will get you there," Ethan said, hauling him half onto his shoulder.

Walking out of the room, Clovis felt Mika take up his other side, and together, they all headed toward their quarters. As they passed through the castle, their footsteps echoed loudly in the eerie silence that now filled the halls. The once peaceful ambiance of the outside world filtering in seemed to cease, as well as the maids that usually lingered in the hall.

"Something isn't right," he thought, gripping his sister's shoulder just a little tighter.

"Clovis?"

"Something isn't right," he muttered.

Nearing their hall, Ehiliana rounded the corner with a tray and nearly dropped it at the sight of them. "Prince! you're awake," she shouted.

"What's going on?"

"I just ran food to Zeppo. He is getting ready to come check on you. Kilgi just left for the mission you gave her."

"This, this is bad. Something is wrong," Clovis said as they walked into his room.

Clovis let him go and pulled himself into the bathroom to clean up while the others sat around his lounging area.

A nervous anticipation ran down his spine as he took the quickest shower of his life. Throwing on a simple black short-sleeved shirt and matching slacks, he walked out of the bathroom, wet locks clinging to his face as he grabbed some socks, his belt, and shoes. Sitting down beside Mika, he finished getting dressed while talking.

"Am I the only one who feels like something bad is going to happen soon?"

"No, we know an attack is coming," Ehiliana said.

"You mean the air feeling buzzy?" Mika asked.

"Yeah," he said, lacing his boots.

"What better time to attack than when we are weak? Kilgi is gone, and we don't know what is going on with Iathos."

"You think it's about to happen?" Ethan asked.

"Yes, so first things first. Mika, go put on something easier to move in. Ethan will go with you. We will still be here."

"O-Okay," she stuttered out, moving to the door.

Clovis watched as Ethan followed behind, and he stood to put on his belt and place his spell book in it.

"Fuck, Kilgi has my book," Clovis said.

"Is that problematic for us?"

"Let's hope we don't need any complicated spells." Is all he said, running a hand through his hair.

After a few minutes, Mika came back in some simple pants and a long blue blouse. Nodding, she moved to sit as Ethan closed the door.

"The guards are going to try their best, to keep an attack from happening. We need to prepare though, if possible."

"There isn't time," Mika said, dazed.

Everyone's heads turned to meet her. "What?" they all said.

Shaking her head, she said, "They're already here. The wards snapped; monsters are coming."

Everyone was weary, tired, and scared. Staring at Mika, he gathered what strength he had and said, "You know this how Mika?"

"My fate told me, and I felt the magic snap. Someone broke the runes on this side so they could get in."

"Oliver, I bet," Zeppo said.

"Or Noa," Ehiliana chimed in.

"There isn't time to speculate it seems," Clovis said, standing tall.

"We move as one from this moment forward, no one splits. We start moving who we can to the dungeons to leave through the siege tunnels. We are going to have to hope Colkirk has competent guards."

Without much thought, all six of them stood, moving for the door. Spreading out in the hallway, Ehiliana summoned her bow seemed to flicker, and handed Regina a knife that had been strapped to her thigh. Zeppo pulled a band of wrap from his med kit and wrapped his hands as they moved.

Meeting his gaze, Zeppo said, "It will help me not mess up my hands and wrist."

"I'm not going to question what you do if it keeps up alive," Clovis said, his gaze shifting back ahead.

Seeing a few guards, Clovis grabbed their attention with a whistle. Turning to him, he said, "There is an attack coming now, start moving people to the dungeons and siege tunnels."

"Prince, with all due—"

"Then go die," he said, passing the pair with his group.

Everything seemed to blur as they knocked on doors with bad news. Many of them grumbled but moved out of fear of disobeying a royal. Servant halls were being opened for a quicker getaway. Only when a high-pitched scream echoed through the castle did everyone start moving. Gasps of shock ran through the crowd of nobles and maids. Clovis could feel Mika's grip on the back of his shirt to not lose him in the new chaos of the crowd.

"We need to get out of the hallway, we are asking to die here," he stated low enough for only his sister to hear.

"Ehiliana sent Regina with the first round of nobles to the dungeons, the rest of us are still here."

"Okay, we are moving to the ballroom."

"Why?"

"All the idiots will take shelter there."

"Oh."

"I wouldn't mind if you hid, Mika, it would make me feel better."

"I'm not leaving you. Because then you may be reckless and leave me for good," she said, tightening her grip.

"Then watch my back as best you can."

"I will, we're stronger together."

"We're stronger together," Islas' voice echoed in his head.

As Clovis reached the staircase, the sound of banging was almost deafening in the open hall. The front doors had been barred, and bulges stuck out from where it had been repeatedly hit. Many knights stood at the ready just a few feet away, their armor reflecting the chandelier's light. As they moved down the stairs, one of the knights called out for the prince.

"Your king is presumably safe. Fight for your kingdom like you mean it, this could be your last night, men. Buy your people time to escape, if push comes to shove, survive," he said.

"If I stop, I will see their faces forever in my dreams. Their fears are loud."

Feeling Mika's hand adjust on his back, he knew she was trying to comfort the both of them. Her fear of losing him is a reminder to not let her lose him. It wasn't until they were moving toward the stairs leading to the ballroom that the door gave out. A loud crash came from behind them, and on instinct, Clovis moved Mika behind him as he whirled around. Many men had been crushed and flung by the door. Blood splattered across the pristine walls and floor, and their screams echoed the terror that had torn into the room.

"They don't stand a chance."

Jesatyl mercenaries moved in around the monster, pulling the knights into a fight. Without thinking, he felt Ethan slap his forehead before moving on to the rest of the group. A warmth tingling through all of them.

"It's a rune to make you immune to their power, it would be pretty fatal for one of us to get caught up in their magics."

"Good work Ethan. Keep moving for the ballroom. Let's go," he commanded.

Ehiliana let off arrows at a rapid rate as they moved backward. She dropped a few mercenaries, but they were closing in fast. One with thinning brown hair managed to get within fighting range, aiming for Ehiliana, he was caught off guard as Zeppo slammed his fist into the side of his head. He hit the floor with a thud, and the next three came.

Forced to drop the bow, Ehiliana kept the arrow and shoved it through the man's eye before pulling it back and kicking him in the chest. His scream called attention to the monster as Zeppo dodged around the other two. Clovis was calling magic to him, but his body was too drained, and the fear from everyone around him was firing around his brain like an echo chamber.

"It's okay, I can help, gather your strength," Mika said, stepping in front of him.

Her hair was wild, and he could see over her short stature as she shot her hand out and blocked Zeppo from a deadly attack, then let it shatter like glass into his assailants' faces. He could hear it in her head: *They can't die, I can't be useless, I can't fail Clovis.* Placing a hand on her shoulder, he walked her backward with the group. The monster was now running full speed at them.

Everything around them exploded as Mika lost control, her fear making her spiral. Placing her hands up flat, she screamed out at the monster, and a shimmering wall appeared, the beast smashing into it. Oily sludge slid down the invisible wall as it staggered back. Up close, it was as if multiple animals had been sewn together to create it. Horns stuck out from its matted head, multiple eyes darting around, and it had paws made from multiple others.

A shudder ran through Clovis, leaning forward on Mika, Clovis called his magic and slammed multiple strikes of lightning into it, watching as it caught fire and wailed. Slamming harder against the wall, he watched as the mercenaries spread out and moved toward different parts of the castle. Mika pushed her hands forward, struggling to hold the wall. Gripping her again, Clovis whispered words of encouragement to her as the monster burned to death before them.

"We need to move. I am pretty much useless till I can gather more magic," he called.

"Clovis! We need to find a way out; people are running from the ballroom!" Ethan yelled as a body flew down the hall, and the sound of glass shattering rang out.

"Fuck," he said, watching as mercenaries moved to block their path.

"I-I think I can turn the runes back on from here, Clovis, but I need time and somewhere safe," Mika said, sounding out of breath.

"Mika."

"I can do it, Clovis, I have help."

"Her fate," he thought.

"Umbri's room," Zeppo said.

"The castle isn't safe anymore," Ehiliana called.

"Nowhere is safe!" Mika yelled.

"We need to get to the streets, I know a place," Ehiliana said.

"Okay, move, go, we don't have much of a choice do we," Clovis called over the arguing.

Instantly, Mika dropped the wall and let it splinter out at the Jesatyl. After that, she seemed to go slack before straightening her back. The air shifted about her, and suddenly, her hands shot out as if grabbing a handful of rocks and throwing them. She lifted the Jesatyl before her and slammed them into the wall in between the double stairs they had gone down earlier.

As if on cue, Ehiliana fired shots again as Zeppo moved beside Mika. Together, they made their way into the mercenaries. Mika slammed them away while Ehiliana pinned them with arrows. Zeppo knocked anyone who got close, occasionally closing any deep wounds he'd received. Ethan was at their back with a sword that he'd picked up. Thinking it smart, Clovis did the same as they stepped over a fallen knight.

The air smelled thick with blood and ash. Before long, whatever monster had been down the hall appeared. It looked like a giant person covered in fur with a fox head sewn on. A feminine leg hung from its mouth, and blood dribbled down its fiery fur.

"I don't think I will ever sleep again," Ethan said, backing up into Clovis.

"I don't see a way out of this," Ehiliana said.

"Clovis, take my hand," Mika said.

Her hand reached back and grabbed him, intertwining their fingers. He felt a surge of power like he'd never felt in his life. In front of him floated a young man with white hair and skin that was like a purplish sunset. Smiling, he shushed him.

"You can't tell them, but Mika needs her other half for this to work. We are going to split the magic. You protect her while she tries to ignite the runes," Ellis said.

"We got this." She smiled.

"I can't lose him; he's all I've got." He heard her say in her thoughts.

Letting his mind settle, he turned to the monster and felt the tingle as he lifted the monster and slammed it into the ground. Ehiliana, Ethan, and Zeppo covered them the best they could. The monster roared as Clovis sent waves of ethereal fire at it. As it thrashed and howled in pain, the few mercenaries in its range got taken out by its sharp claws.

A cold feeling swept up the room with a darkness-like smoke blowing in the wind. Moving to stand in a circle, backs facing one another, a laugh rumbled through the air.

"My, you all are quite formidable. Even managed to turn the runes back on. I have to admit that's pretty impressive for a girl who struggles so much to be worthy of any real accomplishments. Then again, anything is possible when stealing magic from your brother, huh."

Clovis gripped his sister's hand tighter, and as the room darkened, no one answered.

"Do you think he can keep you safe, little girl?"

"Yes," she answered.

Clovis waited to hear the fear come through, but it never did. *She believes in me that much.*

"He's too late." Merkth laughed.

The darkness subsided, and as Clovis turned, a spray of blood hit him. Seconds later, a blood-curdling scream came from his sister. Stumbling back, he peered through bloody vision and felt his heart skip multiple beats.

"Mika! Mika," he said, stumbling forward, his hand still interlocked with hers.

Chapter Twenty-Nine

<u>Kilgi</u>

With the sunset casting its evening glow, Kilgi approached the historical building. Still seeming under construction, the area was quieter than on a normal day. Her gaze roaming around for danger, Kilgi found she was luckily and suspiciously alone in her approach to the building. Slipping through the door, she was met with a destroyed room. Papers, books, tables, shelves, and pillars around the room were still in a disastrous state.

"Did they not start fixing this place up? Why the hell would they even leave it unattended? Something about this feels wrong," Kilgi thought as she descended to the lower depths, following Ehiliana's instructions.

As Kilgi ventured deeper into the underground archives, a palpable tension hung in the air as she reached the bottom of the stairs. The chasm seemed to yawn wider, the shadows growing darker and more foreboding. The stone pillar, though impressive, felt like a sentinel of an ancient and forgotten realm, its presence imposing and unyielding.

The bridges, while functional, exuded an eerie silence, broken only by the soft echo of Kilgi's footsteps. Each step seemed to reverberate through the chamber; the worn stones beneath her feet felt uneven, with occasional loose fragments, adding an unsettling unpredictability to the path.

Peeking into the door along the left side wall, Kilgi saw a room filled with knowledge that exuded an air of neglect and abandonment. Dust and cobwebs clung to forgotten corners, shrouding the volumes in a veiled obscurity. The torchlight's dance took on a sinister quality, casting elongated, shifting shadows that seemed to hide unseen presences. Now and then, a faint rustle or distant drip seemed to break the stillness, leaving Kilgi's senses on edge, acutely aware of their vulnerability in this ancient, forgotten sanctum. Kilgi's presence felt like a disturbance, a ripple in the stagnant waters of the archive's seclusion.

"The weight of the past is heavy here. The knowledge within these walls is probably exactly what we are trying to find, yet it's abandoned. Why?"

Continuing into the depth of the chasm, Kilgi's mind raced. *"Ehiliana had said there were guards here last time, yet nothing now. This must be some kind of trap. There is no way it's that easy for me. There must be a slumbering beast or something down here."*

The air grew heavy and stale as Kilgi approached the prison-like chamber, the atmosphere suffused with a noxious scent that hung on the fringes of her senses. The doors before her were imposing, their surfaces marred by grotesque etchings that seemed to writhe and contort in grotesque patterns. The metal seemed to ooze a sickly sheen of red as if someone had bled the doors.

"I have a really bad feeling about all of this."

Each hinge groaned with reluctant resistance as Kilgi pushed the doors open, revealing the grim tableau within. The room was a cavern of suffering. The walls seeped with dampness, their surface pockmarked and disfigured. Jagged iron bars enclosed a series of cells, their openings yawning like hungry maws, revealing the darkness within.

Within those cells, shadows clung to the corners like specters, obscuring the horrors that lay within. The remnants of forgotten souls, emaciated and contorted, were huddled in corners or slumped against the damp stone. Their eyes, hollow orbs of resignation, stared out into the void, mirroring the desolation of their surroundings.

The floor was a mosaic of filth and decay, a collage of stains and detritus that bore witness to the countless indignities suffered within this wretched place. The echoes of distant drips seemed to resonate with a morose rhythm, punctuating the oppressive silence that hung over the room like a shroud.

Flickering torches lined the walls, their flames casting elongated, dancing shadows that seemed to mimic the twisted forms within the cells. The light played cruel tricks on the eye, casting a surreal, nightmarish pallor over the scene.

As Kilgi stood on the threshold, the air seemed to grow colder as an invisible weight settled on her shoulders, raising the hairs on the back of her neck. The room exuded a malevolent energy of despair. Hearing a whimper from further in the room, Kilgi drew a blade and moved closer to the sound.

"Fuck this is like the horror novels Kimon likes so much. Maybe if I'm lucky, someone will write a book about this horror—oh, wait, no one is here to witness my potential demise."

Reaching the cell that the whimper had come from, Kilgi locked eyes with shockingly white eyes that were flaked with bits of red. What should have been the whites of his eyes were instead inky, as if swallowed by shadows. The chains around him rattled as he curled in on himself and moved further away from her despite being behind bars. Lifting a hand, she summoned some orbs of light and set the torch down. Studying him in the light, he was like a ball of lanky limbs with tattered, almost nonexistent clothes. His head was hidden behind his knees, black and white shaggy hair covering parts of his shoulders and legs.

Pulling on the bars a little bit, Kilgi shook her head and took a step back before pulling the orbs of light to her. Changing the light into a long strip, she waved her hand, letting the hot light slice through the lock.

"One step at a time. I am still learning how to do this magic stuff, and I am tired from helping Clovis this morning."

Opening the cell, Kilgi took a step inside and raised a hand, "Are you Silas?" Kilgi watched as he pushed further into the wall. Kneeling, she said, "Silas, my name is Kilgi, and I am here on behalf of your mother and your friend Wren. We are here for you and your book."

Peeking at her through puffy eyes, he gripped his legs tighter.

"Silas, we need to get moving before something bad happens."

"This is another trick," he said.

"It is no trick, Silas."

"Prove it? He hasn't been able to yet."

"Who hasn't? What am I proving?"

"If you're not him, if you are here to help me. Tell me who is Wren?"

"I see. Wren is like me, Silas," Kilgi said, pulling her braid over her shoulder.

Watching as he took in the sight of her hair, he gave a curt nod. "Okay, I believe you. But he did something to me."

"Do you know what?"

"I don't know."

"Okay. Well, let's get you out of these chains then."

"The book is in the room with golden leaves on the door."

"We will try to find it on the way back," she said as she worked on opening his chains.

"You said you are Kilgi?" he asked, sounding horse.

"I am," she said, setting down the last cuff.

Silas's matted locks hung limp around his tanned but thin face, she saw upon closer inspection, that he had high cheekbones that made him seem ghostly from starvation. His thin, chapped lip was between his teeth as he peeked nervously at her.

"This poor guy."

"He said, he had plans to eat the light and take away hope. He called the light Kilgi," he whispered.

"Well, we will just have to prove him wrong. Let's get moving," Kilgi said, grabbing his wrist to pull him up.

As she did, the world seemed to slow for a second, as she spotted a black pawn on his forearm. It was mechanical, but unlike the others, his tattoo had a rook in its shadow. Kilgi nodded her head and turned to walk, together the pair made their way back into the stony hall. Wrinkling her nose between Silas's bad smell and the halls, they made their way back toward the upper levels.

"They can't open the book without the key," Silas said as they limped along.

"I see."

"Why do they need the book?"

"It contains part of his prison, the last piece before he can walk among us again." Feeling a shiver up her spine, Kilgi frowned. "This is really bad news."

"He won't be free if we unlock the book, it contains him and other important things. He can only be free if he has all the pieces of his prison, and all twelve fates have bled on it."

"How do you know this?"

"My family has been protecting Ligh for ages."

"You mean you are hiding a fate?"

"Used to be, it's a long story, but I am now that fate," Silas said in between coughs.

"This is a mess. Do you think he could have gotten their blood already? Why does he need their blood?"

"He must have most somehow if he is saying he plans on killing you. My guess is, because the fates made the prison, their blood is probably a way to unlock it."

"Seems like we are screwed."

As they reached the upper levels, the sound of a door echoing a few feet to their right made them jump. Letting go of Silas, Kilgi drew her other sword and pushed him behind her. Watching as a figure stepped out with a blue book in hand, Kilgi met Iathos's eyes.

"No," she thought.

"Kilgi," He breathed.

"Iathos, what are you doing here?"

"I came for the book," he said.

"We need to go, Iathos, something isn't right here."

"Kilgi, everything is going to be okay. I am not going to hurt you."

"Iathos, that book needs to go home with Silas."

"This book needs to go to the guy who can stop all of this."

"Iathos, please listen to me, I have no reason to lie to you," she said, stepping forward and lowering her swords.

"You do though."

"What? What are you talking about, Iathos?"

"You are blinded by the dark prince; you do not see that he is using all of you. I am going to free you all from his spell, Merkth wants to help."

"No, no, no, no, no, this is bad," Kilgi thought, panic rising in her chest.

"I don't want to hurt you either, Iathos, but I can't let you bring that book to him."

Neither moved for a few seconds as they sized each other up. When Iathos moved to run toward the stairs, Kilgi gave chase and shot her hand out to slam a bolt of light into Iathos's side. Knocking him into the wall, Kilgi caught up to him as he stood back up. Going for the book, the world blurred as he grabbed her head and crashed it into the spot he had just stood from.

"Fuck," she bit out, feeling dizzy.

"Kilgi, let me go," he said softly.

"I can't. You are making a mistake, cousin; you are going to get us all killed."

"No, Kils, I'm not. This is for everyone's sake, and I care about you and your brothers too much to give up," he said, gripping her hair tighter.

"Luella would be appalled," Kilgi whispered.

Kilgi kicked her leg out from under her and into his knee. She felt his grip leave her head and his sharp intake of breath. Grabbing the book as he fell, Kilgi raced back toward Silas, shoving the book into his arms.

"We need a fast way out of here," she said, summoning platforms made of light that flickered weakly.

"That's it?" he asked.

"I am a little low on the magic stuff currently. It's what we got," she said, keeping an eye on Iathos.

"I can maybe jump us out of here at least," Silas said, gripping the book.

"No time to waste then, get us out of here," Kilgi said, putting a sword away and grabbing his arm.

"No! Kilgi, you are making a mistake!" Iathos yelled, running toward them.

"I'm sorry, Iathos. I am," she said, tightening her grip on Silas.

Feeling a rush of cold, the world around her blurred as her feet hit solid ground. They stood at the market square near the fountain. Letting go of Silas's arm, Kilgi gave him a curt nod.

"I feel sick," he said, blanching.

A feeling of unease swept up Kilgi's spine as she faced the palace. A cloud of shadows seemed to swirl around the area, blotting out light. The echo of fighting, monstrous roars, and screaming echoed through the vacant city.

Why is there no one else around? Kilgi thought.

Silas met her gaze with a terrified one. "We should run," he whispered.

"I can't, my friends are in that castle, and I doubt you are in a position to run well."

"You are going to go toward the danger?"

"Yes, you should get back to your family. We will be meeting you shortly, more than likely, with the way things are going," she said, gripping his shoulder.

"Here take this," he said, picking up a stone from inside the fountain.

Watching as he clasped his hands together, a bead of light peeking in between his fingers for a few seconds. Swaying a little, he put a handout and steadied himself against Kilgi while pressing the stone in her hand.

"What is it?"

"It's a warp stone. They are hard to make, I guess I am a little special, but that's the rest of my energy. It has one use, when you get them, it will take you to the shop along with anyone who touches you."

"You are fantastic, Silas," Kilgi said, stepping from his grasp.

"Please, get home safe and quick," she said before sprinting in the direction of the castle.

Kilgi's breath came in ragged gasps as she sprinted through the desolate streets, her footsteps echoing in the oppressive silence. The cobblestones seemed to blur beneath her, each stride a desperate plea for swift passage. The once-familiar alleyways, now eerily vacant, felt like a haunting labyrinth, their usual bustle replaced by an unsettling emptiness.

Suffocating weight of dread pressed against her chest, her heart pounded, and a frantic cadence mirrored the urgency that pulsed through her veins. Fear for her friends pressed at the edges of her thoughts, a relentless undercurrent to her determined stride. Every corner turned, every alley traversed, held the potential for a terrible revelation, a glimpse of the danger that threatened those she had come to care for.

A roar echoed through the noble's quarters, forcing Kilgi to halt her run at the sight of the monstrosity before her. Unlike the monsters from the first attack, this one seemed to have a vastly different appearance. It had milky white skin and stood unnaturally tall, with bony arms that led into long sharp points covered in blood. Its razor smile widened as it met her horrified gaze. Falling on all fours, it charged at her at a frightening pace.

"This is bad! okay, don't die. Don't think about why it has horns for eyes."

There was no time to dwell on fear; she needed to survive. With every fiber of her being focused on the approaching nightmare, Kilgi steadied herself with muscles coiled like a spring ready to release its pent-up energy.

As the monstrous being lunged forward, its bony limbs propelled by an unnatural strength, Kilgi reacted with a lightning-quick instinct. She ducked to the side, narrowly evading the creature's deadly charge. The air whooshed with the force of its passing, carrying with it a putrid scent of decay.

"I need to end this as soon as possible."

Gritting her teeth, Kilgi turned on her heel, her movements fluid and deliberate. She had to find a way to exploit this creature's grotesque anatomy. With a surge of adrenaline-fueled strength, she lunged forward, Pushing the little amount of magic she had left into striking at the monster's exposed flank. Her blade met resistance, the impact reverberating through her arms as she drove the weapon home.

The creature emitted a guttural, inhuman sound, a mixture of pain and fury. Its milky skin seemed to ripple and contort, the wound oozing a noxious ichor that sizzled on contact with the cold stone floor.

Undeterred, it retaliated with a vicious swipe of its blood-soaked appendage.

With a deft roll, Kilgi narrowly evaded the deadly strike, feeling the rush of air as the creature's arm sailed past. She needed to keep moving, to stay one step ahead of this relentless foe. Adrenaline surged through her veins, sharpening her focus and heightening her senses.

"Just a little more."

Kilgi's breaths came in ragged bursts; her body pushed to its limits as she pushed for more magic. She knew that she couldn't afford to falter, that every strike needed to count. With a final, calculated thrust, Kilgi drove her blade deep into the creature's core as it swung for her. The abomination let out a final, anguished wail, its form convulsing before collapsing in a heap.

"I need to reach the others," she thought, feeling tired.

The castle loomed ahead; its towering spires etched against the darkening sky. Its once-impregnable walls were now crumbled, a bastion of peril. Kilgi's breath misted in the chill, the icy tendrils of air a biting reminder of the urgency of her mission.

"We aren't in the cold season yet; there is something off about this."

As she approached the castle gates, the weight of her apprehension bore down upon her, a crushing burden that threatened to engulf her. Kilgi pushed through the gates with every nerve on edge.

The castle's front door was gone, and the sound of yelling, roars, and the clashing of metal filled her ears. She tightened the grip of her sword and kept moving forward, prepared to fight despite her exhaustion. As she climbed up the steps, Kilgi couldn't help but let out a breath of relief.

Everyone was circled up together, fending off mercenaries and a monster on the upper level.

"I made it in time. Now I just need to draw some attention to me, to give them an opening."

"You're too late," Merkth's voice whispered, brushing past her ear.

Darkness surged forward, blinding her completely.

"My, you all are quite formidable; you even managed to turn the runes back on. I must admit that's impressive for a girl who struggles so much to be worthy of any real accomplishments. Then again, anything is possible when stealing magic from your brother, huh." His voice rang out.

"No, no, no, no, no," she thought, gritting her teeth, pushing forward.

"Do you think he can keep you safe, little girl?"

"Yes," Mika answered.

"He's too late." Merkth laughed.

Like a receding tide, Merkth's shadows let go of Kilgi. He rushed forward toward the others. A scream echoed across the room with a spray of blood.

Chapter Thirty

<u>Zeppo</u>

"You couldn't save your family; you couldn't save your friend. You are the biggest failure of your divine race, a blue-collar, locked in chains, never able to do more. Let me, and I will end it for you. Just step from the pool." Merkth's voice replayed in Zeppo's head.

Mika's bloody form flashed through his mind as the fighting continued. Feeling the cool prickle of dread travel up his spine, Zeppo turned to face Mika the minute Merkth's voice rang through the darkness.

"This is what is in store for you. Her life will end in your hands, but if you let me end your life, I can stop this tragedy."

"No, no, not this, not that vision," Zeppo thought as the shadows surged back.

The thrumming of adrenaline filled his ears, his breath quickening as the shadows receded from the room. Turning to his left, he saw a flash of purple moving in their direction.

"No."

Moving toward Mika, he flinched at her piercing scream. Blood poured from her arm as she dropped to her knees, clutching where her arm had been cut off. The sound of Clovis dropping her arm and screaming her name stirred Zeppo from his daze. As he rushed toward her, he ripped his shirt and pulled it off himself. The air was buzzing with energy, and every hair on his body felt like it was raised as he dropped down next to the princess.

"Calm down. You need to think clearly."

He saw a broken sword hilt on the ground a few feet away. As he went through the motions of wrapping the beginnings of his makeshift tourniquet around her upper arm, his mind began to race.

"This is bad."

"Here," Ethan said, pressing the broken sword hilt into the side of his arm.

Zeppo took the hilt and twisted it into the tourniquet. He glanced at the princess as she seemed to go quiet. When he finished cutting off the blood flow, he pressed his fingers to her skin to make sure he couldn't feel a pulse.

"How is she doing," Ethan called from behind him.

"Alive. I managed to stop the bleeding but if we don't get her out of here . . ."

"Yeah."

"Mika, can you hear me?" Zeppo asked as he maneuvered her into his arms.

Dropping her head to his shoulder, she whispered, "It hurts."

"We'll take care of it," he said, standing up.

The others formed a protective circle around him and the princess. Everyone was exhausted and on their last legs, and they were outnumbered.

As if reading his mind, Kilgi yelled, "Is she safe to move?"

"Yes!" he called.

"Everyone, move in and grab onto Zeppo, now. I have a way out," she commanded.

"What?"

He felt four pairs of hands grab onto his shoulders, and a cold wave swept over his body as the world shifted around him. Suddenly, they were in a bookshop, the smell of paper mixing with blood.

"Follow me," Kilgi said, walking toward a narrow hallway near the back of the shop.

Quiet but hurriedly, the group followed Kilgi through the dark hallways. Moving a hand to Mika's neck to check her pulse, Zeppo pressed his chin against the top of her head.

"I am going to take care of you, Mika, I won't let you die. Be strong for me, okay?" he whispered to her.

Spilling out into a large kitchen, Kilgi wasted no time searching for a pot to boil water. Moving to the open counterspace, Zeppo laid Mika down. Clovis moved to the end of the counter where her head rested and gripped the edge as he peered at her with concern.

"What can we do?" Ehiliana asked.

"We need medical supplies, boiled water, and clean hands from everyone," Ethan responded.

Ethan and Zeppo needing no words, nodded their heads at one another. Zeppo watched as Ethan went to wash his hands, then he grabbed one of the cushions from a nearby stool and placed it to slightly elevate Mika's feet.

"This will help prevent shock, depending on how clean the wound is once we clean it up, we will sew it up right away or leave it open for a few days to see if there is any tissue that needs to be removed."

"This is my fault," Clovis said, touching his forehead to Mika's.

"It isn't any of our faults. She was supposed to die on that floor, and she is here still breathing. We aren't going to lose her; I will do everything I can."

"Can you bring her arm back?"

"I'm not that powerful. If I could, I would."

Going to wash his hands as Ethan came back, Ehiliana arrived with three more people. Setting a large medical kit on the far end of the counter, the older woman with black and white hair started laying items out on the counter. The tall, lanky man, who looked a lot like her, came over to examine Mika, and the blue-haired woman stood on the other side of the room.

"At least he is wearing gloves," he thought.

"Who are you?" Ethan asked, rifling through the medical supplies.

"I'm Octavia, this is my son, Silas, and the girl over there is Wren."

"Pleasure. I am impressed with your stuff. It will be a lot easier putting her under for this."

"My son is a magical engineer. Perhaps if her wound is manageable, he can make her a new arm. It wouldn't be his first."

"Let's get her to a more stable state first," Ethan said, moving back over, his eyes glowing with determination while prepping to heal her.

Following his lead, Zeppo met him on the other side, both feeling tense.

"We can do this."

"If this is the beginning of what Merkth can do, how are we supposed to survive him coming to full power?" Ehiliana asked.

"I don't know." Clovis breathed, dropping his forehead to Mikas.

www.ingramcontent.com/pod-product-compliance
Lightning Source LLC
Chambersburg PA
CBHW051436050726
47593CB00005B/1801